"*Psychoanalytic Credos* is an extraordinary psychoanalytic book. Editor Jill Salberg has assembled a group of highly influential psychoanalysts who have played a major role in shaping what we think of as contemporary psychoanalytic thought. They are wonderfully candid in describing their personal journeys. Indeed, many of them are personal friends of mine, yet I found myself reading fascinating stories that I had never heard before. All describe their struggles to define what kind of analyst they would ultimately become. I was deeply moved as I heard their stories and found myself identifying with so much of what they said. This book is a must read for those who care about the future of psychoanalysis. I consider *Psychoanalytic Credos* one of the major contributions to our field."

—Glen O. Gabbard, MD, Author of *Love and Hate in the Analytic Setting*

"*Psychoanalytic Credos* is a beautiful and embracing book. Inviting analysts to reflect upon their evolving mission and vision, its query is located at the nexus of ethics, theory, culture, reason and faith. In welcoming commentary from diverse perspectives, international thinkers, eminent elders and from more youthful social critics, this text is both broad and deep. Salberg's notion should be taken up by us all: let's keep writing, reading, and teaching these credos throughout our professional lives."

—Dr. Sue Grand, faculty and supervisor at the NYU Postdoctoral Program in Psychotherapy and Psychoanalysis; a fellow at the Institute for Psychology and the Other, and a visiting scholar at the Psychoanalytic Institute for Northern California

"Jill Salberg provides a rare opportunity to listen in as 27 psychoanalysts, spanning 5 decades, across 4 continents, share how they think about their development and work. The credos assembled here vividly convey the fashioning of psychoanalytic identities and what each analyst holds dear. A wonderful way to hear the prosody of psychoanalytic practices."

—Dodi Goldman is a Training and Supervising Analyst at the William Alanson White Institute and author of "A Beholder's Share: essays on Winnicott and the psychoanalytic imagination"

"In Jill Salberg's lovingly curated collection of credos, we have a veritable Canterbury Tales of psychoanalysis. Each voice in turn holds us in its spell as we hear of the roads these pilgrims have traveled. To accompany all twenty-seven wayfarers on their journeys spanning more than fifty years of psychoanalytic history is to witness the intergenerational transmission of ideas as well as the transmigration of souls in our field."

—Peter L. Rudnytsky, University of Florida and Chicago Psychoanalytic Institute

Psychoanalytic Credos

Developing a psychoanalytic credo, a set of beliefs that inform how you listen and approach the analytic enterprise with patients, is in many ways the scaffolding of psychoanalytic training. Drawing upon Mannie Ghent's original Credo essay, 27 psychoanalysts were asked to write their credo and/or their psychoanalytic journey. This book represents a multi-theoretical and multi-generational grouping, trained at different institutes, during different eras (grouped by decades 1960–2000) and across cultures. They are drawn from analysts identified with Relational, Object Relations, Contemporary Freudian and Kleinian/Bionian perspectives as well as those who don't easily fit categorization. This book serves to provide companionship to analysts in training, as part of reading lists in institutes as well as analysts post-training and yet still evolving in their psychoanalytic journey.

Jill Salberg, Ph.D., ABPP, is Faculty at the NYU Postdoctoral Program in Psychotherapy and Psychoanalysis. She edited *Good Enough Endings: Breaks, Interruptions and Terminations from Contemporary Relational Perspectives*, and co-edited with Sue Grand, *The Wounds of History: Repair and Resilience in the Transgenerational Transmission of Trauma*, and *Transgenerational Trauma and the Other: Dialogues Across History and Difference*, both of which received the Gradiva Award for best edited books (2018). She is in private practice in Manhattan.

Relational Perspectives Book Series

Adrienne Harris, Steven Kuchuck, & Eyal Rozmarin
Series Editors

Stephen Mitchell
Founding Editor

Lewis Aron
Editor Emeritus

The Relational Perspectives Book Series (RPBS) publishes books that grow out of or contribute to the relational tradition in contemporary psychoanalysis. The term *relational psychoanalysis* was first used by Greenberg and Mitchell[1] to bridge the traditions of interpersonal relations, as developed within interpersonal psychoanalysis and object relations, as developed within contemporary British theory. But, under the seminal work of the late Stephen A. Mitchell, the term *relational psychoanalysis* grew and began to accrue to itself many other influences and developments. Various tributaries—interpersonal psychoanalysis, object relations theory, self psychology, empirical infancy research, feminism, queer theory, sociocultural studies, and elements of contemporary Freudian and Kleinian thought—flow into this tradition, which understands relational configurations between self and others, both real and fantasied, as the primary subject of psychoanalytic investigation.

We refer to the relational tradition, rather than to a relational school, to highlight that we are identifying a trend, a tendency within contemporary psychoanalysis, not a more formally organized or coherent school or system of beliefs. Our use of the term *relational* signifies a dimension of theory and practice that has become salient across the wide spectrum of contemporary psychoanalysis. Now under the editorial supervision of Adrienne Harris, Steven Kuchuck, and Eyal Rozmarin, the Relational Perspectives Book Series originated in 1990 under the editorial eye of the late Stephen A. Mitchell. Mitchell was the most prolific and influential of the originators of the relational tradition. Committed to dialogue among psychoanalysts, he abhorred the authoritarianism that dictated adherence to a rigid set of beliefs or technical restrictions. He championed open discussion, comparative and integrative approaches, and promoted new voices across the generations. Mitchell was later joined by the late Lewis Aron, also a visionary and influential writer, teacher, and leading thinker in relational psychoanalysis.

Included in the Relational Perspectives Book Series are authors and works that come from within the relational tradition, those that extend and develop that tradition, and works that critique relational approaches or compare and contrast them with alternative points of view. The series includes our most distinguished senior psychoanalysts, along with younger contributors who bring fresh vision. Our aim is to enable a deepening of relational thinking while reaching across disciplinary and social boundaries in order to foster an inclusive and international literature.

A full list of titles in this series is available at https://www.routledge.com/Relational-Perspectives-Book-Series/book-series/LEARPBS

Note

1 Greenberg, J., & Mitchell, S. (1983). *Object relations in psychoanalytic theory.* Cambridge, MA: Harvard University Press.

Psychoanalytic Credos

Personal and Professional Journeys of Psychoanalysts

Jill Salberg

LONDON AND NEW YORK

First published 2022
by Routledge
2 Park Square, Milton Park, Abingdon, Oxon OX14 4RN

and by Routledge
605 Third Avenue, New York, NY 10158

Routledge is an imprint of the Taylor & Francis Group, an informa business

© 2022 selection and editorial matter, Jill Salberg individual chapters, the contributors

The right of Jill Salberg to be identified as the author of the editorial material, and of the authors for their individual chapters, has been asserted in accordance with sections 77 and 78 of the Copyright, Designs and Patents Act 1988.

All rights reserved. No part of this book may be reprinted or reproduced or utilised in any form or by any electronic, mechanical, or other means, now known or hereafter invented, including photocopying and recording, or in any information storage or retrieval system, without permission in writing from the publishers.

Trademark notice: Product or corporate names may be trademarks or registered trademarks, and are used only for identification and explanation without intent to infringe.

British Library Cataloguing-in-Publication Data
Names: Salberg, Jill, editor.
Title: Psychoanalytic credos : personal and professional journeys of psychoanalysts / edited by Jill Salberg.
Description: Abingdon, Oxon ; New York, NY : Routledge, 2022. | Includes bibliographical references and index. |
Identifiers: LCCN 2021027487 (print) | LCCN 2021027488 (ebook) | ISBN 9781032072708 (hardback) | ISBN 9781032054728 (paperback) | ISBN 9781003206248 (ebook)
Subjects: LCSH: Psychoanalysts--Anecdotes. | Psychoanalysts--Attitudes. | Psychoanalysis--Philosophy. | Psychoanalysis--Vocational guidance.
Classification: LCC BF175 .P783 2022 (print) | LCC BF175 (ebook) | DDC 150.19/5--dc23
LC record available at https://lccn.loc.gov/2021027487
LC ebook record available at https://lccn.loc.gov/2021027488

ISBN: 978-1-032-07270-8 (hbk)
ISBN: 978-1-032-05472-8 (pbk)
ISBN: 978-1-003-20624-8 (ebk)

DOI: 10.4324/9781003206248

Typeset in Times New Roman
by MPS Limited, Dehradun

Contents

List of Contributors	x
Acknowledgments	xx
Editor's Introduction JILL SALBERG	1

Section I
1960s   **7**

1 My Journey   9
  SHELDON BACH

2 My Journey: Haydée Faimberg Interviewed by and in Conversation with Graciela V. Consoli and Ezequiel A. Jaroslavsky   14
  HAYDÉE FAIMBERG

Section II
1970s   **29**

3 What After Pluralism? Ulysses Still on the Road   31
  RICARDO BERNARDI

4 What is theory?   41
  CHRISTOPHER BOLLAS

5 My Psychoanalytic Journey   51
  STEPHEN A. MITCHELL

6 An Autobiographical Fragment   59
  JAY GREENBERG

7	Credo: Psychoanalysis as a Wisdom Tradition NANCY MCWILLIAMS	70
8	Becoming the Analysts That We Turn Out to Be MICHAEL PARSONS	78

Section III
1980s   87

9	Credo: Mutuality and Asymmetry LEWIS ARON	89
10	Credo: The Sufferings of the World JESSICA BENJAMIN	96
11	Credo: Playing and Becoming in Psychoanalysis STEVEN H. COOPER	105
12	Credo ADRIENNE HARRIS	113
13	Reflections on the Way I Practice Psychoanalysis THOMAS H. OGDEN	121
14	Toward a Humanistic Psychoanalysis DONNA ORANGE	128
15	Becoming and Being a Psychoanalyst: Credo as Ongoing Journey JILL SALBERG	134
16	Against the Grain: On Challenging Assumptions, Bridging Theories, Practicing Self-Critique, Exposing Underbellies, and Doing the Right Thing JOYCE SLOCHOWER	142

Section IV
1990s   153

17	Learning to Surf: Analyzing Adolescents MARY T. BRADY	155

Contents ix

18	Credo: So Our Lives Glide On KEN CORBETT	160
19	Peasants, Fields, and Expanding Horizons in Psychoanalysis ELIZABETH A. CORPT	169
20	Analytic Eroticism DIANNE ELISE	176
21	Credo quia absurdum BRUCE REIS	184
22	Working It Out: Development, Politics, Multidisciplinarity STEPHEN SELIGMAN	191
23	Credo: In Search of Transformation MELANIE SUCHET	200

Section V
2000s   **207**

24	On Truthlessness—Or, All in the Game STEPHEN HARTMAN	209
25	My Psychoanalytic Search for Freedom ILANA LAOR	218
26	The Risk of Analysis AVGI SAKETOPOULOU	226
27	Credo: Relationality and the Collective—A Psychoanalytic Journey in Context CHANA ULLMAN	234

Index   243

Contributors

Lewis Aron, Ph.D., ABPP, was an internationally recognized psychoanalyst, sought after teacher, lecturer, and the Director of the New York University Postdoctoral Program in Psychotherapy and Psychoanalysis. He was a past President of the Division of Psychoanalysis (39) APA; founding President of the International Association for Relational Psychoanalysis and Psychotherapy (IARPP); founding President of the Division of Psychologist-Psychoanalysts of NYSPA. Aron was also the co-founder and co-chair of the Sándor Ferenczi Center at the New School for Social Research, and Adjunct Professor, School of Psychology, Interdisciplinary Center (IDC) Herzliya, Israel; a co-founder of *Psychoanalytic Dialogues* and the co-editor of the Relational Perspectives Book Series. He is the author and editor of numerous articles and books, including *A Meetings of Minds, A Psychotherapy for the People* (co-authored with Karen Starr) and *Dramatic Dialogue* (co-authored with Galit Atlas). **Training: NYU Postdoctoral Program in Psychotherapy and Psychoanalysis (1980–1985)**

Sheldon Bach, Ph.D., was an Adjunct Clinical Professor of Psychology at the New York University Postdoctoral Program for Psychoanalysis and Psychotherapy, Training and Supervising Analyst at the Contemporary Freudian Society, and a Fellow of The Institute for Psychoanalytic Training and Research. He was the recipient of the Heinz Hartmann Award (2007) from the New York Psychoanalytic Institute for "outstanding contribution to the theory and practice of Psychoanalysis." He was the author of numerous articles and books: *Narcissistic States and the Therapeutic Process* (Jason Aronson, 1993), *The Language of Perversion and the Language of Love* (Jason Aronson, 1994), *Getting From Here to There: Analytic Love, Analytic Process* (Routledge, 2013), and *The How-To Book: For Students of Psychoanalysis and Psychotherapy* (Routledge, 2018). **Training: NYU Postdoctoral Program in Psychotherapy and Psychoanalysis (1961–1968)**

Jessica Benjamin, Ph.D., is the author of *The Bonds of Love* (1988), *Like Subjects, Love Objects* (1995), *Shadow of the Other* (1998), and most recently *Beyond Doer and Done To: Recognition Theory, Intersubjectivity and the Third* (2018). She is a supervising and teaching faculty member of the New York University Postdoctoral Psychology Program in Psychotherapy and Psychoanalysis and at the Stephen Mitchell Center for Relational Studies in New York where she practices as an analyst. In 2015, she was awarded the Hans Kilian prize at the University of the Ruhr in Bochum, Germany, the largest European award for work that joins psychoanalysis with the humanities. From 2004 to 2010, she initiated and directed "The Acknowledgement Project" involving Israeli and Palestinian mental health practitioners and peace workers, since then continuing her interest in the area of collective trauma and acknowledgment. She originally studied social theory with an emphasis on its relation to psychoanalysis, then worked on Beatrice Beebe's research project on mother-infant interaction. She is in private practice in Manhattan. **Training: NYU Postdoctoral Program in Psychotherapy and Psychoanalysis (1980–1986)**

Ricardo Bernardi, M.D., Ph.D., is an Honorary Member of the Uruguayan Psychoanalytic Association, where he has completed his training and has subsequently performed supervisory, analytical, and teaching functions. He has been a member of the Board (ex-Council) of the International Psychoanalytic Association and a member of the Research Committee and the Clinical Observation Committee, among others. He has received the Sigourney Award and the Fepal Award. His current publications are related to the evaluation of clinical evidence in a plural context. He proposed to the Committee for Clinical Observation, the Three-Level Model, currently used in different regions of the API, which allows exploring and refining the inferential process of clinical discussion groups. The model guides the group discussion "from the bottom up," that is, from the analytical resonance of the material in the participants to more abstract and general levels of conceptualization. The discussion aims to explore changes in the patient but also shows where a clinical common ground is strongest among analysts with different theoretical approaches. He is also an Emeritus Professor of the Faculty of Medicine of the National University of Uruguay, Honorary Member of the Society of Psychiatry, and a member of the Academy of Medicine. He is currently a member of the Honorary Scientific Advisory Committee (GACH) advising the Uruguayan government in relation to the COVID-19 pandemic. **Training: Uruguayan Psychoanalytic Association (1975–1980)**

Christopher Bollas, Ph.D., in English Literature, has been visiting lecturer at the University of Buffalo, the University of East Anglia, and Brunel University, and was Professor of English at the University of

Massachusetts from 1983 to 1987 and Visiting Professor of Psychoanalysis at the University of Rome from 1978 to 1999. He trained in psychoanalysis at the Institute of Psychoanalysis in London and in Adult Psychotherapy at the Tavistock Clinic in London. His first book was *The Shadow of the Object: Psychoanalysis of the Unthought Known* (1987) and his most recent work is *Meaning and Melancholia: Life in the Age of Bewilderment* (2018). He is the author of many works of non-fiction, three novels, and five plays. Two books have been written on his work: *The Vitality of Objects: Exploring the Work of Christopher Bollas* edited by Joseph Scalia (2002) and *The Metapsychology of Christopher Bollas: An Introduction* by Sarah Nettleton (2016). He has been described by The Townsend Center (UC-Berkeley) in 2016 as "the most influential psychoanalyst writing in English today," by Al-Haaretz in 2010 as "one of the two most important living theoreticians in the world of psychoanalysis" and by Adam Phillips as "the most evocative psychoanalytic writer we have." **Training: Institute of Psychoanalysis, London (1973–1977)**

Mary T. Brady, Ph.D., is an adult and child psychoanalyst in private practice in San Francisco. She is on the Faculty of the San Francisco Center for Psychoanalysis and the Psychoanalytic Institute of Northern California. Her books, *Analytic Engagements with Adolescents: Sex, Gender and Subversion* and *The Body in Adolescence: Psychic Isolation and Physical Symptoms* were published by Routledge in 2018 and 2016, respectively. She is a member of the Committee on Child Analysis (COCAP) of the International Psychoanalytic Association. She also co-leads a private study group on *The Treatment of Adolescents and Young Adults* and another group, *Trauma on Film*. **Training: San Francisco Center for Psychoanalysis (Adult Program 1993–1998; Child/Adolescent Program 1998–2003)**

Steven H. Cooper, Ph.D., is a Training and Supervising Analyst, Boston Psychoanalytic Society and Institute; Clinical Associate Professor of Psychiatry, Harvard Medical School, and Chief Editor Emeritus, *Psychoanalytic Dialogues*. He has written on a range of topics that include concepts such as the psychic future, evolving conceptualizations of defense, mutual forms of containment in the therapeutic situation, and how to understand the depressive position within both the patient and analyst. He has often explored object relations concepts and theory from the point of view of the analyst's participation. Most recently, he has explored play in the analytic situation, examining in particular how limit is constitutive of play and how play and mourning are linked in paradoxical elements of psychoanalysis. He is the author of *Objects of Hope: Exploring Possibility and Limit in Psychoanalysis* (2000), *A Disturbance in the Field: Essays in Transference-Countertransference*

(2010), *The Analysts's Experience of the Depressive Position: The Melancholic Errand of Psychoanalysis* (2017), and his forthcoming book *Playing and Becoming in Psychoanalysis* will be published by Routledge in 2021. He is an avid fly fisherman and finds it as humbling as being a psychoanalyst. **Training: Boston Psychoanalytic Society and Institute (1980–1986)**

Ken Corbett, Ph.D., is a supervising and teaching faculty member of the New York University Postdoctoral Psychology Program in Psychotherapy and Psychoanalysis. He has published numerous articles in psychoanalytic journals on the topics of gender, queerness, sexuality, and development. He is the author of *Boyhoods: Rethinking Masculinities* and *A Murder Over a Girl: Justice, Gender, Junior High*. He is in private practice in New York City. **Training: NYU Postdoctoral Program in Psychotherapy and Psychoanalysis (1994–1999)**

Elizabeth Corpt, M.S.W., L.I.C.S.W., is a former Past-President, Supervising Analyst, Faculty Member, and Board Member at the Massachusetts Institute for Psychoanalysis, and a Teaching Associate, at the Harvard Medical School, Department of Psychiatry at the Cambridge Health Alliance Program for Psychotherapy. She is currently the Co-Chief Editor of the journal *Psychoanalysis, Self and Context*. She has written, published, and presented nationally and internationally on topics such as clinical generosity, the impact of social class on the forming of an analytic identity, and relational ethics. Ms. Corpt maintains a private psychoanalytic practice in Arlington, MA. **Training: Massachusetts Institute for Psychoanalysis (1995–2001)**

Dianne Elise, Ph.D., is a Personal and Supervising Analyst and Faculty member of the Psychoanalytic Institute of Northern California, a Training Analyst member of the International Psychoanalytic Association, and has served on the Editorial Boards of the *Journal of the American Psychoanalytic Association* and *Studies in Gender and Sexuality*. Her over 30 publications include wide-ranging papers on the subjects of gender, sexuality, and erotic transference, appearing in the *Psychoanalytic Study of the Child*, *The Psychoanalytic Quarterly*, *Journal of the American Psychoanalytic Association, Psychoanalytic Dialogues, Studies in Gender & Sexuality,* and *Psychoanalytic Inquiry,* as well as several book chapters. Elise's book, *Creativity and the Erotic Dimensions of the Analytic Field* (Routledge, 2019) expands her work in innovative ways and presents her contemporary thinking on erotic life in psychoanalysis. She is in private practice in Oakland, California. **Training: Psychoanalytic Institute of Northern California (PINC) (1994–1998)**

Haydée Faimberg, M.D., is a Training and Supervising Analyst at the Paris Psychoanalytical Society, APA (Argentina), International Distinguished Fellow (British Society). She created the Conference on Intracultural and Intercultural Psychoanalytical Dialogue; Co-chaired the British-French clinical annual meeting (1994–2004). First Chair of the First Working Party on Clinical Issues, in the European Federation (EPF), followed (among other Working Parties created afterwards) by the Working Party on Faimberg's method (practiced in the three IPA continents), using in another field her clinical concept "listening to listening" (1981) (always used with the *psychoanalytic method*). She is the first author to publish on Melanie Klein's "case of Richard" in the light of certain Lacanian concepts (1976); first author to link ([1998] 2012) the concept of *après coup* with "Fear of Breakdown" (Winnicott); and first author to discover (2013) Winnicott's use of the Paternal function as early as 1955. "The Snark Was a Boojum" ([1977] 2005) reads nonsense as the *logic of the unconscious.* Her principal book is *The Telescoping of Generations: Listening to the Narcissistic Links Between Generations* (2005). She received The Mary Sigourney Award 2013 for outstanding contributions to psychoanalysis. Dr. Faimberg is in private practice in Paris. **Training: Asociación Psicoanalítica Argentina (IPA) (1964–1970)**

Jay Greenberg, Ph.D., is a Training and Supervising Analyst, William Alanson White Institute; former Editor, *The Psychoanalytic Quarterly;* former Editor for North America, *International Journal of Psychoanalysis*; former Editor, *Contemporary Psychoanalysis*; Co-author with Stephen Mitchell, *Object Relations in Psychoanalytic Theory*; author, *Oedipus and Beyond: A Clinical Theory*. Author of more than 80 papers on psychoanalytic theory and technique. Recipient, 2015 Mary S. Sigourney Award for Outstanding Achievement in Psychoanalysis. In Private Practice in Manhattan. **Training: William Alanson White Institute (1974–1978)**

Adrienne Harris, Ph.D., is Faculty and Supervisor at New York University Postdoctoral Program in Psychotherapy and Psychoanalysis. She is on the faculty and is a supervisor at the Psychoanalytic Institute of Northern California. In 2009, she, Lewis Aron, and Jeremy Safron established the Sandor Ferenczi Center at the New School University. She writes about gender and development, analytic subjectivity, ghosts, and about the analysts developing and writing around the period of the First World War. She, Lewis Aron, Eyal Rozmarin, and Steven Kuchuck co-edit the Book Series *Relational Perspectives in Psychoanalysis,* which has published over 90 books. She is an editor of the IPA ejournal, *Psychoanalysis Today* and serves on the Editorial Boards of *Psychoanalytic Dialogues, Studies in Gender and Sexuality,* and *Psychoanalytic Perspectives*. She is the author of *Gender as Soft Assembly,* co-edited over seven books with other authors, and has been co-editor with Lewis Aron of the Relational Psychoanalysis

Series Vol. 2–6 (Vol. 3 included Melanie Suchet as co-editor). **Training: NYU Postdoctoral Program in Psychotherapy and Psychoanalysis (1980–1985)**

Stephen Hartman, Ph.D., is an executive editor of *Psychoanalytic Dialogues* and a co-editor of *Studies in Gender and Sexuality*. He practices in San Francisco and New York City, and teaches at the Psychoanalytic Institute of Northern California (PINC) and on the Relational Track at the NYU Postdoctoral Program in Psychotherapy and Psychoanalysis. Stephen is the author of several articles and book chapters that address object relations theory from the standpoint of emerging technologies, the socio-politics of psychoanalytic encounter in an intersectional matrix, and the interface of digital culture and the practice of psychoanalysis. His recent publications include *Hashtag Mania or Misadventures in the #ultrapsychic* as well as essays and blog posts that explore working in a psychoanalytic frame mediated by COVID-19 and the politics of race. Stephen is an avid long-distance cyclist and a Yoga Alliance certified Kula Vinyasa Yoga instructor. **Training: NYU Postdoctoral Program in Psychotherapy and Psychoanalysis (1998–2006)**

Ilana Laor, Ph.D., is a clinical psychologist and group analyst. Currently, she is a board member and the president of the Israeli chapter of IARPP. Laor teaches and supervises at the Psychotherapy Program: Core and Relational Track at Tel Aviv University, Sackler School of Medicine. Laor also initiated a special project called "Chavruta" (ancient Hebrew for "in company") at the relational track Tel Aviv University. For four consecutive years, she conducted the project, bringing together artists, writers, film directors, bible scholars, judges, and brain researchers, who met with psychoanalytically oriented professionals, in order to share thoughts and hold discussions that were of mutual benefit. She was the former owner and Director of Ramat Aviv Institute, a private clinic certified by the Israel Ministry of Health for internship in clinical psychology, for analytical therapy for children and adults, individual, group, and couple therapy, relationally oriented. She writes on the relational consulting room, and the analytic process and has been published in professional journals, in both English and Hebrew, and has published "relational" children's books. She is in private practice in Tel Aviv. **Training: Group Analytic Institute, Tel Aviv (2001–2004)**

Nancy McWilliams, Ph.D., teaches at Rutgers University's Graduate School of Applied & Professional Psychology and practices in Lambertville, New Jersey. She is the author of *Psychoanalytic Diagnosis* (1994, rev. ed. 2011), *Psychoanalytic Case Formulation* (1999), and *Psychoanalytic Psychotherapy* (2004) and is associate editor of both editions of the *Psychodynamic Diagnostic Manual* (2006, 2017). A former president of Division 39

(Psychoanalysis) of the American Psychological Association, she has been featured in three APA videos of master clinicians. She is on the Board of Trustees of the Austen Riggs Center. Her books are available in 20 languages; she lectures widely both nationally and internationally. She is currently working on a book on psychoanalytic supervision. **Training: National Psychological Association for Psychoanalysis (1973–1978)**

Stephen A. Mitchell, Ph.D., was a clinical psychologist/psychoanalyst and considered a founder of Relational psychoanalysis. Mitchell was Faculty and Supervisor at New York University Postdoctoral Program in Psychotherapy and Psychoanalysis and one of the founders of the Relational Track, Founding Editor of Psychoanalytic Dialogues, a highly influential scholarly quarterly that continues to bring Relational Psychoanalysis to a wide audience and was a supervising and training analyst at the William Alanson White Institute where he had trained. Mitchell served as Editor for the journal's first 10 years (1990–2000) and of the International Association of Relational Psychotherapy and Psychoanalysis (IARPP). His first book was co-edited with Jay Greenberg, *Object Relations in Psychoanalytic Theory* (1983), became a classic textbook in graduate schools and post-graduate institutions. He went on to author numerous articles and books: *Relational Concepts in Psychoanalysis* (1988), *Hope and Dread in Psychoanalysis* (1993), *Influence and Autonomy in Psychoanalysis* (1997), *Relationality* (2000), *Can Love Last?* (2001), and, with Margaret Black, *Freud and Beyond: A History of Psychoanalytic Thought* (1996). **Training: William Alanson White Institute (1972–1977)**

Thomas Ogden, M.D., is the author of 12 books on the theory and practice of psychoanalysis, as well as literary readings of Frost, Borges, Kafka, and others. His recent volumes include *Reclaiming Unlived Life*; *Creative Readings: Essays on Seminal Analytic Works*; *Rediscovering Psychoanalysis*; *This Art of Psychoanalysis*; as well as two novels *The Parts Left Out* and *The Hands of Gravity and Chance*. His work has been published in more than 20 languages. Ogden's honors include the 2004 International Journal of Psychoanalysis Award for the Most Important Paper of the year; the 2010 Haskell Norman Prize, an international award for Outstanding Achievement in Psychoanalysis; the 2012 Sigourney Award; and the 2014 Hans Loewald Award for Distinguished Contribution to Psychoanalytic Education. He teaches, supervises, and practices psychoanalysis in San Francisco, where he also teaches creative writing. **Training: San Francisco Psychoanalytic Institute (1979–1986)**

Donna Orange, Ph.D., Psy.D., was educated in philosophy, clinical psychology, and psychoanalysis. She is faculty at New York University Postdoctoral Program in Psychotherapy and Psychoanalysis and at the

Institute for the Psychoanalytic Study of Subjectivity, and teaches in private study groups. She held the Freud Fulbright in Vienna in 2018. Recent books are *Thinking for Clinicians: Philosophical Resources for Contemporary Psychoanalysis and the Humanistic Psychotherapies* (2010), *The Suffering Stranger: Hermeneutics for Everyday Clinical Practice* (2011), *Nourishing the Inner Life of Clinicians and Humanitarians: The Ethical Turn in Psychoanalysis* (2016), *Climate Justice, Psychoanalysis, and Radical Ethics* (2017), and *Psychoanalysis, History, and Radical Ethics: Learning to Hear* (2020). **Training: Institute for the Psychoanalytic Study of Subjectivity (1987–1991)**

Michael Parsons, M.D., is a Fellow of the British Psychoanalytical Society and a member of the French Psychoanalytic Association. His first degree was in philosophy, classical literature, and ancient history, after which he trained as a doctor and became a psychiatrist. His analytic training was at the Institute of Psychoanalysis in London where he became a Training Analyst of the British Psychoanalytical Society. He worked in private psychoanalytic practice in London and is now retired from clinical work. He has strong links with psychoanalysis in America and Europe (he was elected to membership of the French Association in 2009), and is internationally known as a teacher and lecturer. He has a particular interest in links between psychoanalysis and other fields such as art, literature, and religion. He is the author of *The Dove that Returns, The Dove that Vanishes: Paradox and Creativity in Psychoanalysis* (Routledge, 2000) and *Living Psychoanalysis: From Theory to Experience* (Routledge, 2014), and co-editor of *Before I Was I: Psychoanalysis and the Imagination. Collected Papers of Enid Balint* (Free Association, 1993). **Training: Institute of Psychoanalysis, London (1978–1982)**

Bruce Reis, Ph.D., FIPA, is a Training and Supervising Analyst and Faculty Member at the Institute for Psychoanalytic Training and Research, New York; an Adjunct Clinical Assistant Professor in the New York University Postdoctoral Program in Psychotherapy and Psychoanalysis; and a member of the Boston Change Process Study Group. He is Regional North American Editor for the *International Journal of Psychoanalysis* as well as the North American book review editor. He has previously served on the editorial boards of *The Psychoanalytic Quarterly* and *Psychoanalytic Dialogues*. He is the co-editor (with Robert Grossmark) of *Heterosexual Masculinities* and author of *Creative Repetition and Intersubjectivity* (2020). **Training: NYU Postdoctoral Program in Psychotherapy and Psychoanalysis (1996–2002), Institute for Psychoanalytic Research and Training (2011–2013)**

Avgi Saketopoulou, Ph.D., is a Greek and Greek-Cypriot analyst, trained at the NYU Postdoctoral Program in Psychotherapy and Psychoanalysis.

She is on faculty at her home institute as well as the William Alanson White Institute, the New York Psychoanalytic Institute, and other NYC-based training programs. She serves on the editorial boards of several analytic journals. Her writing orbits around psychosexuality, race, and consent, and she is currently at work on a solicited book manuscript provisionally titled "Overwhelm: Risking Sexuality Beyond Consent." With Jonathan House, she co-planned the event called "Laplanche in the States: The *Sexual* and the Cultural," (Fall 2021) the first conference in the United States dedicated to the work of Jean Laplanche. **Training: NYU Postdoctoral Program in Psychotherapy and Psychoanalysis (2003–2014)**

Jill Salberg, Ph.D., ABPP, is clinical associate professor, consultant/supervisor at the NYU Postdoctoral Program in Psychotherapy and Psychoanalysis, faculty/supervisor at the Stephen Mitchell Relational Study Center, Institute for Contemporary Psychotherapy, and member of IPTAR. She is the editor of and contributed to *Good Enough Endings: Breaks, Interruptions and Terminations from Contemporary Relational Perspectives* (2010). She has co-edited with Sue Grand, *The Wounds of History: Repair and Resilience in the Transgenerational Transmission of Trauma* and *Transgenerational Trauma and the Other: Dialogues Across History and Difference* (2017), both won the Gradiva Award (2018). She has conceived of and co-edits the Book Series, *Psyche and Soul: Psychoanalysis, Spirituality and Religion in Dialogue* at Routledge/Taylor&Francis Group. She is in private practice in Manhattan. **Training: NYU Postdoctoral Program in Psychotherapy and Psychoanalysis (1982–1989)**

Stephen Seligman, Ph.D., is Clinical Professor of Psychiatry and Behavioral Sciences at the University of California, San Francisco; Joint Editor-in-Chief Emeritus of *Psychoanalytic Dialogues*; Training and Supervising Analyst at the San Francisco Center for Psychoanalysis and Psychoanalytic Institute of Northern California; and Clinical Professor at the New York University Postdoctoral Program in Psychotherapy and Psychoanalysis. He is the author of *Relationships in Development: Infancy, Intersubjectivity, and Attachment* (Routledge) and co-editor of the American Psychiatric Press' *Infant and Early Childhood Mental Health: Core Concepts and Clinical Practice.* **Training: San Francisco Center for Psychoanalysis (1991–1997)**

Joyce Slochower Ph.D., ABPP, is Professor Emerita of Psychology at Hunter College & the Graduate Center, CUNY. Joyce is faculty and supervisor at the NYU Postdoctoral Program, Steven Mitchell Center, the National Training Program of NIP (all in New York), Philadelphia Center for Relational Studies, and the Psychoanalytic Institute of Northern California in San Francisco. Joyce has published over 100 articles on various aspects of psychoanalytic theory and technique.

Second Editions of her two books, *Holding and Psychoanalysis: A Relational Perspective* (1996) and *Psychoanalytic Collisions* (2006), were released in 2014 by Routledge. She is Co-Editor, with Lewis Aron and Sue Grand, of *De-idealizing Relational Theory: A Critique from Within* and *Decentering Relational Theory: A Comparative Critique* (Routledge, 2018). She is in private practice in New York City where she sees individuals and couples, runs supervision and study groups. **Training: NYU Postdoctoral Program in Psychotherapy and Psychoanalysis (1982–1987)**

Melanie Suchet, Ph.D., is Clinical Associate Professor, NYU Postdoctoral Program in Psychotherapy and Psychoanalysis and Faculty member at the Stephen A. Mitchell Center for Relational Studies. She is an associate editor of *Psychoanalytic Dialogues* and a contributing editor of *Studies in Gender and Sexuality*. She is the originator and co-editor of *Relational Psychoanalysis: Volume 3* dedicated to bringing to the fore newer ideas, especially political and social issues. She is co-editor of the Routledge book series Psyche and Soul. She works and has written articles on the edges of psychoanalysis, attempting to bring into the center what has been excluded and dissociated. Her interests also lie in the analyst's subjectivity, and specifically in the subject positions the analyst holds with respect to race, class, gender, and sexuality. Her private practice is in Manhattan. **Training: NYU Postdoctoral Program in Psychotherapy and Psychoanalysis (1994–2004)**

Chana Ullman, Ph.D, is a Clinical Psychologist, a Training Psychoanalyst, and faculty at the Tel Aviv Institute of Contemporary Psychoanalysis. Dr. Ullman is faculty and supervisor at the Relational Track, the School of Psychotherapy, Sackler School of Medicine at Tel-Aviv University, and faculty at the doctoral program of Psychoanalysis at Tel Aviv University. Dr. Ullman is past-president of the International Association of Relational Psychoanalysis and Psychotherapy. She is the author of the book *The Transformed Self: The Psychology of Religious Conversion* (Plenum Press, 1989) and of numerous publications regarding witnessing, political context, and the psychoanalytic process from a relational perspective. She lives and practices in Rehovot, Israel. **Training: Tel Aviv Institute for Contemporary Psychoanalysis (2002–2007)**

Acknowledgments

Over the years, there have been close colleagues who have been important to my growth and development and have also been good friends. My dialogues with them, both real and imagined, always engage me, and result in enlarging my thinking and work. My appreciation and affection to Lew Aron, Seth Aronson, Galit Atlas, Andy Druck, Sue Grand, Melinda Gellman, Dodi Goldman, Linda Jacobs, Bruce Reis, Joyce Slochower, and Melanie Suchet. I have been part of a wonderful writing group for nearing two decades and it has transformed me and my writing. I remain indebted to Carole Maso, our writing teacher and a good friend, and to members Annabella Bushra, Anita Herron, Linda Luz-Alterman, Melanie Suchet, and Alexandra Woods whose support and intimacy make writing possible.

Additionally, my first edited book was part of the Relational Book Series and was overseen by Adrienne Harris and Lew Aron, each offering me mentorship, warmth, and guidance. Lew's friendship was mutually supportive and his interest in my Credo project helped spark this book; while his death has been a loss, his love for psychoanalysis and his friendship will always endure within me. Adrienne's guidance continues to be a wonderful ballast helping me discover my ideas and my voice. Her support for this book has been invaluable.

My student's engagement with the task of creating their psychoanalytic sensibility early in their training has encouraged me to keep formulating my own. I have great appreciation for their openness and their new vision of what psychoanalysis could be. While it is often said that we learn from our patients, I sincerely feel a debt of gratitude to those people who trusted me and the process, allowing me to keep learning through our time in conversation and in silence.

Lastly, I am indebted to my husband Michael whose supportive acceptance of the many hours spent up close to my computer working on the writing and editing work of this book has been profoundly important. His love and care allows me the fortitude to keep growing.

Editor's Introduction

Jill Salberg

The Latin word *credo* means a statement of the beliefs or aims which guide someone's actions. It can be extended to how someone lives or works. Developing a psychoanalytic identity, a set of beliefs that inform the analytic enterprise is, in many ways, the scaffolding of psychoanalytic training, although neither the development of this identity nor a credo has been a focus in the literature. I imagine it has been implicitly assumed as a byproduct of the study of theory, of supervision, and of clinical work with patients.

In all likelihood, this nascent identity and early credo does not become fully inhabited until one has been working as a psychoanalyst for some time. When I asked my analyst when I would feel more confident working as a psychoanalyst, his response suggested that it would take 10 years postgraduation from the institute. Many in my generation remember having been told something similar, that it takes time and years of experience and personal growth.

In my involvement with teaching and coordinating the First Year Introduction to Contemporary Psychoanalysis at my institute, NYU Postdoctoral Program in Psychotherapy and Psychoanalysis, I have seen our role as faculty to be the task of ushering in and welcoming candidates into psychoanalysis. Beginning psychoanalytic training can be daunting and I remember wanting to learn and rely on theories and the history of psychoanalytic ideas—to find the facts or rules to follow. Now, after 40 years of working as a psychoanalyst and teaching, I understand it is perhaps best to start analytic training with questions, with issues in the clinical work that need to be sorted out, thought through differently. It is in so doing, hopefully, that curiosities are opened up, and that the need for answers to fade.

A number of years back, I began assigning an assortment of articles from the literature that are personal credos and ones on developing a psychoanalytic identity. Every year I found the entering candidates responding enthusiastically to these pieces. They are hungry to learn from analysts about how they formed their ideas and thinking, what influences have shaped those ideas, what theoretical leanings have been important, and what aspects of personal life have informed and shaped them. It is with this in mind that I conceived of a book that would include reprints of some of these important papers/credos while also inviting other analysts to write new pieces. I wanted to include selections across the theoretical spectrum of what might be loosely considered an American version of the British "middle school,"[1] drawing from writers identified with Relational, Object Relations, Contemporary Freudian, and Kleinian/Bionian as well as those who don't easily fit categorization.

In this volume, I felt that a broad section of writers would be crucial and ones that cross other domains: multi-theoretical, multi-generational, trained at different institutes and different eras, and across cultures. The layout of the book speaks to generations and decades of analysts' training and includes the following: 1960s (Sheldon Bach and Haydee Faimberg); 1970s (Ricardo Bernardi, Christopher Bollas, Stephen Mitchell, Jay Greenberg, Nancy McWilliams, and Michael Parsons); 1980s (Lewis Aron, Jessica Benjamin, Steven Cooper, Adrienne Harris, Thomas Ogden, Donna Orange, Jill Salberg, and Joyce Slochower); 1990s (Mary Brady, Ken Corbett, Elizabeth Corpt, Dianne Elise, Bruce Reis, Stephen Seligman, and Melanie Suchet); and 2000s (Stephen Hartman, Ilana Laor, Avgi Saketopoulou, and Chana Ullman).

Additionally, I felt it would be interesting to have essays from people early on in careers, in mid-career and later in their careers. It certainly makes a difference when you write a credo, whether you are looking back over a career or just setting on a path and looking around to contemporaries or even looking ahead. The era that one trains in will clearly have an imprint, but *when*, in one's professional career one writes a credo, becomes another vector in terms of their focus. Interspersed among these decades you will also see International (UK, Israel, Argentinian/France, and Uruguay) and North American analysts, a cross-fertilization of the socio-cultural and psychoanalytic cultures which is often interesting in terms of the zeitgeist in which ideas are formed, taught, and reformulated. While some people name their influences, it is also interesting to notice how similar ideas take hold in different locales and cultures.

I suggest you also look to see with whom they are in dialogue, whose thinking have they dwelled upon or diverged from, and where they have taken a theory and changed it in some personal way. For many of us, it is our contemporaries/peers—with whom we are meeting in peer supervision, discussing cases with or in reading groups with—who become influential in crucial ways. While not always explicitly stated, we are often actually in dialogue with peers and write from that position and, in this way, a kind of cross-pollination occurs. This mutual influence is deeply important and, as a female analyst, I have found it an important form of mentorship. Analytic work is fraught with anxiety and isolation; we have to absorb and carry our patient's traumas, sufferings, longings, and hopes. Having colleagues with you in the trenches has been enormously important and sometimes under-recognized. No less poignant is the extent to which individual sensibilities come into play. Even analysts from the same generation sharing similar theoretical orientations often diverge in how their personal sensibilities (Goldman, In Press) inform their relationship to their own theory and what draws them to or what is most salient in their work.

I find that when I write I often try to discover what it is I actually think and know. Not infrequently I am surprised by how much further I can take a thought if I commit to writing about it as if I'd hadn't quite known that a spring of an idea might, with immersion, reveal a deep, expansive source. Something may also change in the writing, in the attempt to fully explicate what you believe in. In struggling to articulate what I am thinking about, the writing moves me to form the ideas that have, thus far, been unformulated. It is almost an act of creative will that summons into being what I have been thinking. It is an exercise worth the difficulty, and one that additionally adds to the formation of a psychoanalytic identity.

First Psychoanalytic Credo

In psychoanalysis, many of us associate a credo with Ghent's (1989) article, "Credo: The Dialectics of One-Person and Two-Person Psychologies." This article was Ghent's bold announcement of having formed a new set of beliefs, a new credo and psychoanalytic identity. For a few years prior he was, with Stephen Mitchell, Philip Bromberg, Bernie Friedlander, and others, working to establish the Relational Track within the NYU Postdoctoral Psychoanalytic Training Program. The article and the track were birthed simultaneously. But that would be a limited understanding of this article, only as a declarative statement of a new theoretical orientation, although it was very much that indeed. Ghent was enacting simultaneously what he was writing about in his credo.

In his article, Ghent demonstrated an understanding that as analysts we often are operating from a belief system that may be unformulated, existing out of awareness. His urging students to engage in the writing exercise, something I too have tried in the introductory course at the NYU Postdoctoral Program, highlights the difficulty and resistance. There is an odd paradox that he suggests, an assumption that we all have a working credo that can, however, remain unknown.

My experience in encouraging candidates to write their credo, as well as working on writing my own, informs my sense of how difficult it is to reconcile what we consciously think we believe with what we implicitly operate from: our unconscious intuitive beliefs and biases. I have the sense that for Ghent his writing expanded what he initially saw as a shift in theoretical orientation, a moving to a more expansive, integrative point of view. As the article continues, we see him systematically review theorists and theories that have been important and influential in his thinking. In some cases, he dismantles the theory, revealing its limitations, in others he demonstrates what he believes holds the greater value.

Ghent also posed, "How does one choose one's theory? Or is it that, unbeknownst to ourselves, we are chosen (p. 173)?" This question is elegant in its simplicity and also its complexity. How do we sort through all the theories we encounter, landing upon what speaks to our understanding of people; their difficulties in living and loving, in thwarted and stalled development, and in finding and sustaining satisfaction in work? Our psychoanalytic world has broadened, theoretically, internationally, and interdisciplinary in its reach and scope.[2] Our influences, both inside and outside the field, are varied and I believe need to be more saturated by history—past and current—and engaged with the very changes that are currently occurring within the culture and the social and political realm. We need to be sensitive to how complex our identity formation can be. If it takes a village to raise a child, it certainly necessitates a wider lens to understand a person in their culture, of a particular moment in history, within racialized and class/caste social structures that include fluid and non-binary gender and sexual expressions.

Ghent's article and ideas became imprinted in many who trained with him and in 2012 *Psychoanalytic Dialogues* launched a series entitled "Credo," referencing Ghent's earlier paper. The editors Anthony Bass and Hazel Ipp saw it as, "an ongoing feature in the journal, where we will publish brief essays by psychoanalysts around the world in which they will formulate their current thinking about the fundamental values, idea, observations, and beliefs that shape their approach to clinical work (p. 1)." I have used many of these Credos when teaching and, while Ghent urged his students to write a credo at the beginning and ending of his course, my own appeal to candidates is that they write one during the Introductory course and then again when they are graduating from the institute. *When* during your professional career you write a credo fittingly suggests that it is an evolving process and that you are always growing as a candidate and later as an analyst, and this will be reflected in changes in one's credo. Adrienne Harris suggests writing a credo at the beginning of one's career and then late in the career (Personal Communication), suggesting not only that one is evolving but also that experience and the stage in your life itself will change what you believe and will be reflected in your credo.

Earlier than the Dialogues project, *Psychoanalytic Inquiry* (starting in 2002 and completing in 2009) dedicated four entire journals to writers throughout the world asking their authors to write about how they became the analysts they are today. (First Issue (2002, vol. 1): psychoanalysts trained within the American Psychoanalytic Association (APA); Second Issue (2004, vol. 4): psychoanalysts in the USA trained outside of the APA; Third Issue (2005 vol. 5): psychoanalysts trained in South America; Fourth

Issue (2009, vol. 3): psychoanalysts trained in the British Psychoanalytic Society and practice in Britain.) I also included some of these papers in my teaching since the emphasis was on the development of the analyst. Many of those writers felt that particular theories and theorists directly influenced them, while others found that their work with patients enabled them to listen and to evolve a more personal psychoanalytic sensibility.[3]

There have been two other books that, in some way, also suggest the desire for analysts to write from their own experience and learn from reading about other's. These books, *Psychoanalytic Conversations: Interviews with Clinicians, Commentators and Critics* (2000) by Peter L. Rudnytsky and *The Voice of the Analyst: Narratives on Developing a Psychoanalytic Identity* edited by Hillman and Rosenblatt (2018), have been formative in creating what might be considered a genre in psychoanalytic literature which this book will join and expand to include credos.

It was my aspiration in editing this book to provide companionship to analysts in training and analysts still evolving in their psychoanalytic journey. Here, in these pages, you will find credos of great interest: intelligent, poignant, filled with struggle, and hard-earned insight. The hope is that each might in some way provide company, illumination, and inspiration. These essays reflect a compelling record of the journey: where we have come from, what we grapple with now, and where we might be going next. To read and find inspiration in someone else's essay is to see a path, to learn how a credo was built and perhaps see new ways forward aided and lit by the journey of others.

Notes

1 Spezzano (1995) first describes and refers to "American Middle School might be the school of affect, representation, and intersubjectivity (p. 23)," while Chodorow (2004), in a slightly different vein, refers to an American Independent Tradition.
2 Psychoanalysis has been greatly influenced by neuroscience, infant-mother research, critical theories on gender and race to name a few.
3 See Bott Spillius (2009) and Johns (2009), respectively.

References

Bass, A., & Ipp, H. (2012). "CREDO": Editor's Introduction to a New Series of Essays. *Psychoanalytic Dialogues*, 22(1), 1.
Bott Spillius, E. (2009). On becoming a British psychoanalyst. *Psychoanalytic Inquiry*, 29(3), 204–222.
Chodorow, N. (2004). The American Independent Tradition: Loewald, Erikson and the (Possible) Rise of Intersubjective Ego Psychology. *Psychoanalytic Dialogues*, 14(2), 207–232.
Ghent, E. (1989). Credo: The Dialectics of One-Person and Two-Person Psychologies. *Contemporary Psychoanalysis*, 25(2), 169–211.

Goldman, D. (In Press). Winnicott's Moon. In J. Aguayo (Ed.), *Winnicott in America*. Oxford, UK: Oxford University Press.

Greenberg, J. R., & Mitchell, S. A. (1983). *Object Relations in Psychoanalytic Theory*. Cambridge, MA: Harvard University Press.

Hillman, L., & Rosenblatt, T. (2018). *The Voice of the Analyst: Narratives on Developing a Psychoanalytic Identity*. London and New York: Routledge.

Johns, J. (2009). How Do You Get Where You Want to Be When You Don't Know Where You Want to Be? *Psychoanalytic Inquiry*, 29(3), 223–235.

Mitchell, S. A. (1995). Commentary on "Contemporary Structural Psychoanalysis and Relational Psychoanalysis." *Psychoanalytic Psychology*, 12(4), 575–582.

Rudnytsky, P. L. (2000). *Psychoanalytic Conversations: Interviews with Clinicians, Commentators and Critics*. Hillsdale, NJ: The Analytic Press.

Spezzano, C. (1995). "Classical" Versus "contemporary" Theory: The Differences That Matter Clinically. *Contemporary Psychoanalysis*, 31, 20–46.

Section 1

1960s

Chapter 1

My Journey*

Sheldon Bach

The integration and disintegration of mind and body has fascinated me ever since I began to study psychology more than half a century ago. Even as a child I was curious about how it was that some people seemed so at home in their bodies while others seemed to inhabit their bodies with ill grace, as if they were on temporary loan.

As a young man I witnessed the devastation of minds and bodies and of bodies politic in Europe during World War II. After the war ended I lived, worked and studied in Paris for a number of years. My sense of my own un-integration that began in my childhood and my interest in altered states and transformations was compounded by my disruptive experiences as a GI: the sudden confrontation with life and death and the abrupt immersion in the strange and unfamiliar culture of a war-torn Europe.

I remember the culture shock that I experienced after the war when I was going to school on the GI Bill at the Sorbonne. In the United States, I had been given a taste of English literature from Beowulf to Thomas Wolfe in one crowded freshman semester. In Paris, the professor wrote one line of poetry on the blackboard and this line, examined from many aspects, was our text for the year. As an impressionable young man, I was smitten by what I saw as the European outlook on life, and it took me a long time to integrate these two different perspectives.

But the existence of multiple perspectives became a given in my own life, and my thought was fueled by the postwar thinkers, political scientists, and poets who were each, in their own ways, trying to see if any sense could be made of the great psychological traumas of the war and the Holocaust. I thus became interested not only in Freud, at a time in the 1950s when his presence dominated American psychiatry, but also in the great analytic

---

* Reprinted with kind permission: This chapter was first printed as part of the Introduction of Sheldon Bach's book, Chimeras: and Others Writings: Selected Papers of Sheldon Bach which was published by IPBooks in 2016.

DOI: 10.4324/9781003206248-1

traumatologists, such as Ferenczi and Winnicott, who seemed to me to be dealing with the very issues that I found so pressing.

When I returned to America I tried my hand at a number of pursuits, including writing, comparative literature and film making, all of which I found fascinating but at none of which I excelled. To help understand what was going on, I began my first analysis, and this soon inflamed me to become a psychologist.

Both luckily and unluckily, my first analyst was not formally trained, so he neither interpreted this desire away nor dissuaded me from my ambition. I enquired and learned that the NYU Clinical Program was at that time considered tops in the country, so I applied there despite never having taken a course in psychology and despite assurances from the person who interviewed me that my chances for admission were infinitesimal. I afterwards learned that in the end I had been accepted under their policy of admitting one "oddball" each year.

At NYU I happened by good luck to stumble into the Research Center for Mental Health where George Klein, Robert Holt, David Rapaport, and others were conducting cutting-edge research into psychoanalytic theory.

I was excited and fascinated by the ongoing studies of alternate states of consciousness, of dream imagery, of LSD trances and of subliminal stimulation. I was intrigued also by our unsuccessful attempt to increase the sale of popcorn at movies by subliminally projecting EAT POPCORN! onto the screen. The atmosphere in which we all thrived was that of an academic, grant-supported and research-oriented thinktank with a slightly nutty character, exemplified to my mind by a distinguished-looking Middle European psychiatrist who used to come to his laboratory cubicle on occasional afternoons, unpack an ancient violin, and dreamily play selected arias to experimental subjects while releasing vials of perfume in pursuit of his investigations into sensory synesthesia.

By contrast, the seminars that David Rapaport gave us on Freud's dream book were unparalleled examples of Old World scholarship. Rapaport would distribute two or three questions about the two pages of Chapter VII that were our text for the week. Although our small group was composed of some of the most distinguished scholars around, including George Klein and Robert Holt, to the best of my recollection hardly anyone ever answered a question to Rapaport's satisfaction, and he would then bolster his arguments by quoting Freud chapter, page and verse from memory. Two years later when I applied to be his research assistant at Austen Riggs and told him that I had spent a month reading Erikson's *Childhood and Society* with Robert Holt, he responded that he himself would read that book with his class at the New England Institute, but of course they spent a whole year reading it during which time they usually only finished the first chapter or two.

When in 1957 I interned at Jacobi Hospital in the Bronx, I had a chance to experience not only the immense variety of pathology on display in a city hospital, but also to encounter many of the greatest analysts of the day including Mahler, Greenacre, Jacobson and Hartman, some of whom would frequently come up to do Grand Rounds. The training I received at Jacobi and Einstein was first-rate and absolutely invaluable and I became best friends with two psychiatrists there, William Grossman and Lester Schwartz with whom I later wrote the paper on the Marquis de Sade. But I also had my first taste of discrimination against non-medical people there because of the rigid hierarchical system that then prevailed in most all hospitals and institutes. There were many restrictions on psychologists doing psychotherapy and even after I became licensed it took about two years of active politicking before I was given permission, as an exception only, to open a private practice while still at the hospital. How much this situation has reversed itself in only 60 years might give us pause to contemplate the relationship between science, politics, morality and money.

Working with the extraordinary analytic thinkers whom I met there was a heady experience. When I finished my doctorate, I wanted to apply to the New York Psychoanalytic Institute for training but found that as a psychologist I could only be given "research" training and would have to sign a pledge never to actually practice psychoanalysis. At that time a number of my colleagues went along with this requirement, received excellent if rigid training and, of course, are now practicing, but somehow I found this requirement unacceptable and instead enrolled in the NYU Postdoctoral Program in Psychoanalysis that was just opening. This was, I believe, the first University-based psychoanalytic program in the country. Its initial class enrolled some candidates who had been waiting for years for the opportunity to obtain this kind of official training in psychoanalysis, an historic event for psychologists.

The moving force behind NYU Postdoc was Bernie Kalinkowitz, although many others, including a number of medical analysts, worked very hard to make it happen. Many of these early candidates were more mature and experienced than typical postdoctoral students at the time and among them I was lucky enough to find my peer group, which has met once a month for over fifty years. We have voraciously consumed large tracts of the psychoanalytic literature and also discussed many of our own papers, for we turned out to be a productive group. Over the years we have also voraciously consumed large quantities of food and good wine for, as Heinz Hartmann noted in a letter to Kohut, one of the few compensations for the discomforts of aging is that the wines you drink tend to get better and better.

As for my personal views on psychoanalysis, I was trained in the Freudian tradition and still feel that my roots grew there, and that a developmental and dynamic way of thinking remains essential for what I consider to be analysis. If Freud were alive today he would be writing very differently than he wrote in 1939, for he understood the very provisional nature of his thinking better than most of his followers did. Some other great influences on my thinking and practice have been Ferenczi, Balint and Winnicott, many poets and artists of all descriptions, and the infant researchers and observers who have begun to discover the non-verbal rhythms of life and to translate them into ways of being with our patients.

When I first opened my private practice in 1962, I worked for a few hours into the night after a full day at the hospital. Naturally, my first referrals were recently-discharged patients, so I found myself treating severely disturbed people before the advent of psychotropic drugs. Amazingly, these people appeared to get better at a rate that seems little different from what it is today, but of course I have not done a controlled study and perhaps my memory fails me here. We should recall, however, that there is now considerable hard evidence that being with people and talking with them in the right way can change their brain chemistry and architecture in ways similar to psychotropic drugs, sometimes with fewer negative side effects.

My early experience with patients usually regarded as difficult or intractable influenced me enormously because I found that the model of classical psychotherapy I had been taught worked well enough with certain people but was ineffective or even downright harmful with others. Not wanting to be in the position of asserting that my treatment was correct and that it was the patient who was either faulty or untreatable, I began to explore different ways of viewing the therapeutic situation.

I was impressed primarily with my mishandling of narcissistic vulnerabilities and as I was trying to reflect on this I stumbled first upon Kohut and then upon Winnicott. Kohut's work was an immediately accessible revelation to me and seemed to spell out the direction my thoughts had been taking. I later had the privilege of meeting him and of speaking at some self-psychology conferences. When Mahler somehow heard that I was going to Chicago, she summoned me to her office to tell me to explain to "Heinz" that she, Margaret Mahler, thought he was wrong about separate lines of narcissistic development. She seemed convinced that if I reported to him what she thought, he would certainly change his mind!

As important as Kohut's writings were, to me the picture always seemed a bit more complicated and eventually I turned to Winnicott for guidance. I was there in 1968 when he gave his famous talk at the New York Psychoanalytic Society on "The Use of an Object," a talk that was met with incomprehension and bewilderment, even by Edith Jacobson whom I so much admired. I also found the paper intriguing but confusing, primarily because I had not yet amassed enough experience of the way he was managing patients to fully comprehend his theory.

Eventually I tried to formulate my evolving understanding in the paper, "The Narcissistic State of Consciousness" and in a book, *Narcissistic States and the Therapeutic Process* in 1985. I focused on issues of both the "inflated" and the "deflated" narcissist, a concept of narcissism that some have found useful. It seemed that working with narcissism led inevitably to dealing with sadomasochism and classical "perversions." After seeing many people with both and thinking it over for a number of years I published my tentative views in *The*

Language of Perversion and the Language of Love in 1995. While I have always been primarily interested in how one works with challenging patients in the clinical situation, treating sadomasochism and perversions unsurprisingly led to questions about the nature of love and the particularly vexing question of love in the analytic situation. That is the subject matter of my later book, *Getting from Here to There: Analytic Love, Analytic Process.*

Over the course of time, I have encountered children and adults of all ages who suffer from disorders of the self; ranging from Kohut's delineated narcissistic character disorder which requires a coherent self to be analyzed, to psychotic-like disorders where the patient lacks the feeling of any sense of self or identity, has little or no connection to his body or to authentic or enduring feelings and often has only a flickering awareness or none at all that the self he might experience was externally imposed or imitated by him and is not an authentic growth from the inside of his being.

Much of this I discuss in *Chimeras*, including the crucial issue of how it is that one person can take in another person's different views, thoughts, and body feelings in such a way that they become an authentic part of his true identity, and not just a submission, an idealization, a projective identification or an addenda to a false self.

All in all, I have been working in the area of psychology for more than sixty years now. I continue to practice, teach and supervise because I find it utterly fascinating and, aside from plentiful vacations, I cannot imagine what else I could be doing with my time that would be more gratifying. I think that we in this field have very special obligations but also very special privileges, and that one of our privileges is the opportunity to obtain a unique view of the human mind at work, as well as the opportunity to further our own self-improvement while being paid for the privilege.

Contrary to the usual pessimism encountered these days, I am optimistic about the future of psychoanalysis because I cannot believe that our method of healing people by talking with them is ever going to disappear, not-withstanding the current co-optation of the field by the pharmaceutical-industrial complex. Psychoanalysis has long remained in a self-imposed isolation from which it now seems to be emerging. Today it is forging ties with neuroscience, academic attachment research, traumatology, early infancy programs and other real-world involvements. We have amassed over a hundred years of reflection, experience and research by some of the best scientists of the time on the subjective aspects of the human mind, and we have inherited an incomparably diverse literature. I believe that so long as people continue to think, that effort will not be lost.

Chapter 2

My Journey: Haydée Faimberg Interviewed by and in conversation with Graciela V. Consoli and Ezequiel A. Jaroslavsky*

Haydée Faimberg

Ezequiel A. Jaroslavsky (EAJ):

Some time ago you published an article, and recently a book, on *The Telescoping of Generations*, based on the case of Mario, who underwent psychoanalysis with you in Buenos Aires. It seems to me that this led to your subsequent theorizing about the telescoping of generations. What could you tell us about this?

Haydée Faimberg (HF):

On account of two patients who were in analysis with me in Buenos Aires in 1970, Mario and Jacques, I began looking for an adequate theoretical framework for the clinical situations that they presented. It became clear to me, perhaps because I started to listen in a different way at that time, that the evolution of those two patients provided a clinical response to theoretical issues and questions that I had *not yet* formulated.

Mario is an exemplary case: psychically, he remained a huge distance away. He was psychically *absent*, but it made no sense to interpret that absence because he was not there to listen to me. At a crucial moment, when he came to a session to announce that he had to interrupt his analysis, paradoxically, we came closer to one another than at almost any other time. It was in that session, I can say now, which changed the course of my analytical thinking.

I will synopsize what occurred with Mario. At the time he announced that he had to interrupt his treatment (as inflation was gnawing away at his small income and not leaving him enough to live on until the end of the month), Mario expressed distress, interest and an obvious desire to continue. I was

---

* Reprinted with kind permission: This interview was first published online with the same title in Publicada en la Revista Psicoanalisis e Intersubjetividad No. 4 (online) December 2008 – ISSN No.: 1850-4116 https://www.intersubjetividad.com.ar/entrevista-a-haydee-faimberg/

DOI: 10.4324/9781003206248-2

surprised, since he seemed so far from any relationship with me or with reality. He told me that a friend had suggested that he buy dollars (which we did at that time in Argentina to protect ourselves from spiraling inflation causing the peso to be greatly devalued.) As to the question from his friend as to whether he knew how much a dollar was worth, Mario had answered that a dollar was worth two pesos. As he was telling me that, Mario smiled affectionately and, by a gesture, seemed to be checking that something was still in his pocket. He then added in a completely offhand and casual way that his friend had told him that a dollar was worth 5,000 pesos. What caught my attention was both the enormous disparity between the two dollar values and the discrepancy between his detached way of telling me about this and the affectionate concern that he showed about something that he seemed to have in his pocket.

Fearing that this was his last session, I felt compelled to say something to him, while at the same time finding it hard to put into words what I wanted to say. What Mario was saying was enigmatic in the twofold sense that I did not know what he meant and that what he was saying brought me surprisingly closer to him than ever before.

The first line of approach that I found consisted in my telling him *how I was hearing what he was saying*. I formulated something that I later considered to be a construction: I said to him that there must be something very important in his pocket, something that referred to another time and another era, and that perhaps it was related to dollars that were worth two pesos. This I inferred from the smile and the gesture that I have just described to you. I also added that *I didn't know* what he was talking about, but that *perhaps he knew*. In that case, I was wondering if he had any idea who those dollars were for.

After saying this, I felt deeply shaken, *because I was talking about something and I did not know what it was, although I was reassured to think that I had told him that I did not know: ethically I felt at peace with the idea that we did not know, but that perhaps he knew, and in that case we could find out who the dollars were for*. To my surprise, Mario immediately replied, "I know who those dollars are for", showing an emotion *that I had never seen in him*. After adding, "those dollars are for my father's family", he began to tell me the story of his father, a Polish Jew who had migrated to Argentina in the 1930s, who had sent dollars to his family in Poland during the war until one day the money order was not cashed. Mario commented, "My mother says the whole family must have been wiped out. And that my father was never the same, he never spoke of the family again and never told us anything: it was my mother who told me all this".

So that session posed a key problem for me, because I realized that the patient was not really absent, *he was in another place and in another epoch*, in another time and in another space, I did not have an analytic theory to account for what had happened in that session.

Mario was able to continue his analysis. A year and a half later, he told me that he had asked his mother where Aunt Rita was; and that his mother had been surprised that Mario knew of the existence of that aunt. He continued: "Then my mother told me that when she was pregnant with my brother..." (Mario had never told me that he had a brother, he had never talked to me about a brother.)

I learned that about his brother, and that his sister was born later. Mario continued: "My mother told me that when she was pregnant with my brother (and clarifying for me, said: I was five years old), Aunt Rita had a fit of madness (she was his mother's sister, he said) and they put her into a home: she was never spoken of again. I asked about her and I went with my brother (who was now a doctor), to visit her. I told her everything that had happened in the last 25 years, I brought her to my house and now I have her at home; I set myself as an example to teach her to wash herself and I am connecting her with the world. This happened three months ago, but I couldn't tell you until today".

Then I said to him that he did not know how to *talk to me* about a secret, that the only thing he could do was put me in the same secret position that he had been in and in which he did not speak, did not play, was not the same (these were the same words used by his mother to describe the father's situation).

On the basis of the twists and turns of that analysis, I wondered what theory could account for what had happened to us clinically. (This is the subject of chapter 1 of my book.)

Then again, in 1970, a very creative patient, Jacques, a writer who was in his fourth year of analysis, began the session by narrating a dream. He said that he had dreamed of a lunar landscape; time seemed to have stopped; there was a grotto from which a very curious man came out, as though sewn together from different pieces. (I thought of Frankenstein.) Jacques added: "It was as if it was me and not me at the same time." He remained silent and associated: "it makes me think of a Russian landscape". As he is a very intelligent man, with a great capacity for symbolizing, I was struck by the realism with which he added: "It cannot be... it is a Russian landscape *and I have never been to Russia*, so it is very strange that there was a Russian landscape in my dream". For my part, I associated his description with Chagall's paintings. As I said, I was surprised by his realism in saying, "I was never in that place." Jacques went on to say (with the same realism), "My father and my grandfather must have known that landscape because they are both Russian." For me, the sense of an enigma grew, the sense that something was happening that I could not theoretically account for.

In chapter 9 of my book, (chapter 10 in the Argentine edition) I return to that case and show how, by narcissistic resistance, an analyst can block listening to new material. I could not account at that time, either theoretically, or in the transference, for what was happening. But at the same time, I *could not not say* that I was hearing *something new*. I therefore devoted an entire chapter of the book to talking about the analyst's narcissistic resistance to listening to new material that he cannot account for: either because his theory cannot contain it, or because in his own transference he has not experienced it, or again because the institutional context and the psychoanalytic culture in which he was trained do not contain it either.

Despite all this narcissistic resistance studied *après-coup* or retroactively, I was able to interpret that what he was telling me was formed of different pieces and that those pieces belonged to different times, different spaces. We were talking about his associations, about the realistic way in which he spoke of the Russian landscape, of the fact that his father and grandfather were both Russian and how he then began for the first time to tell the story of his family. He said that his father, the youngest of several brothers in a Jewish family in Russia, had been destined from the beginning to be a laborer, and excluded from the possibility of studying. The patient entered treatment with the problem of writer's block; after four years of analysis, he had achieved a very important unblocking, he had gone back to writing, to creating; and as a result of his psychic changes, he had married and, one year earlier, had become a father. But all these changes had been accompanied by an anxiety crisis, by a real negative therapeutic reaction: the better he became, the worse he became, his anxiety increased.

I told him that he was saying in a dream, through the associations he presented, that he was composed of pieces from different times and spaces, and that a part of him seemed to be telling me that he was, like his father, condemned to not being able to do the things he most liked doing in his life. Additionally, Jacques had brought another important association. He had said to me: "Do you remember when I told you that my father was always going to swallow me, that he wanted to drink me all up? Now I realize that what I really mean is not that he was going to eat me up, but that I am angry that he never wanted to go beyond the position that his father had assigned to him."

At that point I formulated the interpretation that I have just spoken of.[1] With these two patients, I felt that I had found "*answers to questions that I had not yet formulated*" (as a say in the introduction to my book): and I carried this problem with me when I emmigrated to France, like an enigma in my mental baggage. I was very interested in reviewing the theories of Winnicott and Melanie Klein in the light of Freudian theory, revisiting Freud and all the Argentine analysts who are so dear to me. Among them I include Enrique Pichon Rivière, José Bleger, Willy Baranger and Jorge Mom, (who was my analyst). They have been my pillars. David Liberman has also been very important to me. (I mention them in the acknowledgments part of my book as the interlocutors with whom I maintain an uninterrupted dialogue. This ongoing internal dialogue was not only crucial for me, but is vital for all analysts to have sustaining them in their work and continuing development.)

Following my immigration to Paris, I was led to compare psychoanalytic cultures. But already in Argentina it went without saying that cultures were compared, this was how studying and learning occurred. I hope that it is clear that Bleger and Pichon Rivière knew all the international books that were written, and felt at home with all the British, French, and American authors. You can see this in the 1947 study by Enrique Pichon Rivière, in which he compares types of delirium according to the German classification and the French classification. He revisits Lacan's ideas (about paranoia), the views of Rouart and others, and takes a fresh look at the work of Lagache, concluding that *all this reading gives grounds for thinking that the structuralist conception is the right one at this time for thinking about psychiatry psychoanalytically*. And Bleger, in his 1955 work where he talks about the glischrocaric nucleus, refers to the work of Pierre Marty on the allergic personality (published that same year in the *Revue Française de Psychanalyse*).

I was immersed in that culture, and studied from 1959 at the School of Dynamic Psychiatry created by Enrique Pichon Rivière, where all medical students had the huge good fortune to study psychiatry in the light of psychoanalysis. They even looked kindly on students who, like me, had not finished medical studies, requiring only that we were in analysis. I inquired if I could attend when I had not yet studied psychiatry, and Bleger's response was: "Indeed you can, you have not yet been deformed by traditional psychiatry, and those are the kind of students we want, in addition to those who are already analysts." Suddenly I, who was a medical student and had not yet studied psychiatry, would attend courses at the School of Dynamic Psychiatry every Monday where, in the first course, Pichon Rivière expounded his single-disease theory; then Bleger, Liberman, Rolla and Taragano would speak. For example, Rolla spoke about epilepsy and Dostoevsky, Liberman about hysteria. Bleger was very interested in making methodological distinctions and in working on psychotic and non-psychotic functioning. We split into discussion groups that lasted more than two hours. I was incredibly lucky to find myself with Bleger.

So for a year we viewed dynamic psychiatry in the light of psychoanalysis. The dialogue that we had in that School formed the very core of the internal dialogue that I referred to, a dialogue that continued in me when I left Argentina and moved to France. Crucially, in that dialogue our 'not-knowing' was respected. Bleger valued above all our ability to ask questions, he helped us put into words questions about what we did not know, and we pursued a dialogue that reached far and embraced much... it was a deeply moving enterprise. And so suddenly I knew about Kanner's autism as if it was the most natural thing in the world, whereas later I came to know that it had been very little written about before. I knew about Kanner's autism before I even knew how the psyche was formed, but then from that time on we would talk to Bleger about the formation of the psyche. These are absolutely unforgettable things, because respect for not knowing is part and parcel of this internal dialogue; it opens up the possibility of approaching someone who knows and with whom together we can find the words for the situation and the words of dialogue (a dialogue still ongoing today without Bleger, who died when he was just 49 years old).

This internal dialogue continued, allowing respect, not shame, for what I did not know and what I did not understand in the session. Because I knew there was someone inside, Bleger, Pichon Rivière and my other teachers, who allowed me, in my not knowing, that I could only come to know with the patient, and that was the essence of the situation. I believe that without the support that this type of dialogue gave me, my emigration would have been very different.

When I arrived in France, I started to think about how I could develop a dialogue with the members of the Paris Psychoanalytic Society where I had to give my lecture. In 1981 I gave my first lecture and the following year was appointed Titulaire en Fonction Didactique, which in France at that time was the equivalent of a training and supervising analyst. To that end, I presented together two pieces of work: one, *The telescoping of generations*, in which I included the case of Mario, the case of Jacques and a third French case, but for the purposes of this situation I presented only Jacques, despite the fact that Mario was much more eloquent. Then I presented *Narcissistic resistance to listening*, from which emerged a more structured exposition of the concept of the function of "listening to listening" (1981). Listening to how the patient listens to the analyst's interpretations and silences ("listening to listening") enabled me to listen to the narcissistic identifications of the telescoping of generations. And that led me to link clinical concepts to theoretical concepts that are important to me.

In order to link the Mario case and the Jacques case to theoretical concepts that I had not yet developed, the study that I had carried out in Buenos Aires with Guillermo Maci on the work of Freud was important to me. In particular "Instincts and their vicissitudes" (1915), and also of "On narcissism: an introduction" (1914). Those articles were central to the realignment of analytical thinking that I had already studied in Argentina, where all the Anglo-Saxon authors were naturally included, but also the French. Besides the people already mentioned, whom I consider teachers (in the particular sense of teaching a way of thinking, of dialoguing), let us not forget Willy Baranger (who also was my supervisor) with whom I studied for many years in private seminars on Melanie Klein and Lacan; as with Liberman (who also was my supervisor).

With Bleger I must add that, in addition to taking his seminars and being supervised by him, I studied Introduction to Psychology and the Psychology of Personality in the Department of Psychology where he taught, and I also led discussion groups with students for the Introduction to Psychology (which included mostly but not only psychoanalysis).

So, picking up the thread of what I was saying, in that 1981 lecture, whereby I introduced myself to the Paris Psychoanalytic Society (the lecture was entitled *Narcissistic resistances to recognizing otherness and the difference of generations*), I combined two papers. One was *The telescoping of generations* (in which I could only talk about the case of Jacques), and the other which was published the following month in the *Revue Française de Psychanalyse* was a study entitled *Narcissistic resistances to recognizing otherness*. The second part (*and the difference of generations*) was very long and was not published on that occasion.

Graciela V. Consoli (GVC):

Was the Mario case published in the APA Revista de Psicoaálisis as well?

HF: It was published in the *Revista de Psicoanálisis* (Argentine Psychoanalytic Association) after I presented it again in Hamburg (1985). The International Congress that took place in that city was an extraordinary experience, because it was the first to be held in Germany after the war. *The telescoping of generations* that I had presented for the IPA Congress in Helsinki (1981) was not accepted on that occasion. I put it in a drawer and four years later I decided to present it in Hamburg when I saw that the topic was "Identifications and their vicissitudes", considering that my central thesis on telescoping refers to alienating identifications combining three generations, which is the mode of transmission. I was faced with the problem of language. The work for Helsinki had been presented originally in English. For Hamburg in 1985 I felt more at home in French. I also presented it in English, but with some misgivings.

What was it then that I had touched on in my unpacking of that text? I consider that I had touched a crossroads where many currents of analytical thought were coming into being, emerging ideas *which, however, I had not yet read*, that fitted in with my thinking. And it was then, in the discussion, that I first encountered Ferenczi's work, because when I attended seminars in Argentina almost no one was reading Ferenczi. He had been erased from the history of psychoanalysis by what Jones had referred to as Ferenczi's psychosis, until later when he was rehabilitated, in particular through the influence of Balint. However, we did read some of his clinical texts. For example, Ferenczi's (1949) work on the confusion of languages I did not know. When I wrote for the *International Dictionary* directed by Alain de Mijolla an article on intergenerational relations, I looked exhaustively into what had been done up to that time and discovered that Ferenczi was at the origin of a way of seeing how the adult intervenes in the structuring of the psyche. His article on the confusion of languages was a radical turn in our thinking about how the psyche is structured.

So, going back to Hamburg, after my presentation of *The telescoping of generations*, I saw people I did not know greeting me in a friendly way. Then an analyst approached and told me that listening to my work made him understand something very important about his own analysis. I asked him what that something was. There is a point when you discover that you are saying things that you do not know you are saying, and when you are saying more than you think you are saying. This is the point where "listening to listening" becomes so important to me. That person had heard something being said in my work that I had not *yet* heard. He said to me: "I know now why I never spoke in my analysis of what my parents had done in Germany during the war: your presentation gave me the key." I kept silent and did not discover what key I had given him. He continued: "Now I found out why, it was because I knew the answer; unconsciously I knew what they had done and that is why I did not want to know, because I unconsciously identified with them." And this is very interesting to me, helping me formulate something. Many years later, in 2001 I think, the 50th anniversary of the German Psychoanalytic Association (DPV) was celebrated and I was invited to participate. The event took place in Frankfurt. They asked me to talk about the psychic consequences of Nazism on the basis of the ideas I developed in the book. And in that presentation of mine in Frankfurt, who did I see in the front row? – Why, that same German analyst!

GVC: In other words, you had given him the key.
HF: *And he had given it to me, to me too, a key that I consider even more interesting.*
EAJ: Another question, Haydée, concerns your ideas, which were put forward a long time ago. Those ideas grew out of the permeable relationship that you developed with your patients and from the openness to theory of your teachers who helped you, as well as your own openness to what you did not know. But how do you see this confluence of ideas, which was also evident here in France with Abraham and Torok (1994) regarding transgenerational relations, and later authors such as René Kaës, Micheline Enriquez? How do you see this question that in some way has become an object of study, namely, different ways of considering the links between generations?
HF: That is an important question. You know, I wrote a chapter that was added to *The Telescoping of Generations* in the Amorrortu edition, (added: and published in Reading French Psychoanalysis; complete bibliography) which does not appear in the original English edition, nor in the Italian one. And that was because I was very interested in publishing that chapter, which was not accepted for the English edition as it was considered superfluous. I specially asked Horacio de Amorrortu to include it in the Spanish edition and I am very happy that he was kind enough to agree. The chapter is titled "Listening to the telescoping of generations" (1988),

chapter 3 in the Spanish edition. That text was intended for a seminar that did not take place owing to the tragic death of Micheline Enríquez. Micheline was a profound analyst and a person of great value. She had invited me to her seminar (the fourth group, Piera Aulagnier's group) to discuss a topic that we both deal with, from our different perspectives. She had very generously stressed to me the importance of après-coup reconstruction in my approach, which I had not compared from different points of view. Micheline had stressed to me the value it had for her, and that was why she invited me to the seminar, because of the concept of *Nachträglichkeit*, of *après-coup*, which I brought to bear on the problem (of alienating identifications combining three generations).

Actually, I must make it clear that if I approached it in this way, it was because the relationship between generations (until I was faced in 1970 with the two clinical examples already mentioned) had never previously held my attention as such in itself (I had no expectation in that regard). So because of a problem, which I could call a *clinical methodological* problem, I discovered (without having previously considered the matter) that alienating identifications combining three generations represent an unexpected and surprising retroactive discovery, about something that was silently happening during the analytical process, at a key moment, following the appearance of a story pertaining to another generation (the story of the father told by Mario or what Jacques related by association from the dream).

Surprisingly, a patient's association with a story that belongs to another generation leads to the discovery of alienating identifications that are then reactivated (but that were mutely present all along). So that led me to understand and write that the telescoping of generations and alienating identifications are a retroactive, *après-coup* discovery. Micheline Enriquez had particularly appreciated my approach and invited me to discuss our ideas at her seminar. A week before the date set for the seminar, she died in a tragic car accident, at a very young age. Micheline was an extraordinary person. When a tribute was organized the following year, I was invited to participate, both in the day-long event that I attended, and in a publication in *Topique* (the journal directed by Piera Aulagnier). At that point I realized that I could not recreate a seminar that had not taken place or imagine a dialogue that tragically had not occurred (even though I imagined what that discussion might have been like). I therefore chose to reflect on the case of a patient of Micheline Enriquez, Catalina, included in another contribution to *Topique*.

In that article, which was my tribute to Micheline, I noted that although my ideas had been compared with those of Nicolás Abraham and María Torok, at the time that I had presented them in those texts I had not been aware of those authors' contributions (I thought that they were Kleinians, because the translation into French of one of Melanie Klein's books contains an introduction by María Torok, on mourning). Nicolás Abraham had died a year before I arrived in France; Maria Torok, for her part, had left the Paris Psychoanalytical Society, and was a member of the group "Confrontation" (with Serge Leclaire among others). So I did not know them personally nor had I read their texts. When I presented my ideas about the telescoping of the generations, Alain de Mijolla compared them with those of Abraham and Torok (de Mijolla, whose ideas followed on from theirs, had written about the unconscious fantasies of parents).

Retroactively, I felt compelled to compare my ideas with theirs and asked myself how we were the same and how we were different. Irrespective of whether or not we had read one another, they (more exactly Maria Torok, since Nicolás Abraham had passed away) *had not read me and I had not read them.* I then discovered the differences. I was coming from a country where we had given so much attention to the depressive position and mourning (which are important I must add) and projective identification, I found it interesting to set aside those concepts to investigate in a new epistemological space. As an illustration of the problem of grief, the Mario case is ideal; so ideal that saying that it is an unfulfilled grief is obvious. What happens, I wondered, if I force myself not to think of it as obvious and try to discover something else. Insofar as the problem of grief arose only through the father's story, I found it interesting to put it aside methodologically, both the concept of grief and that of projective identification: two concepts that I could have drawn on to get around the enigma. Having left those three concepts out, I followed a totally different path from that of Abraham and Torok whose work follows upon ungrieved losses.

When I began comparing the work, I realized that, having consciously set aside those two concepts, it was clear that I was not coming to any of the conclusions regarding grief that they uphold through the concept of the crypt. But what interested me was that I had singled out *Instincts and their vicissitudes* and *On narcissism: an introduction* for the reasons I said and, of course, they had also singled out *Instincts and their vicissitudes.* So we had chosen the same article for different but convergent reasons and we seized on a number of very interesting common elements. Later I discovered why they had singled out *Instincts and their vicissitudes*; I it was because Freud introduced the concept of introjection that he took from Ferenczi, which I had not noticed because I was not familiar with Ferenczi's works at the time. We drew upon the same article, but our readings or understandings had been different.

EAJ: I am interested in the link to a particular Hungarian school of thought because I know that Nicolás Abraham had been in analysis with Béla Grunberger. Grunberger had been in analysis with

Ferenczi. Additionally, Ferenczi had also had as a disciple Imre Herman, who in 1942 published an article on dual unity that influenced Bowlby and Melanie Klein. Imre Herman's model is very similar to J. Bleger's model of the glischrocaric position, of symbiosis, that is, the idea of an initial narcissistic fusion. I say this as a digression because I find it interesting to think about how similar theoretical developments are articulated, which originate from different authors without having been linked to each other.

HF: Speaking of similarities and differences, I said to myself that it was important to specify, retroactively, *what lay at the core of my own thinking*. And this analysis appears in the chapter "Listening to Telescoping of Generations." I came to the conclusion that the essential thing in my reasoning is to propose the concept of Oedipal Configuration (by convention I capitalize this concept), where, on the one hand, we find an expression of the child's desire for his or her parents, which constitutes the Oedipus Complex, and on the other hand, the type of relationship that the parents had with the child, as reconstructed in the analytic session. In the Oedipal Configuration, as I propose it, there is a place for the discovery of the "*object of the object*" (for example the father's father, that is to say, the child's grandfather), in other words, of three generations. The concept of the Oedipus complex is not broad enough for this operation. If we continue with this comparison, I also realize that, for methodological reasons, by setting the concept of mourning aside (phenomenological *epoché*), I was intent on studying in particular "the narcissistic dimension in its linkage with the oedipal conflict", a linkage that I propose through the concept of the Oedipal Configuration. The telescoping of generations is a particular case of the narcissistic dimension of the Oedipal Configuration.

If I reconstruct the history of my debt regarding these concepts, I can say the following. Enrique Pichon-Rivière said something at a time when I could not yet grasp its full implications. I am referring to two comments that stayed in my mind to be understood "later". There came a time when I was able to penetrate the enigmatic character of Pichon-Rivière's two statements. The first comment was as follows:

In an informal conversation, Enrique had said that it was probably necessary to accept that the triangle, the triangular relationship, constitutes the epistemological limit of knowledge. When I found myself able to begin working through certain ideas and, in the light of what I saw in respect of narcissistic functioning, I conceived and then developed the idea that *a triangle can function as a narcissistic triangle*. The fact that the relationship is triangular is no guarantee that it is oedipal in nature (these ideas are developed in chapter 2 of the book).

Additionally, the other idea of Pichon Rivière was that in the consulting room there are more protagonists than there are official protagonists. By this he meant that both the patient and the analyst bring their own Oedipal constellation.

I wish to add something about countertransference. It is a complex relationship between what we do as analysts in working psychically with our patients and the simultaneous functioning of our unconscious. How can we set the limits of this obsessively delicate balance (as analysts) between intrusion and appropriation, which patients already suffered in their object relationships with their own parents,[2] and how this gets repeated in the analytical relationship? Nor should we isolate our unconscious obsessively, since it is good for us to draw on what we perceive and think and on our experience of countertransference.

In this connection, I have a story to tell you about Bion that I consider to yield an essential truth. In 1968 when we were students at the Institute of the Argentine Psychoanalytic Association, we supervised in a group in Buenos Aires a presentation given by one of us after listening to Bion's lecture entitled "Without memory or desire". The situation which was presented to Bion was one in which the analyst interpreted on the basis of an association that he made with something that had occurred in another session and therefore the interpretation emerged from that association. We expected a very severe criticism from Bion, because we had taken at face value the idea that we must listen 'without memory or desire.' But Bion strongly agreed with our fellow student's interpretation. We looked at each other in surprise and we asked him how it was possible for him to accept such an interpretation based on the analyst's memory. Bion replied, that the analyst's memory of prior sessions should not be carried as if to know or be predictive. However, if in the session the analyst has an association that the patient has encouraged, why shouldn't we take it into account, it's the psychic work of the analyst listening to the patient. In response to the "without memory and without desire" Bionian myth, I understood that Bion had not said something impossible, such as not having any desire or memory, he had spoken of a *listening position.*

When, in turn, I speak of a listening position, I am referring to the active position proposed by Bion when he uses the term (taken from Keats) of "negative capability". Returning to the Mario case, clearly my countertransference position made me listen to what I was listening to. When I spoke to Mario about pesos and dollars I ended my speaking with, "I don't know what I'm talking about but perhaps you do." We see here a very curious encounter, between my own personal knowledge, going back to when I was a child, and all the rest; in my words to him, I stripped away the personal elements of mine that could have led me in a completely different direction. What is more, I would say that I didn't understand him when he told me that the dollars were for the parents' family in Poland, I said to myself as I was listening to him: But why? What happened? I hadn't even yet realized that the family had emigrated. So my insight, my openness to that idea, was effected by a personal association about the value of the dollar from a long time ago. But there was an openness to listening, clearly there was an openness to listening and that marks out the road between: What does the analyst contribute and what does the patient contribute? I am thinking of *open-ended, non-saturated interpretations, where not knowing can be heard*, where the patient would have to fill the gaps, where I listen to how my patient listens, completes, rectifies, makes me think otherwise.

I very much regret that I did not explicitly develop the concept of the link as I learned it from Enrique Pichon Rivière, but it is always implicit in my thinking, as is also the concept of *unconscious family inscription*, which exists in the Mario case because he is unconsciously inscribed in a family structure. Starting from the concept of unconscious family inscription, colleagues who work with families were very appreciative of what I brought from individual analysis. Because even in individual analysis, unconscious family inscription can be detected.

EAJ: What do you think about whether the unconscious (also the family unconscious) is more easily able to express itself according to the organization of the session? I know that you addressed this issue in your treatment of the individual cure, in a flawless, beautiful and very readable style, but it seems to me that in a family setting, family therapists are advised to look out for the emergence of situations involving, in addition to the generations of parents and children present in the family, one or two preceding generations.

HF: I will answer by quoting myself from the introduction in my book:

"Freud constructed a new theoretical object: the concept of the Unconscious and a new method for gaining access to this world...In most of the chapters, answers from different perspectives are attempted to the following key questions: Can we propose a theory for listening to narcissistic links between generations without the Ego's narcissistic beliefs of being, as Freud puts it, the 'monster in its own house'? Can we propose a, so to speak, 'non-narcissistic theory' (i.e. a theory that studies narcissism but does not espouse the Ego's narcissistic beliefs) of listening to narcissism?

EAJ: I think it's an excellent answer, what is more I think it could be the last word...

CODA

My affiliation gave me different psychoanalytical languages to be in dialogue with, in recognition of otherness (in opposition to the narcissism of the small differences).

I was both honored and touched to receive in 2013 the Mary Sigourney Award, given that year for Europe– an award that for nine years had not been bestowed on an analyst in France (after J.-B. Pontalis and Joyce McDougall in 2001 and Alain de Mijolla in 2004).

In the preface of my book I say "This book describes a journey that I compare to my quest for the 'Snark'. For those readers who do not remember too clearly what kind of object a Snark is and how it may be hunted, I recommend that they read the final chapter, 'The Snark was a Boojum'. Among other 'instructive lessons', they will see the important role played by nonsense in revealing the existence of other types of logic – *the logic of the unconscious, and its trademark, humour*."

I had published in 1976 in the Revista de Psicoanalisis the case of Richard published by Melanie Klein in the light of the three register of Lacan, the war (Richard was following the war, where was the father) and the non-unilineal temporality (*après-coup*). My idea of a broader concept of *Nachtraglichkeit* has its origin in that very first publication.

And my very dear French colleagues recognized this and gave their time to personally discuss both articles with us. I wish to thank them: J.-B. Pontalis, J. Laplanche, A. Green, S. Leclaire, P. Aulagnier, M. Neyraut,V. Smirnoff, J. McDougall, M. de M'Uzan, C. Racamier (who had studied Spanish to read Marie Langer!), D. Widlöcher, S. Viderman, G. Rosolato and Christian David (to whom I am so grateful because he accepted my proposal to publish in 1981 Simbiosis y Ambiguedad in the collection he directed, fil rouge, PUF with Viderman. He trusted my judgment, knowing that the reviewers were not prepared yet to understand Jose Bleger at that time.

My article on Klein led to Pontalis and Gantheret inviting me to teach in discussions groups on Melanie Klein at the University, only one year after arriving in Paris.

My studies and case researches on the telescoping of generations with the unconscious narcissistic alienated identifications where three generations are condensed, was recognized and appreciated so that I was honoured to be a guest speaker at the thirtieth anniversary of the Psychoanalytical Association of France. I was to rethink and speak as to why the concept of unconscious identification was considered in France as a pre- Freudian concept. Jean Florence wrote an excellent thesis on identification in the work of Freud. He was the first person coming from abroad that I invited to my seminar at the Societé Psychanalytique de Paris.

My very first seminar was given on the article of Psychoanalysis of the psychoanalytical frame by Jose Bleger, which was worked on the whole year.

I proposed an adventure to Christopher Bollas: he would be the first foreign analyst invited to give a lecture in the Paris Psychoanalytic Society. And he was, with the friendly help of André Green. Then came others...I close this credo sharing how intensely valuable my early training was in turns of being encouraged to not know the answer, to be listened to in a way that allowed me to think and to treat my patients with the respect that my teachers, supervisors and analyst gave to me.

References

Abraham, N. & Torok, M. (1994). *The Shell and the Kernel Vol.1*. Chicago: The University of Chicago Press.

Faimberg, H. (1981). "UNE DES DIFFICULTÉS DE L'ANALYSE: LÀ RECONNAISSANCE DE L'ALTÉRITÉ L'écoute des interpretations. *Revue Française de psychoanalyse*, 45 (6): 1351–1367.

Faimberg, H. (1996). "Listening to Listening." *The International Journal of Psychoanalysis*, 77: 667–677.

Faimberg, H. (1998). "The Telescoping of Generations: Genealogy of Certain Identifications." *Contemporary Psychoanalysis*, 24: 99–117.

Faimberg, H. (2005). *The Telescoping of Generations: Listening to the Narcissistic Links between Generations*. London and New York: Routledge, Taylor and Francis Group.

Ferenczi, S. (1949). "The Confusion of Tongues Between the Adults and the Child: The Language of Tenderness and of Passion." *The International Journal of Psychoanalysis*, 30: 225–230.

Freud, S. (1914). On Narcissism: An introduction. *S.E.* Vol.XIV: 67–102.

Freud, S. (1915). Instincts and their Vicissitudes. *S.E.* Vol.XIV: 109–140.

Pichon-Rivière, E. (1947). "Psicoanálisis de la Esquizofrenia." *Revista de Psicoanálisis*, 5 (2): 293–304.

Section II

1970s

Chapter 3

What After Pluralism? Ulysses Still on the Road*

Ricardo Bernardi

IT IS NOT EASY TO CONVEY WHAT IT MEANS TO BE A PSYCHOANALYST in Montevideo. I do not refer to the problems of understanding and explaining it, but to something much simpler. After saying "Montevideo," very frequently there comes—especially if our interlocutor is from another continent—a long silence that is embarrassing for me. Should I say where Montevideo is? If I do, my interlocutor may feel I do not trust his knowledge of geography. But if I do not, the misunderstanding may be major. So I decide to say very quickly that Montevideo is the capital of Uruguay, a little country between Argentina and Brazil located on the Río de la Plata.

More or less the same thing happens when I have to refer to my psychoanalytic identity. Some 15 years ago I was part of the scientific committee of the International Congress of Psychoanalysis and somebody asked me what my approach was in psychoanalysis. At that moment, I did not know what to say. Obviously I had thought about it—I had just written something on the topic—but I realized that the defining elements of identity probably meant very little to someone coming from a different cultural context. I said, "Freudian, but actually trying to recover elements of a local tradition that has undergone a strong British influence on one side and French influence on the other." And fortunately, at that point I decided to stop talking. Too many words for a question apparently so simple. But now it is time to deal again with that question, which never really was a simple one, and to relate episodes of a personal and collective odyssey around pluralism. In my personal journey, pluralism was a point of departure, not of arrival. This forced another question to take the leading role: once a plurality of theoretical and technical options is admitted, what direction should we take?

To fully understand my odyssey into psychoanalysis, it will be useful for me to impart some aspects of the history of psychoanalysis in River Plate.

---

* Reprinted with kind permission: This chapter was originally published as an article with the same title in *Psychoanalytic Inquiry* (2005), 25 (5): 654–666.

Interest in psychoanalysis first appeared in cultivated circles of Buenos Aires and Montevideo in the first decades of the 20th century. In 1938 the Psychoanalytic Association of Argentina was formed, and it developed quickly. In 1956, Willy and Madelaine Baranger, a couple of psychoanalysts of French origin, came to live in Montevideo, where they stayed until 1965, to help the Uruguayan group form its own psychoanalytic society. During this early period, psychoanalysis was clearly Kleinian oriented both in Buenos Aires and Montevideo. It is not easy to say why this is so. The analysts who had come from Europe (A. Garma and C. Cárcamo) had not had Kleinian training there, and the local group was at first interested in various authors. However, in the first issue of the Argentinean *Journal of Psychoanalysis* a chapter of Klein's (1932) book *The Psycho-Analysis of Children* is included. Translated by Arminda Aberastury, it promoted her thinking in Buenos Aires and Montevideo. Kleinian theory, especially the fantasies and primitive mechanisms, quickly became the key to helping neuroses, as well as children's analysis, psychosis, psychosomatosis, group therapy, and so on. Klein's ideas progressively dominated the institutes of the River Plate and some other groups in Latin America. They also spurred original contributions—some of which contain intuitions not completely developed yet—by E. Pichon Riviére, E. Racker, W. Baranger, J. Bleger, D. Liberman, H. Etchegoyen, and others. The Kleinian hegemony continued until the late 1960s, when the influence first of British authors (Bion, Winnicott) and then French authors (especially Lacan) began. By the 1970s, a plurality of approaches was seen in River Plate.

I started my practice as a psychiatrist in the 1970s, and did my psychoanalytic training. I graduated at a time when a new curricular program began in our medical school at Universidad de la República. This change introduced a psychodynamic perspective in the conception of the patient-physician relationship. It was led by Uruguayan psychoanalysts (J. C. Rey, M. Viñar, etc.), with the participation of Argentinean analysts (J. Bleger, H. Etchegoyen). When I got my degree as a doctor in 1969, I was proud to work with this group of analysts. These changes in medical education encouraged the student to take a more active role in his education, following ideas that still exist today. During these years, the Psychoanalytic Association of Uruguay also underwent a process of education reform, in a somewhat similar spirit. This was not coincidence; many of the analysts were working in both institutions. The category of training analyst was replaced by three distinct groups—analysts, supervisors, and professors of the institute—that functioned like faculties with a certain degree of autonomy and separation of functions. An analyst could be part of the three groups or only of one. Candidates had direct representation in some of the meetings of the board of the institute, as was the case at the National University. These changes are still in force and their effect has been positive. Of course, they have not solved all the problems, but they have limited the accumulation of power by small groups and have kept the plurality of orientations open.

While my psychoanalytic training was taking place in an institute where freedom of thought prevailed, in Uruguay, in one of those contrasts so frequent in Latin America, the opposite process was taking place. Loss of democratic freedoms created serious social commotions in Uruguay as well as in Argentina: urban guerrilla movements first, followed by a military dictatorship in power between 1973 and 1985 in Uruguay. It brought about serious human rights violations, and some analysts left the country. I stayed in Uruguay, but I was fired from the university because I did not support the new authorities. This expulsion prohibited my entering any university facility, so I lost my teaching positions as well as my work as a researcher in the Centro Latinoamericano de Perinatología y Desarrollo Humano (CLAP) of the United Nations (PAHO-WHO), which was placed inside the university hospital. The situation meant a civil death: I could not obtain a passport, hold any position in government-funded institutions, direct civil societies, and so forth. It is hard to believe today, but all citizens were classified into three categories (A, B, C); only those acceptable for the government (category A) enjoyed all the civil rights. For example, during those years the Psychoanalytic Association of Uruguay had two lists of authorities: a formal one with the few persons accepted by the police, and an informal one with those who actually did the work but could not do it openly. This makes me praise freedom of thought much more, in society as well as in the psychoanalytic field.

I married Beatriz de Leon (literature teacher and then psychoanalyst), and we had three children. My parents died during this period. The Psychoanalytic Association of Uruguay was very important for me as it was the only scientific group I could be part of. Intellectual endeavors had always had an important place in my life, partly because I was an only child of a middle-class family that regarded professional development highly. I underwent psychoanalysis, which helped me overcome hindrances in my affective life. My first experience was a group psychoanalysis. When I was still training to become a psychiatrist, I participated in a psychoanalytic group treatment that strictly followed the Kleinian and Bionian approaches prevalent in River Plate at the time. The therapist (J. C. Rey) favored interpretations of the group fantasy in the transferential here and now. The group fantasies of a destructive type were given special relevance in the interpretations; this was not arbitrary, since one of the group members died in a car accident, profoundly affecting the group. Many things shocked me in this first contact with psychoanalysis. The interpretations in the here and now made me pay more attention and understand in a different way my feelings as well as those of others. By the time the group finished, something had definitely changed in me. I next underwent analysis for some years with Mercedes Garbarino, with whom I felt united in a quest, difficult at times, in which I experienced great internal freedom. Our psychoanalytic group with its many referential theories favored a less dogmatic attitude on the part of the analyst when facing problems that could be approached from various perspectives. I had a similar feeling during two shorter reanalyses that I underwent later with Sélika Mendilaharsu during hard times in my life. I believe that this freedom during analysis develops a positive disposition toward self-analysis, or at least more tolerance toward what we do not understand in ourselves or in others. This developed tolerance toward uncertainty, plus a less credulous attitude about the explanations that we give ourselves, is a great help in confronting the hardships of everyday life. At moments when my internal problems were more important, this was not enough and I had to go into reanalysis. These re-analyses were short and of low frequency, but they were very useful—an opinion shared by many colleagues in my country.

Between 1975 and 1980, I completed my psychoanalytic training in the Uruguayan Psychoanalytic Association. At that time there were controversial opinions about how convenient it was for an analyst to be entirely devoted to psychoanalysis, leaving aside all other activities. As I said before, the dictatorship forced me to work exclusively in my private practices of psychoanalysis and dynamic psychiatry, while in previous years I had held teaching positions at the medical school, had studied psychology and the philosophy of science, and had held teaching positions in the Psychology Department as well as the Philosophy Department. This is why my admission as a candidate was debated, and as I was accepted, I was told that my multiple interests could be a potential problem. Some years later a colleague in another association brought up the same idea, telling me that he did not think a person could keep his hands suitable for surgery while working as a bricklayer. This seemed to me to be a deeply mistaken conception, for I believe that patients benefit from analysts who keep an active interest in knowledge developed in related areas. Psychoanalytic training around the world sometimes seems more concerned with defending the purity of certain ideal models than with investigating the real benefit patients obtain from these models. It is often assumed that following the ideal model is necessarily the best for the patient and no further search takes place to see to what extent this is so.

Pluralism allows us to recognize that there are different ideal models of "true psychoanalysis"; psychoanalysts must choose the way of working that we consider beneficial for each patient. I appreciated the bright side of pluralism as a candidate and then as a member of my psychoanalytic association for its advantages to the patient. But there is also a dark side of pluralism that appears when it is chosen without adequate critical analysis of the advantages and disadvantages of its different theoretical and technical approaches.

The benefit of pluralism is the freedom to connect with different ways of thinking and of practicing psychoanalysis. An attitude of research—leaving theories standing by—is then necessary. It was fostered among us by Marta Nieto, though it was present throughout the institute already. To be accepted as an Associate Member, I had to present a theoretical-clinical work; I chose a patient who had been for two years especially difficult to approach, for me and for the supervisor. This led us to discuss during supervision the usefulness of continuing with analysis. In that moment I was, by chance, reading a work by Kohut (1971) that turned out to be extremely enlightening regarding this case, and that, with my supervisor's consent, led me to start to interpret in a different way what so far was a narcissistic position impossible to approach. To my surprise and that of my supervisor, this opened the analysis to a series of dreams and grandiose fantasies, what Kohut described as mirror transference, which made the analysis progress. The supervisor became interested in the ideas and encouraged me to present the case. I compared my approach to other theoretical and technical approaches more usual in our community. I tried to show the similarities and differences of Kohut's approach with the Kleinian perspective and with the ideas of some French authors. I never again had a patient with such clear features, and I did not become a supporter of self psychology, even though I always found its ideas very useful in clinical work. But as time went by, I became more critical of the way in which our theories may influence the clinical work.

Each theory tends to generalize its hypotheses, thus making us see the whole analytic field from that perspective. This is why debates that allow confronting various approaches are important. But these controversies are difficult for historical and psychological reasons. When I joined the Psychoanalytic Association, Kleinian dominance had decreased and the most experienced Uruguayan analysts became more and more interested in other approaches, generating different areas of specialization around different authors. So colleagues with special interests in the works of Bion, Winnicott, certain French authors, and others appeared. As time went by, more personal positions, theories, and ways of researching the clinical material were developed. This situation allowed the candidates to get in touch with different ways of thinking since there was always enough freedom to choose analyst or supervisor. Of course, there were also pressures brought about by fashion or by the action of certain partisan groups, but these pressures were not too strong if you did not want to give in to them and this was not really a serious hindrance.

Nor was there a tendency to splitting inside the association. Freud's work, though interpreted in different ways by different trends, served as a shared language, allowing communication among different trends. I believe that the more restricting factor was our tendency to look for similarities among the various orientations, rather than methodically discuss similarities as well as differences. In general—and this is probably something that happens with all publications—psychoanalytic works quote only convergent comments without equally examining alternative hypotheses. In this way, the possibilities of conflict among colleagues were diminished, but so were the stimuli for critical thinking and for contrastive research of the effects on patients.

At a deeper level, pluralism might promote functioning of the type of "fraternal clan" like the one mentioned by Freud (1913) in "Totem and Taboo." When W. and M. Baranger—undoubtedly leaders of their group—returned to Buenos Aires in 1965, the Uruguayan group underwent a new balance of power and influence among its senior analysts, choosing different areas of specialization. This was good for us candidates, but it also tempted us to affiliate with certain authors whose ideas were believed unquestionable. When identity relies excessively on adhesion to a certain author, a situation like the one described by Freud as the "neurotic's family romance" is produced. That is, the dominance of a fantasy makes us come in a direct line not from our real analysts and masters, but from distant figures that we idealize (Lacan, Klein, Winnicott, etc.—and, of course, Freud). This is part of a larger problem: that of the identity of Latin American psychoanalysis and its position opposite the centers of theoretical production in the Northern Hemisphere. Then, as different "families" are made around fantasized affiliations—since there was no real or sustained exchange with the authors or groups taken as reference—the link with the local tradition is cut, and the creativity and production of new ideas diminish.

When I finished my psychoanalytic training, I had acquired theoretical and technical knowledge that was essential to my professional practice. Theoretically I was familiar with the fundamental concepts of some theories (Freud, Lacan, Klein, Bion, etc.), and there were in Montevideo or Buenos Aires colleagues or study groups with whom I could go deeper into the ideas that interested me. Studying various authors, if a clear discrimination of their ideas is reached, is extremely useful in providing the personal flexibility necessary to create the metaphors or "linguistic games" that allow us to approach what is particular in each patient and to promote personal ideas in the analyst. But for these ideas to develop properly, a collective process of critical analysis of the coherence of the different ideas is necessary to help determine when an idea no longer applies and when one is more useful than another and why. Analysis or self-analysis of the unconscious meaning of theories is also necessary (Bernardi and De León, 1992).

This was the point I was the most dissatisfied with: pluralism was undoubtedly superior to any dogmatic position (Bernardi, 1992), but at times the peaceful coexistence of different approaches was a political coexistence rather than a scientific one. When reading the psychoanalytic literature from all over the world, it was not easy to say to what extent the various theories coincided, were complementary, or were opposed—or if they were really talking about different things with different languages. The basic concepts (Oedipus, castration, narcissism, etc.) could be used by all of them as long as they were used in a lax way, which was pointed out at that time by J. Sandler

(1983). For these reasons, I supported the idea that psychoanalytic theories, in certain aspects, were incommensurable. That is, it was not certain that there could be logical compatibility and semantic congruence between the different approaches. In other words, it could not be said that they were speaking of the same things in the same language. To say they were, I relied on the ideas of the epistemologists like T. S. Kuhn. Since I retained my interest in the philosophy of science, I took these ideas to a congress of epistemology of psychoanalysis in Buenos Aires in 1983; attending was a group of analysts and philosophers interested in the topic. In 1987, I presented a longer work (Bernardi, 1989) at the International Congress of Montréal. This was the same congress where Wallerstein, talking about the problem of pluralism, asked in his presidential address the question: "One Psychoanalysis or Many?" Wallerstein emphasized the unity of the clinical theory as a common ground for all psychoanalysts (Wallerstein, 1988). But at the time I was not satisfied with this spin, since psychoanalysis behaved like a science with multiple paradigms, conditioning goals, and techniques (Bernardi, 2001).

During the 1980s, the French influence became more and more important and the Uruguayan analysts, interested in the patient's verbal discourse and less prone to interpret the emotional contact in the here and now of the session, more silent. A qualitative and quantitative contrastive study of the interpretations in the works presented in our association showed significant changes between the 1960s and the 1990s. In fact, interpretations varied significantly in different aspects (global frequency; emphasis on transference, aggressiveness, etc.), but this could not always be predicted through theoretical changes. I believe that original developments appear in the implicit theories of the analysts rather than in the official theories.

I had also become more attentive to the patient's free association. But I found that my practice did not improve with these changes. When an attitude of self-analysis prevailed in the patient, a silent and receptive attitude by the analyst was useful, but it was not enough when a more intensive work on the patient's defenses and primitive mechanisms, was required, as well as when the patient was undergoing critical situations. So with a theoretical concern for the conceptual aspects of different psychoanalytic models, I started to become concerned about the different results of these models in clinical practice. This made me reconsider authors of the River Plate tradition (e.g., E. Pichon Rivière, H. Racker, J. Bleger, D. Liberman, W. and M. Baranger, H. Etchegoyen) who had praised an intersubjective perspective that I think still holds true today in discussions about the interpersonal aspects of psychoanalysis. The works of my wife, Beatriz de León, were very important for me in this reconsideration. I was surprised to find a line of thought in the River Plate that had worked for more than half a century on the need to give greater empirical support to psychoanalytic hypotheses by testing the interpretations during session as well as by searching indicators that assess change in the patient. I was surprised at the way many of these ideas were cast aside later in the Río de la Plata and replaced by others without proper discussion of the reasons for such change.

After the dictatorship period ended in Uruguay in 1985, I went back to my university activities. This marked quite a change for me since I had been exclusively devoted to my private practice. With democracy, a total reconstruction of the university began, and it required a lot of work. I became head of the Department of Medical Psychology at the medical school and a professor at the psychology school. My work at the university was demanding and not well paid, but it was a very stimulating period. On one hand, it allowed me to apply ideas of psychoanalysis to new problems; on the other hand, it forced me to get in touch with new knowledge and methodologies that challenged my usual ways of thinking. Soon after returning to the university I represented the medical school in a task force commissioned by the government to make a National Program of Mental Health, which required considering psychoanalytic problems from new perspectives. The need to develop different research fields with new challenges arose many more times. Teams were formed to consider early mother-infant issues, the problems of development of children from poor areas, the vulnerability of facing organic diseases, the mechanisms of defense, and the quality of life. In the following years, I got into topics like the advances of clinical epidemiology and of evidence-based medicine and into the discussion of practice guidelines on psychotherapy. The contact with academic analysts from other regions was a great help; work agreements were established that turned out to be very stimulating for the younger doctors and psychologists researching at the university. We had an active exchange with colleagues at various centers—University of Ulm, University College of London, Cornell University, and others—who were also working on the interface between psychoanalysis and neighboring disciplines. It is not easy to integrate psychoanalytic knowledge with that of other methods and disciplines, and my first reaction was to keep a "splitting" of the two types of knowledge. However, as time went by, it became more useful to look at the phenomena from multiple perspectives, without expecting to be all-encompassing, but allowing the different approaches to interact.

Pluralism appears in a different way when we consider it from a relativistic postmodern perspective rather than from health sciences. From the latter perspective, a couple of unavoidable questions come up: What changes when we work with different technical and theoretical approaches for the patient? Can we really say that some patients benefit more from one psychoanalytic model than from another? These questions cannot be left aside when we discuss the reasons to prefer one technical theoretical model or another. But it is also true that no infallible procedures to solve these questions are available. We can neither conciliate all theories nor choose at will how to work with each patient. Our resources are limited. There is no single discipline or procedure that answers all questions, but rather there are multiple methods for multiple questions, and we know that no answer is forever.

Psychoanalysis must face questions of a different nature. Some are clearly empirical—such as how change takes place in psychoanalysis, which aspects, in what kind of patients, studied in which way. Other questions are hermeneutic in nature—we wonder, for instance, about the meaning of a dream. Others are unanswerable, at least for the current state of the art—we can only make conjectures, as when we wonder about the nature of many meta-psychological concepts. We cannot then resolve the questions posed by pluralism in a simple manner. But I believe that it is possible to foster procedures that advance valid procedures for answering them. Clinical research is the main support of our hypotheses, but we have to examine how this evidence is influenced by the explicit premises of our theories and by the implicit theories of each analyst that are closest to his real work (Sandler, 1983). This does not mean falling into relativism or fragmentation. Different experiences, especially as chair for the Committee of the Scientific Program of the New Orleans Congress, showed me that our discipline gets stronger as we openly discuss our differences and uncertainties.

We do not even need very demanding agreements at the epistemological level, which do not even seem possible. Just think of the hardships to make compatible the traditional epistemological approaches with poststructuralist and postmodern positions. I believe ordinary language is enough for the different psychoanalytic approaches to develop their arguments, thus showing their strengths and weaknesses. I have become more and more interested in studying the debates in psychoanalysis and especially the conditions that allow the establishment of a shared argumentative field that allows more fruitful controversies and better grounded comparisons between hypotheses (Bernardi, 2002, 2003). From this perspective, incommensurability between different positions can be considered a defensive strategy to avoid confrontation between various perspectives rather than as an obstacle impossible to overcome. My journey, then, has taken me from pluralism to seek the reasons to ground the preference of one choice or another, knowing that these reasons are never final.

In the Prologue of *Psychoanalytic Inquiry*, Volume 22, Issue 1 ("From Ego Psychology to Pluralism and Diversity: An American Psychoanalytical Odyssey"), Melvin Bornstein says, "We need chronicles like the one that Homer left about the motivations, adventures and responses to events of our own last half-century" (p. 1). Reading this reference to Ulysses brought back memories from my childhood, since Ulysses was one of my favorite heroes. I had come across *The Odyssey* in my father's library as a child and I avidly read the work, identifying alternatively with Ulysses and with his son. I read the book again many times, and it always seemed great the way Ulysses came back home and, after drawing his bow, hit the target and defeated

Penelope's candidates. After recalling these memories, I started having unwanted thoughts that took me far away from my infantile memory of Ulysses. I became aware, with a certain disappointment, that in relation to pluralism the end could not be the same as in the *The Odyssey*. We may be able to defeat the Cyclops, leaving behind the temptation of a unilateral perspective on problems. We may as well avoid the mermaids singing, giving up the appeal to conciliate all theories, without realizing that in doing so we are cannibalizing all ideas. It is also possible to resist the temptation to live in the land of the lotus eaters, where the contributions from the past are forgotten and only new fashionable ideas are interesting.

Up to this point I believe we can be victors. But I believe we must give up the idea of getting to a mother land in which truth has no other claimants. Neither can we, with perfect marksmanship, hit the target for all questions. But we may still have something else. When Ulysses reveals himself to Penelope, he finds that the best way to do so is recalling the way he made their bed in the trunk of a tree that is still rooted in the land in which it grew. In the same way, there is not a better way for us to reveal ourselves than by showing, as best we can, the ways in which we have made the hypotheses on which we rely.

References

Bernardi, R. (1989), The role of paradigmatic determinants in psychoanalytic understanding. *Int. J. Psycho-Anal.*, 70: 341–347.
Bernardi, R. (1992), On pluralism in psychoanalysis. *Psychoanal. Inq.*, 12: 506–525.
Bernardi, R. (2001), Psychoanalytic goals: New and old paradoxes. *Psychoanal. Q.*, 70: 67–98.
Bernardi, R. (2002), The need of true controversies in psychoanalysis: The debates about M. Klein and J. Lacan in the Río de la Plata. *Int. J. Psycho-Anal.*, 83: 851–873.
Bernardi, R. (2003), What kind of evidence makes the analyst change his or her theoretical and technical ideas? In: *Pluralism and Unity? Methods of Research in Psychoanalysis*, ed. M. Leuzinger-Bohleber, A. U. Dreher & J. Canestri. London: International Psychoanalysis, pp. 125–136.
Bernardi, R. & De León, B. (1992), Does our self-analysis take into consideration our assumptions? In: *Self-Analysis: Critical Inquiries, Personal Visions*, ed. J. W. Barron. Hillsdale, NJ: The Analytic Press.
Freud, S. (1913), Totem and taboo. *Standard Edition*, 13: 1–161. London: Hogarth Press.
Klein, M. (1932), *The Psycho-Analysis of Children*. London: Hogarth Press.
Kohut, H. (1971), *Analysis of the Self*. New York: International Universities Press.
Sandler, J. (1983), Reflections on some relations between psychoanalytic concepts and psychoanalytic practice. *Int. J. Psycho-Anal.*, 64: 35–45.
Wallerstein, R. S. (1988), One psychoanalysis or many? *Int. J. Psycho-Anal.*, 69: 5–21.

Chapter 4

What is theory?*

Christopher Bollas

I

When Freud wrote himself into a corner he would engage a literary trope. It would go something like "if you believe what I have been arguing up till now you will have been following the wrong line of thought." Then off he would go on his merry way leaving many a reader flummoxed over why so much time had been spent thinking incorrect ideas. Freud's writing simply demonstrated his view that we think free associatively. Typically, he followed not just one line of thought but scores of "chains of ideas"—a term he often used, like "trains of thought". When these lines of thought were in outright contradiction with one another, Freud would engage the above trope or claim he was stuck and defer the issue until later.

I find a particular moment in *The Ego and the Id* (1923b) touching. Writing about the repressed unconscious, Freud is about to finish up Chapter One when a thought pops into his mind. Not only are the repressed contents unconscious but so, too, is the agency that commits them to the unconscious. He pauses. He states that it would seem that he has several different theories of the unconscious. For a moment he turns to God to see if the issue can be resolved: "A part of the ego too—and Heaven knows how important a part—may be Ucs., undoubtedly is Ucs" (*ibid.*, p. 9). Freud lapses into a very brief literary depression, implicitly wondering if he should scrap his entire theory of the unconscious—"we must admit that the characteristics of being unconscious begins to lose significance" (*ibid.*)—but finishes the chapter with a nod to the future and the hope that somehow this problem can be resolved.

Freud was clear that there were two forms of unconscious: an unconscious *process* and unconscious *content*. Yet, looking back, as no doubt he was in some ways, his prior failure to keep this distinction in mind created a

---

* Reprinted with kind permission: This chapter was first published with the same chapter title in *The Freudian Moment*, by Christopher Bollas (2007) Karnac.

confusion about what he meant when he was referring to *the* unconscious. Was he referring to repressed contents or to the process of repression? But the problem does not stop there. Unconscious processes are not restricted to repressing unwanted ideas. As Freud repeatedly pointed out, there are non-repressed unconscious contents, and so, by implication, there are unconscious processes that do not operate to repress contents but to form contents for other reasons.

Unfortunately, psychoanalysts have tended to focus on the repressed unconscious to the exclusion of the non-repressed unconscious. For decades the non-repressed unconscious has been mischaracterized as simply the "descriptive unconscious", which means that it is not dynamically organized and just rather inert. It could be argued that unconscious memories, for example, are simply part of this descriptive, non-repressed unconscious.

For classical psychoanalysts, the dynamic unconscious refers to the repression of sexual and aggressive drives that seek return to acceptable consciousness in some form or another. *This* unconscious is, by definition, drive-like; it is a pulsion seeking discharge any way it can and when it ropes in thinking it does so rather expeditiously.

Contrast this with Freud's dream work model.

Here the unconscious is an intelligence of form. Its proprioceptive capabilities receive endopsychic data from the storehouse of the unconscious; it also registers "psychically valuable" experiences of the day, sorting them as the day goes on into a kind of predream anteroom, and then it organizes thousands of thoughts, arriving through the intermediate space of lived experience, to be dreamed. The creation of the dream is not only a remarkable aesthetic accomplishment, it is the most sophisticated form of thinking we have. A dream can think hundreds of thoughts in a few seconds, its sheer efficiency breathtaking. It can think past, present, and imagined future in one single image and it can assemble the total range of implicit affects within the day experience, including all ramifying lines of thought that derive from these experiences. With the arrival of the Freudian Pair (see Bollas, 2002) the dream work at last has a companion in the analyst's receptive unconscious and we can see, in the remarkable chains of ideas released through the *process* of free association, infinite lines of meaning. The process of free association is an accomplishment of the ego's work.

It is astonishing, given Freud's emphasis on the dream work (followed by his book on jokes and his book on the psychopathology of everyday life), that he never constructed an explicit theory of unconscious perception. Nor did he spend time indicating how the ego was the vehicle of unconscious organization and communication with the other. I have speculated that Freud, ironically enough, repressed his theory of the unconscious ego. Perhaps he preferred to focus on the repressed unconscious because this seduced the name of the father, the authority *banishing* unwanted ideas. But the ego (the *process* of our mind) is partly formed during the self's relation to the mother within what I have termed the maternal order. The mother *welcomes* the infant into mental life. Banishment of the forbidden is a long way off. Indeed, *this unconscious process* is a long period of fulfilling needs and wishes. When Freud repressed knowledge of the maternal order he also rid himself of a theory of mind that was based not on banishment, but on seduction. He "forgot" that part of our unconscious that creatively fulfils our desires all the time, in daydreams, conversations, relations, creative activities, and whatnot.

In his 1915 essay on the unconscious, however, Freud stuns the reader by stating that it is a remarkable thing that the unconscious of one person can react upon the unconscious of the other without going through consciousness. What is remarkable is that he should throw this observation into his metapsychological essay on the unconscious where there is no conceptual room for this thought. What an arresting return of the repressed!

Had Freud unequivocally stated that the ego was not only mostly unconscious but it also created the dream, the symptom, and all works of creativity, then he would have allowed subsequent generations of analysts to see matters differently. His concept of unconscious communication, de-repressed in the above comment about one person's unconscious reacting upon another, *alluded* to unconscious thinking as a highly sophisticated form of thought.

Instead of recognizing that sophistication, Freud "dumbed down" his theory of the unconscious in the structural model. He tried to transpose his topographic model of the mind into the structural model. Thus, the unconscious of the topographic model morphed into the Id. The unconscious of the topographic model and the Id are *not* the same. What we have is a kind of model molestation as Freud tried to segue one theory of the unconscious into the other. It not only sustained a muddle, it contributed to it. More to the point, by morphing the non-repressed unconscious into the *Id* the unconscious was now an "aboriginal" part of the mind that the ego was meant to somehow tame.

It is not difficult to understand what Freud was trying to work out. On the one hand, he knew that part of a person's unconscious life was primitive. It carried the history of the early species within it, it contained infantile sexual phantasies, and it was also the source of the drives. On the other hand, the work of the dream revealed a highly sophisticated form of thinking. How can one reconcile the primitive unconscious with the sophisticated unconscious? In fact, there is no contradiction if one simply understands that *in the beginning* both the form and the contents—that is the process and its productions—of the infant's unconscious were primitive. During the course of time, however, the self's ego becomes more sophisticated. This does not mean that primitive elements of the unconscious—the drives, infantile fantasies, envy, greed, etc.—cease to exist; it simply means that the unconscious processing of these contents becomes more and more sophisticated. Indeed, right from the beginning of life the self is dream working the primitive, transforming urges into images.

Classical analysts to this day think of free association as returning drive derivatives. They rightly point to Freud's writing to support this view. I do not disagree with this, and certainly it is confirmed in clinical practice. However, the *other* unconscious, the non-repressed unconscious, is of little use to classical analysts.

Contrary to the view that this receptive unconscious is the descriptive unconscious, as opposed to the dynamic, the way we organize what impresses us during the day (what is evoked, and what forms we choose to further think them: dreaming, talking, writing, painting, composing, etc.) is actually a highly dynamic process.

Here, I am condensing two points into one, as I would like them to converge for a while before going separate ways. First, we need to be aware of the continued dynamic implications of repression of this kind. Second, Freud's conundrum serves to highlight the hazards of theory formation and both the reach and the limits of theory.

Freud's topographic model is, for example, the best way for us to conceptualize repression. Even if many would throw out his concepts of cathexes and anti-cathexes as outdated, I would submit that we still do not have a better set of metaphors to conceptualize mental intensity. I do not care if Freud's metaphors are hydraulic or electric any more than I care that the Klein–Bion model of ingestion, digestion, and metabolization is alimentary. The point is, does one understand what the metaphor conveys? *This is the definition of metaphor. It is a mental transportation system.* So, does it tell us what it intends to convey or doesn't it?

The topographic model helps us to see how a repressed idea gathers other repressed ideas into mental clusters and how it returns that idea to consciousness. The structural model is less helpful when it comes to conceptualizing repression. But it "sees" the psychodynamics of certain parts of the human mind. It helps us to imagine the play between our drives represented in the concept of the Id and the psychic organization of the rules of our society, allegorized in the theory of our Superego. The agency given the responsibility for sorting out this play, for negotiating, for making compromises, for allowing relief from the needs of the one or the other, is the Ego. This model, now somewhat out of fashion, is invaluable.

The structural model, however, does not advance the topographic model. Although it is historically further along in Freud's thinking and obviously was hugely popular with Freud's daughter and others, it does not address the same issues as the topographic model any more than the topographic model replaces the dream theory model of the unconscious.

Analysts think of newer models of the mind as "advances" in the wrong sort of way. They do increase understanding of the mind, but they do *not* replace prior models. This skewed modernist bias, that every intellectual development inevitably improves existent views, has unfortunately resulted in abandonment of important prior models of the mind.

In one psychoanalytical society where I spent a week lecturing and supervising, the analysts were topographical folks and hated the structural model. To put it in geo-political context, the structural model is associated with the Americans and the topographical model with the rest of the classical world. It can actually come down to a kind of culture war. In fact, the structural model and ego psychology were popular first with child analysts, because these models "saw" psycho-development. It was not otherwise visible in the other models of the mind. Try imagining psycho-development according to the topographic model. I wish you luck. The French, in particular, saw the concept of ego development as spurious. They craftily pointed out that as the unconscious was timeless, the entire notion of psychodevelopment was based on a false psychic premise. Yes, we did obviously develop—there were outward and inward signs of this—but such development had nothing to do *per se* with unconscious life. Unconscious life does not make temporal distinctions of any kind; indeed, it lives in its own a-developmental temporal kingdom. The idea of a psycho-development was a quaint tale told by those who seemed to have a more commercial notion of the self as progressive product. American analysts were the soft target of this critique because not only were they ego psychologists, but also they were selling psychoanalysis to the medical establishment and insurance companies by removing the more radical features of analysis from their representations. No longer could one find in the major texts of the ego psychologists the passage in Freud stressing that the analyst was to catch the drift of the patient's unconscious with his own unconscious. Had they pointed this out to the people of Blue Cross or Blue Shield it would have been a jaw dropping moment.

II

Freud's topographic and structural models come complete with respective images. This helps one to see what they mean. An image, worth a thousand words, serves unconscious purposes. Like a condensed dream fragment it is rather ready-made for the unconscious. It can be more easily internalized and helps a clinician to think about a highly complex matter.

Lacan's Symbolic, Imaginary, and Real does not come as an image, but once we have this tripartite model of meaning in mind it is not difficult to *imagine* the act of listening as involving an interplay between these three orders. Klein's paranoid–schizoid and depressive position theory comes with a small image of arrows (psarrow and d-arrow) to signify movement between the two positions. Having internalized this image and the concepts, Kleinians often visualize the material from this perspective.

In addition, all psychoanalysts have unconceptualized theories embedded in the way they practise. Setting aside the inevitability that one's character is a complex set of idiomatic theories functioning on the operational level, clinicians each have individual ways of ordering what they hear and what they say.

It will come as no surprise that each of the differing theories of the psychoanalytical experience constitutes a different perceptual category. If we listen to the material through the structural model, rather than the Kleinian, we will see things differently. Lacan's categories of the Symbolic, Imaginary, and Real gave me a new way of seeing my analysands. Before this I had not seen what I could now see.

This led me to appreciate the value of psychoanalytical theories as *forms* of perception. One theory sees something that other theories do not see. Freud's theory of the logic of sequence imbricated in the flow of any person's free talking allows one to perceive that logic. If we have not learned how to see things in this way then sequential logic will go unnoticed and one will miss an incredibly important field of unconscious material. Klein's ps and d allow one to see forms of splitting and integration that are not otherwise observable.

"A system of thought is something we live in", writes the British philosopher Simon Blackburn (1999) "just as much as a house, and if our intellectual house is cramped and confined, we need to know what better structures are available" (p. 10). Blackburn terms such building "conceptual engineering" (*ibid.*, p. 11) and I think this is a good way to describe the acquisition of psychoanalytical perspectives. As theories are forms of perception, if we settle with just one or two theories we live in a confined intellectual house.

How the psychoanalyst sees human life is obviously conveyed to the patient. The theory by which he thinks constitutes a psychic world-view. Upon entering psychoanalysis the analysand may be unaware of that view, akin to someone getting on an aeroplane headed to a country without knowing where they are going: just a country. There is a difference, however, between landing in Baghdad or Beijing. There is an astonishing difference in the worldviews of analysts, just as there are different cities that breed radically different cultures.

Theory, therefore, is not simply a way of perceiving something. It influences the way analysts transform their analysands. Practice follows theory.

Take Freud's theory of free association. If the analyst listens in a state of evenly suspended attentiveness—without trying to concentrate on anything, remember anything, or anticipate anything—his unconscious will occasionally perceive the analysand's unconscious patterns in thought. A form of practice put into place by European analysts, this theory meant waiting, perhaps for long periods of time in sessions, until the analyst got the picture.

They suddenly saw a line of thought, which might lead to a comment, or they might elect to remain quiet, meditative.

One person talking; the other listening.

Contrast this with the British School's view of the transference. *All* the people, places, or events in the analysand's narrative are indirect references to the psychoanalyst. If the analyst remains quiet, while the analysand projects a thought into a surrogate, such silence is understood by the analysand—so it is argued—as agreement with the projection. The analyst must therefore translate each and every reference to, or action upon, the self in order to mitigate such a process.

It would be hard to find two more strikingly different ways of perceiving the psychoanalytical experience or two more radically different ways of being with an analysand.

III

There is an ethics of perception. Theories are not simply forms of perception. When practised they *become* ethical decisions.

The Freudian view, just outlined, implicitly assumes the analysand's unconscious construction of meaning. By remaining silent and ostensibly out of the picture, the analyst attends not simply to a line of thought but many divergent lines.

At this moment a thought may arise. "But what about the analyst as a participant? Isn't this a relationship? The idea that the analyst is neutral is a fallacy, as he is affecting his patient all the time."

True, of course.

However, meditation *is* action. It is intended to affect the analysand. It creates the possibility for free speech. By creating the illusion of neutrality the analyst partly suspends the oversight of consciousness. Analysts who *practise* neutrality enable the patient's free associations to guide the sessions. They are more receptive to the analysand's free talking than analysts who believe that analysis is a highly interactive event. Inevitably, highly interactive analysts will interpersonalize a session. The illusion of neutrality is intended to function as much for the analyst as the analysand. The analyst believes he is just listening. This is not dissimilar to a reader who believes he or she is just reading, or a listener who is just listening to music.

Let us ask a different question. How might one's subjective response to the analysand be discoverable? Setting aside the reality that an analyst—like a reader or listener to music—should be so deeply lost in listening that he would not know how to answer this question, let's still proceed. Where *is* his subjective response to be found? *If* we really do believe in the unconscious, then this question has a most disconcerting answer. Neutrality recognizes a plain fact. Even though we have some conscious responses to what our analysands say and do, we rarely know our "personal" unconscious response. Neutralized by our unconscious, we simply do not have access to the sort of information the question seeks. Frustrating as this fact of our life is, if we cheat—and try to manufacture news from our unconscious, if for no other reason than to come up with some kind of story-line—we deny ourselves and our patients *the fact* of living as an unconscious being.

IV

Theories vary in depth and range of view.

A *psychoanalytical theory* only becomes useful when it has entered the psychoanalyst's receptive unconscious. Joining other theories, it will operate according to the dictates of the analytical experience in a session. Sometimes a theory will pop into consciousness not before the clinician has come to its realization, but afterwards. It functions in much of the way "genera" (Bollas, 1992) work, a concept I coined to identify the arrival of new unconscious realizations that lead to a different way of viewing life.

Some will see here what seems to be a reversal of one of Freud's paradigms: the movement of unconscious issues into consciousness. Freud was rightly concentrating on unconscious conflicts and believed that moving them into consciousness was therapeutically efficacious. That is certainly true some of the time, although I have argued that the greater part of psychic change occurs unconsciously and need not enter consciousness, either in the analyst or in the analysand. My reversal of Freud's paradigm accounts for the obvious and ordinary internalizations of informative models that people absorb all the time to become part of their unconscious structure. Were this not so we would neither learn nor benefit from lived experience.

The legitimacy of any one psychoanalytical theory resides in its function as a form of perception. To plumb the depths of this depth psychology a theory must have a *capacity for* unconscious perception. Some theories obviously have greater depth than others. Therein lies a challenge to all psychoanalysts, because the deeper a theory, the harder it is for a psychoanalyst to embrace it. Not only because it takes longer to acquire and structuralize, but because it inevitably involves the clinician in a more exacting personal experience.

Theories, then, have varying degrees of depth potential.

Freud's theory of the dream work gives meaning to the term depth psychology; indeed, he defined depth psychology as the interpretation of dreams. His understanding of how the dream works the previous day's experiences, guided by the self's psychic history, *is* depth psychology. The dream work theory embraces both the phylogentic and the ontological realms of human subjectivity. His use of free association allows us to see some of the work of that depth psychology, thus enabling us to follow chains of ideas that may occur just for a few seconds in a session, or trains of thought that may be elaborated over a life span.

Freud's dream work theory is a complex perceptual matrix that takes years to acquire. Like Lacan's theory of the Symbolic, Imaginary, and Real, or Klein's infantile mind theory, the analyst learning these models must be patient as the acquisition of a form of perception takes time.

V

Most students seek "super-vision" from a clinician steeped in one model of the mind who is gifted in conveying how one can see the material from his or her particular perspective.

An irony of psychoanalytical practice, however, is that for theory to be effective, once it is grasped it must then drop out of consciousness. For this to happen the supervisor must sense when the supervisee has understood the basic paradigms being taught. Once this has happened it is time to stop.

This does not always happen. While it is understandable that a supervisor or teacher will outline, discuss, and indicate how a theory can help the student comprehend certain clinical material it is not so common for the teacher to indicate to the student that after internalization it is in the best interests of the patient and the analyst for the analyst to be without conscious preconception. To this day it is all too widespread a public practice to hear analysts talking about finding the drive derivative in the material, or the ego position, or the here and now transference, or the true self, extending the idea that one can see these matters *continuously* in consciousness.

One of the most troubling features of psychoanalytical training is the degree to which some theories are meant to reside in the analyst's conscious mind all the time. That may be keeping an eye on the analysand's ego position, or projective identifications in the here and now transference, or the drive derivative, or the analyst's personal effect on the analysand. The retention of such theories in consciousness—not allowed to sift down into the unconscious to join other theories—not only leads to a hypertrophied consciousness, but amounts to an unwitting evisceration of the work with unconscious experience. It is unsurprising that a considerable number of analysts are now wondering if the unconscious exists. Little wonder, then, that there is an embarrassing soap opera romancing of consciousness theory in psychoanalysis.

VI

Schools of psychoanalysis are invaluable. It is an ethical obligation, in my view, for all psychoanalysts to immerse themselves in the theoretical orientation of the major schools of psychoanalysis: Freudian, Kleinian,

Hartmanian, Kohutian, Bionian, Winnicottian, and Lacanian. To do so is to increase one's perceptual ability, to expand one's mind, to greet patients with a wisdom that can only be realized by passage through difference.

A school usually studies the text of one or two seminal thinkers. Students are taught by experts in that school, sometimes by the seminal thinker, and later by those who have carefully read and scrutinized the writing. Great teachers are invaluable because the way they teach sinks down into the unconscious life of a student and is effective for a lifetime.

A theory is a metasensual phenomenon. It allows one to see something not seen by other theories; to have as an unconscious possibility should clinical need for it arise. To declare oneself against other schools of thought is like someone stating that one is an eye person and does not like the ear or auditory sense data, or for someone to declare that they trust what they hear, but never trust what they smell. The metasensual equivalent, operating in psychoanalysis today—where one needs all the differing perspectives one can possibly structuralize in the course of time—is a form of auto-castration. To entirely oppose the Kleinian or Lacanian view of mental life is to wilfully reduce one's psychic capability as an analyst.

Psychoanalysts need to learn all the theories they can so that they may become unconscious perception-structures enabling practitioners to participate more deeply in the psychoanalytical experience. The analysand's unconscious will sense the range of perceptive receptiveness of the psychoanalyst. This will both deepen and broaden the analysand's skill in unconscious communication. While the work of rendering symptoms, character distortions, pathologic structures, and trauma into consciousness remains a crucial feature of a psychoanalysis, *the work of the unconscious* will increase the analysand's capacity for unconscious perception, creativity, and communication. We see this not so much in the removal of a symptom, pathologic structure, or character deformation (although those, too, will go or be modified) we see it in the way the analysand engages life in a more creative way.

If theory is perception, if it indicates an ethics of practice, it also serves as a sign of the limits of consciousness. However much a theory presumes to tell us something about a person, its actual function is less in what it discovers than in how it sees. Klein's theory of what takes place in the first year of life is less significant than the allegoric perceptual structure that permits us to imagine infancy. Lacan's theory of the subject's instantiation through the chain of signifiers is less a theory of found unconscious meanings than a portal to entering a world of linguistic relations.

Even though the psychoanalyst can only ever know unconscious expression through its effects (or derivatives), these complex articulations are the matrix of our being. As psychoanalytic theories are, among other things, forms of perception, each will inevitably be of some use in helping us to unconsciously perceive unconscious processes and their contents.

Chapter 5

My Psychoanalytic Journey*

Stephen A. Mitchell[1]

LIKE MANY IN THE FIELD OF PSYCHOANALYSIS, I WAS FIRST DRAWN to the ideas of Freud himself. I don't remember how I came across Freud's writings, but I spent a good part of the summer between my junior and senior years of high school devouring the five-volume edition of Freud's collected papers. I went to college looking for Freud in psychology courses, only to discover rats (not the Rat Man). I ended up with a wonderful cross-disciplinary major, "History, the Arts & Letters," in which I learned a great deal about structural, comparative approaches to ideas. My major interests, in addition to psychology, were politics and philosophy. Eventually, both began to merge for me back into psychology: helping people change their lives politically and socially required understanding them psychologically, and Nietzsche convinced me that philosophy had made a wrong turn in focusing on how people should be rather than on how people actually are.

I got my doctorate in clinical psychology at New York University (NYU) in the remarkably open and stimulating atmosphere created by Bernie Kalinkowitz and many of his friends, adjunct faculty trained at the William Alanson White Psychiatric Institute. I minored in community psychology. My dual focus on individuals and social processes was maintained in my internship at the Columbia Psychiatric Institute, where I spent half the year on the community service and half the year on the psychoanalytic service.

My conceptual and clinical development in those years reflected that same dialectical tension between the individual and the social, intrapsychic, and interpersonal. Although Freudian ego psychology was very much a presence at NYU (through Robert Holt, Leo Goldberger, and others), I was most drawn to interpersonal teachers and supervisors whose ideas spoke more directly to my own experience and understanding of the world. I read Sullivan and Fromm avidly, and I was introduced (through Bernie Friedland) to Fairbairn and Guntrip. At about the same time, I discovered the existentialist and

---

* Reprinted with kind permission: This chapter was first published as an article with the same title in Psychoanalytic Inquiry 24 (4): 531–541.

interpersonal essays of Leslie Farber, whose thought has had a lasting influence on me. During those years, I was also in a very meaningful and useful personal analysis with a contemporary Freudian.

For me, these various foci deepened during the mid-1970s at the White institute. I was forced to change to a White institute training analyst, which I resented at first. However, the second analysis in some respects had more of an impact on me than the first did, and I have come to treasure the two experiences in tandem as having taught me a great deal about how deeply personal and interpersonal each analytic dyad is. The dominant intellectual influence at White in those years was Edgar Levenson, who greatly transformed and modernized interpersonal theory into its current emphasis on transference– countertransference phenomena. But I was also very lucky to be able to study Freud with Irving Paul and ego psychology with Martin Bergmann. My favorite supervisor, Geneva Goodrich, told me that it takes about seven to eight years to learn to do psychoanalysis, so that took off some of the pressure I put on myself. I had enormously rich clinical experiences with patients and supervisors, and I still find myself thinking about these experiences and people today. I watched my clinical work change from year to year in tandem with changes in supervisors, and I worried about being too easily influenced, as if I were clinically promiscuous. (This was also noted by a couple of my patients!) But I decided again that psychoanalysis was a very personal business and that a kind of surrender to the sensibility of supervisors and teachers was the best way to learn deeply what they had to offer. I stopped worrying.

I had discovered in college that the only way to really learn anything was to study it on one's own, and I began to find that the best way to learn something deeply was to teach it. I taught psychoanalytic ideas and interdisciplinary courses to undergraduates for eight years during the 1970s, and then I began teaching at a wide range of different psychoanalytic institutes. It was in teaching—taking apart, reconstructing, and comparing different theoretical models—that I discovered that I had developed a point of view. And it was in presenting and reflecting on my own clinical work that I discovered that I had indeed developed a coherent style of my own. The teaching lent itself naturally to writing, which I had always loved doing, but until then I had not felt that I had anything particularly useful to say. To the deep satisfactions of doing clinical work were added a passion for both teaching and writing, on which I have continued to spend a major portion of time, to this very moment. For the past 15 years or so, I have been meeting with reading groups to explore both past and present analytic literature. Meeting with these groups has been a rich vehicle for sharing and processing my clinical experiences and ideas. It is difficult for me to imagine doing clinical work without the teaching and writing that have become its counterpart.

Over lunch one day, Jay Greenberg and I discovered that we were both planning to write the same book. We joined forces, and the book eventually became *Object Relations in Psychoanalytic Theory* (1983). We wanted to show that a broad shift (in those days, *paradigm* was not yet a cliched word) had taken place over several preceding decades of psychoanalytic thought—from an understanding of mind as built from drive-based impulses and defenses to an understanding of mind as built from relational configurations. We tried to demonstrate the different strategies for dealing with this shift—from more conservative strategies of accommodation (in Freudian ego psychology) to more radical strategies of clear alternatives (in interpersonal theory and in the object relations theory of Fairbairn). For me, writing this book was extraordinary in many ways. Jay and I often converged in our approaches to issues, but there were some important differences as well. Struggling with those differences and devising a conceptual framework for encompassing them made the book much more balanced and textured than it would have been if either of us had written it alone. That taught me a great deal about collaboration and community. And research into the book sections for which I was responsible deepened my sense that there were fundamental compatibilities among interpersonal psychoanalysis, British school object relations theories (particularly Fairbairn's), and much of the clinical wisdom of contemporary Kleinian theory.

The understanding of the history of psychoanalytic ideas that developed in those years has stayed with me ever since. There had been many innovations and departures from classical Freudian drive theory over the years, but they had remained isolated around different issues in different schools—interpersonal theory, object relations theory, self psychology, existential psychoanalysis, humanistic psychology, and so on. Many of these contributions use different terminology, but they are grounded in common conceptual assumptions. Together, they form a comprehensive alternative to what had increasingly become, for me, the anachronistic features of classical metapsychology.

In the mid-1980s, I began to develop an integrated relational perspective for exploring various major psychoanalytic concerns, including sexuality, development, narcissism, agency, aggression, self, authenticity, the psychoanalytic relationship, and analytic process. The results of my explorations were eventually published in *Relational Concepts in Psychoanalysis: An Integration* (1988), *Hope and Dread in Psychoanalysis* (1993), and *Influence and Autonomy in Psychoanalysis* (1997).

As I was working out my own personal synthesis of concepts and influences, several institutional developments were having an enormous impact on me.

First, the Division of Psychoanalysis (Division 39) of the American Psychological Association began to really take off. After decades of passively waiting and hoping to be taken in by the American Psychoanalytic Association and the American Federation, psychologists began to empower themselves to study, teach, and practice psychoanalysis. I became active in teaching at various "local chapters" in different cities (Denver, Boston, Chicago, San Francisco, and, later, Toronto and Seattle), and these chapters grew into a new generation of psychoanalytic institutes. These teaching experiences—involving marathon weekends, speaker phones, and video cameras—were some of the most exciting I've enjoyed. There seemed to be a synergy between the revolution that was relaxing the tight institutional control that had been strangling psychoanalytic education and the theory and clinical practice revolution that the relational literature was beginning to capture and systematize.

Second, I extended my teaching from the White Institute to the Postdoctoral Program at NYU. I was brought in by Bernie Friedland and Mannie Ghent to teach object relations theory in the Interpersonal/Humanistic track at a time when the Freudian and Interpersonal/Humanistic tracks were locked in a power struggle that prevented either from developing fully. In 1989, various factors converged to end this struggle, and Mannie, Bernie, and I (soon to bejoined by Phil Bromberg and Jim Fosshage) were given the mandate to form a quasi-independent Relational track. Out of the explosion of interest, which was truly unexpected and startling, emerged a community that has been an extremely rich intellectual home for me.

Third, during the fall of 1989, Lew Aron and I discovered (over another fateful lunch) that we both had the fantasy of developing a relational journal. Lew mentioned this to Paul Stepansky of The Analytic Press. Paul, very excited about the idea, approached me to form a small group to develop the journal that would eventually become *Psychoanalytic Dialogues: A Journal of Relational Perspectives.* The extraordinary interest the journal attracted almost from the beginning was extremely exciting, and being its editor gave me the opportunity to work closely with colleagues who have become friends and, each in their own way, major influences on my own thinking over the years—at first, Lew Aron, Phil Bromberg, Mannie Ghent, and Adrienne Harris, and then, over the years, Neil Altman, Tony Bass, Jody Davies, and Muriel Dimen. Most recently, we were joined by Margaret Black, Carolyn Clement, and Jay Frankel. In 199x, The Analytic Press launched the Relational Perspectives Book Series, coedited by Lew Aron and me. Lew and I recently coedited the series volume *Relational Psychoanalysis: The Emergence of a Tradition* (1999).

The overlapping communities that emerged in these organizations have been extremely important in the development of my understanding and clinical sensibility. In a very fundamental way, my psychoanalytic journey has been a "journey with others," and as a result I have learned a great deal about many things, including these few: the dense complexities of the interactions between analysand and analyst (Lewis Aron, Jay Greenberg); multiplicitous self states and trauma (Jody Davies, Phil Bromberg); the pervasive and subtle workings of gender (Adrienne Harris, Muriel Dimen, Virginia Goldner);the ways in which we are saturated in social class and racial meanings (Neil Altman); the richness of the self-psychological approach to experience (Margaret Black, Jim Fosshage); and varieties of authenticity and intersubjectivity in the subtle distinctions among surrender, submission, and recognition (Mannie Ghent, Jessica Benjamin).

As I look back from my current vantage point, I see that the basic interests and values with which I began have stayed with me throughout the years. My early interest in both individual psychology and social problems and processes has led to a relational psychoanalytic vision that emphasizes the interpenetrability of the intrapsychic and the interpersonal. Jay Greenberg and I intended the term *relational* as a bridge concept between interpersonal relations and internal object relations. My subsequent clinical and intellectual experiences have taken me more deeply into both realms. My early education also imparted to me a strong sense of the contextual nature of all human thought—its embeddedness in cultural place and historical time. That commitment has certainly stayed with me over the years and nurtured my involvement in the sometimes hazardous business of "comparative psychoanalysis." It has also girded my conviction that, whereas Freud's psychoanalysis was inevitably both facilitated and constrained by the intellectual milieu of his time, our psychoanalysis must interface with, learn from, and speak to other participants in our intellectual milieu. So, contemporary philosophy, science, philosophy of history, and literary theory have remained to some extent my hobbies. What I have been able to learn about the concerns of scholars in these areas has had an ongoing, living relationship with the evolution of my psychoanalytic ideas and clinical concerns.

In addition to the original formative influences of Freud, Sullivan, Fromm, Farber, Levenson, Fairbairn, Winnicott, and Klein, and the cross-fertilizing exchanges I had with my colleagues on *Psychoanalytic Dialogues,* other analytic authors have also had a major impact on my thinking. Over the past 15 years or so, I have found the contributions of the contemporary Kleinians of great interest and resonance; I've come to recognize Racker's writings on transference and countertransference as a source of great wisdom. In the 1980s, I had the privilege of getting to know both Merton Gill and Irwin Z. Hoffman, and each has had a large impact on me both personally and professionally. Gill's lucidity, incisiveness, and intellectual integrity have become ideals for me, and Irwin's brutally honest, ongoing investigation of the ambiguities of the analyst's participation in the analytic process continues to push me in ways I am not always happy to go but always find very rewarding. I have also found the evolving thought of Thomas Ogden to be always challenging, profound, and inspiring. More recently, I've found that Adam Phillips's aesthetic take on psychoanalysis captures and expands what I've always felt has been the fun in psychoanalytic thought. And, even though I disagree with Roy Schafer, especially on basic issues of technique, I have found his writings over the years to be a source of great riches.

Perhaps the greatest joy in my reading of the psychoanalytic literature in recent years has been my immersion in the work of Hans Loewald. I was asked to be the discussant of a paper he was to present at the White institute in 1981, and, in preparation, I read a good deal of his work. The exchange we had then was stimulating for me, and in a sense his ideas became part of the background of my own thought and writing. Somewhere through teaching in the mid-1990s, however, I began to realize just how powerfully Loewald's vision had influenced my own in many ways I had not directly recognized. This led me to study his work systematically. (I included two chapters on Loewald in my most recent book, *Relationality: From Attachment to Intersubjectivity*.) As Loewald's ideas all developed within the context of his love of Freud and of his extremely idiosyncratic and creative reading of Freud's work, reading Loewald led me back to reread and reconsider Freud. I've found this kind of continual cycling back as probably the best way to both preserve and revitalize analytic traditions.

Several features of the politics of the recent history of psychoanalysis seem worth noting at this point, because they have had a big impact on my experience of and location in the psychoanalytic world. When Jay Greenberg and I began writing about the relational tradition, I regarded relational ideas as an extension of interpersonal psychoanalysis and current relational contributions as continuous with the earlier interpersonal tradition through the bridges created by object relations theories. It was one of the greatest surprises of my professional life to discover that many identifying themselves as "interpersonal psychoanalysts," particularly those of the older generation, did not see it that way. For them, object relations, because of its intrapsychic focus, is incompatible with interpersonal psychoanalysis and is merely an extension of everything that is wrong with traditional Freudian thinking. The title of one of the chapters in Edgar Levenson's *The Ambiguity of Change* (1983) puts the issue succinctly: "Object Relations Theory: Bridge or Detour?" So, even though I have always considered myself both an interpersonal analyst and a relational analyst, relational psychoanalysis began to be regarded by many as a distinct school of psychoanalytic thought unto itself.

On the other side, relational concepts have continued to seep into the contemporary Freudian literature. I use the word *seep* purposely, because relational authors are most often, though with important exceptions, simply not cited. Seepage has occurred in a couple ways. Sometimes, as *relational* became almost a buzzword, the claim has been made that mainstream psychoanalysis has been relational all along. And sometimes relational authors have been caricatured as the wildest sort of "anything-goes" clinicians. These developments have made it very important to try to sort out understandings and terminology in an effort to locate real differences from both false agreements and false polarities.

I now turn to what I find most significant and most pressing in psychoanalytic thought and clinical practice today. In terms of theory, the basic underpinnings of psychoanalytic ideas have shifted broadly in recent decades—from drive-based to relational-based concepts. Concurrently, there has been a marked shift in the center of gravity in analytic thought—from the biology–culture dialectic that Freud explored to the oneness–twoness dialectic that pervades much of the contemporary literature. This is apparent in the ways in which that fundamental psychoanalytic premise, the unconscious, is now used both in theory and in clinical practice.

In Freud's time and in Freud's way of thinking, the unconscious was dangerous because of its primitiveness. The narcissistic blow we suffered with the discovery of the unconscious was, Freud suggested, the horrible truth that we are not masters in our own house. The masters of the psyche are instinctual impulses and defenses against instinctual impulses, in all their complex derivatives and compromises. The unconscious and resistances to the unconscious were understood in terms of the emergence of phylogenetic remnants in the life of culture and the power of biology to destabilize civilization.

This way of thinking about the unconscious surely has enduring relevance for us. But in our time, and in our most recent analytic thought, the destabilizing power of the unconscious, both within our personal experience and as a doctrine, is increasingly understood not so much in terms of biology but in terms of otherness or "alterity"—the ways in which oneness is limited by, in some sense is constituted by, twoness. (Biology is still enormously important, but it is a differently conceived biology, not in contrast to nurture but as partly shaped through nurture.) Our minds are not static structures that we carry around for display in different contexts. What we carry are potentials for generating recurrent experiences that are actualized only in specific contexts, in interpersonal exchanges with others. (Intrapsychic structure is still very important, but it is a differently conceived structure—less static, more contextual, actualizing itself in situations.) Conversely, our very thought processes are composed of language and interiorized conversations with others. Therefore, we are embedded, to a great extent unconsciously, in interpersonal fields, and, conversely, interpersonal configurations are embedded, to a great extent unconsciously, in our individual psyches.

The great nature-versus-nurture, biology-versus-culture dialectic shaped Freud's ways of understanding all fundamental psychoanalytic problems—the unconscious, sexuality, aggression, fantasy, conflict, and so on. For us, these polarities have been deconstructed, rethought in more complex terms. We have come to appreciate the ways in which nature and nurture, as well as biology and culture, continually interpenetrate and mutually shape each other, so that traditional psychoanalytic problems are increasingly reframed in terms of conflictual mental states and organizations, projective–introjective cycles of intrapsychic and interpersonal processes, and conflictual attachments and identifications with different sorts of external and internal objects.

In terms of clinical technique, I believe a very important shift began about five years ago. With the development of interpersonal or relational understandings of the analytic process in the 1970s and 1980s, the analyst's participation in and influence on the analytic process were understood as being increasingly important.

Countertransference was no longer an obstacle but a tool, and neutrality was understood as an influence-masking illusion. The most important contributors to that understanding, in my view, were Edgar Levenson and Merton Gill, and both Levenson and Gill placed great importance on the interpretation of transference–countertransference dynamics as *the* fundamental analytic tool. It is very important not to assume that the patient's experience of the analyst is a distortion, a temporal displacement from early childhood, both argued. The patient reacts to the analyst—through past experience and unconscious dynamics, to be sure—as a real, nontransparent person in the here and now. The analyst has to keep a focus on the patient's experience of the analyst's participation—for Levenson, through Sullivan's "detailed inquiry," and for Gill, through continual interpretation of allusions and resistances to the transference. If the analyst's impact on the process is not made explicit, the process becomes, in Levenson's (1983) terms, persuasion rather than cure, and in Gill's terms, a manipulative transference cure. In this view, the analyst's interactive involvement in the process is an inevitable contaminant, but the patient's autonomy can be preserved by a vigilant analysis of that contaminant.

Over the past five to 10 years, there has been a gradual realization that there is no way to filter out the analyst's impact on the process. Continual inquiry, persistent transference interpretation, and systematic self-disclosure are hardly ways to limit the analyst's influence. They are, in fact, very powerful ways of steering and influencing the process. This realization, I believe, is having a profound impact on the ways we are now exploring the nature of analytic technique.

For previous generations of clinicians, technique referred primarily to behavior. What should the analyst do? What should the analyst refrain from doing? This cannot possibly work for us. We have come to realize that the meaning of whatever the analyst does or does not do is contextual and co-constructed. The analyst cannot decide on the meaning of the "frame" unilaterally. For some patients, silence is a form of holding; for others, it is a form of torture. For some patients, interpretation conveys deep recognition and self-expansion; for others, it is a form of violent exposure. For some patients, the analyst's self-disclosure might offer a unique and precious form of authenticity and honesty; for others, it is a form of charismatic seduction and narcissistic exploitation. For some patients, questions represent a precious willingness to join and know them; for others, questions are a surreptitious invasion. It is no longer compelling to decide that these events are what we want them to be and that when patients experience the otherwise they are distorting. Interpersonal situations are ambiguous and can be interpreted in many different ways, depending on our past and our dynamics.

Note

1 The late Stephen A. Mitchell, Ph.D. was Founding Editor, *Psychoanalytic Dialogues: A Journal of Relational Perspectives.*

Chapter 6

An Autobiographical Fragment*

Jay Greenberg

You couldn't grow up in Brooklyn when I did, in the late 1940s and the 1950s, and not turn out to be at least a little bit of a Freudian. You might never have heard of Freud, of course, and I don't recall that I did. Joseph McCarthy, Jackie Robinson, and Elvis Presley more directly entered into and shaped my life. But, you'd be a little bit of a Freudian nonetheless, whether you knew it or not, because conflict and compromise were the stuff of everyday life. Roy Schafer (1976), in describing Freud's tragic vision, remarked that it sensitizes us to the "inescapable dangers, terrors, mysteries, and absurdities of existence" (p. 35). In Brooklyn, this was the air that we breathed.

What I mean by this is that, in those early years, wherever you looked, especially if you looked beneath the surface, the bad guys were winning.

Prosperity and peace were all around, and there was a great deal of relief about the end of World War II—a relief that seemed like some kind of distant adult experience because nobody born during the war could guess what the great danger had been. But the events of the day—the execution of the Rosenbergs, the conviction of Alger Hiss (in both cases, we all believed passionately in their innocence), the defeat, twice, of the cerebral, liberal Adlai Stevenson, and the ascent of the first Republican president to hold office since our parents were barely out of their teens—made it clear that, however much promise there was in the air, it must be for other people. Our own causes, our own passions, were doomed, and nobody outside our immediate community seemed to care.

And then there were the Dodgers who every year, with the regularity of the seasons themselves, brought tragedy home and reminded us unmistakably and unavoidably what life was all about. The tragedy of the Dodgers played itself out literally outside my window (we lived right next to the ballpark) as well as deep within my heart. The Dodgers—true heroes to a

---

* Reprinted with kind permission: This chapter was first published as an article with the same title in *Psychoanalytic Inquiry* 24 (4): 517–530.

man, including, amazingly, their owner, who took it on himself to break baseball's color barrier just as I was becoming aware of the game—seduced us every spring and betrayed us every fall. Not only did they lose after coming oh so close, but they lost (usually) to the Yankees, that very embodiment of front-running, right-wing, mainstream dominance.

The message was clear: good things may happen, but they happen to somebody else. Our own passions are whetted, teased, and ultimately frustrated. Living repeatedly through the Dodgers' shortfall, I inevitably felt that I'd found a kindred spirit when I read Freud (1912): "however strange it may sound, we must reckon with the possibility that something in the nature of the sexual instinct itself is unfavorable to the realization of complete satisfaction" (pp. 188-189). Desire by its very nature dooms itself to frustration, and it dooms those who feel it to disappointment. The man who wrote this would have felt entirely at home in my Brooklyn Octobers. In the tragic vision, Schafer (1976) reminded us, time is linear and consequences irreversible (p. 36). Despite Yogi Berra's quasi-romantic reassurance that "it ain't over'til it's over," by mid-October it was over, and only the winter lay ahead.

But I suspect that Freud would also agree with what I had more or less preconsciously concluded as I was growing up: knowing that disappointment is coming need not dampen the pleasure of the pursuit. To cite Schafer (1976) again, the tragic vision includes an appreciation of the way in which there are "elements of defeat in victory and of victory in defeat" (p. 35). So, our predictable defeat was, paradoxically, an affirmation of life itself. "Wait'til next year" was the rallying cry for all of us, and we did wait, though we were aware of and enjoyed the irony. And then every April we believed that things were going to turn out differently. So, we loved the ride, even as the rumblings of distant thunder permeated every aspect of the experience.

The appeal of a tragic vision of life drew me not only to Freud but also to the Greeks, who invented tragedy as a dramatic form. I studied ancient Greek history and philosophy in college, and classical plays and epic poems still constitute the bulk of my summer reading. What the Greeks knew, and what Freud learned from them and was able to apply to what his patients were telling him, was that a great deal of the drama of life goes on beneath the surface—fueling social structure but hidden from everyday view. Aeschylus's *Oresteia* tells the story of how the Athenian justice system—in fact, the human capacity to know and to act on what is just—emerged from hundreds of years of acts of greed, lust, blind ambition, parricide, child-murder, and revenge, all within the generations of a single family. Freud's borrowing of the Oedipus story (and his brilliant, world-changing, idiosyncratic reading of it) highlighted the hidden drama beneath the surface of every social organization from family to city state. Recall that the public Oedipus was considered by his subjects to be a wise, virtually godlike king and that Thebes prospered for many years despite his seminal crime.

Of course, it was not just life in Brooklyn, not even mainly my attachment to the Dodgers, that drove home the wisdom and poignance of the tragic vision. Within my family, there was an unmistakable but unspoken tension between the way things worked and the feelings felt. On the surface, everything was calm; desire seemed perfectly matched to available resources. As a result, I never sensed any lack; what my parents wanted, they had. There was never a great deal of anticipation, and there was not very much talk about the future or about the past.

Despite the smooth operation of my family, widely acknowledged and appreciated by their friends and neighbors, the calm did not extend very deeply into my parents' experience. From what I was able to see over the years, disappointment infiltrated their self-consciousness like water that seeps into a wood foundation, eventually rotting it from inside. My father, a more than locally renowned athlete in his youth, was on the cusp of playing professional basketball—admittedly not the big deal in those days that it is today but nevertheless the thing he valued most throughout his life—when he hurt his knee and had to give up his plans. Trained as a lawyer, he practiced with little success for a couple of years during the Depression and then pretty quickly went into my maternal grandfather's small manufacturing business. He hated the business and for various reasons felt betrayed both by his father-in-law and by my mother. This I learned years later through the grapevine; although I knew perfectly well how miserable he was, I never knew anything about why. When he was in the hospital during his final illness (my mother had been dead for 10 years already), I had a chance to look at the chart that included the information he had given to the admissions clerk. My father had listed his occupation as *attorney*, a profession he had practiced for perhaps four years of his 30-year working life. It drove home to me, as none of our time together had, how wasted he felt his life had been.

My mother's story was, in many respects, not terribly different. Also trained as a lawyer—remarkable for a woman of her generation but never impressive to me, partly because so many other women in the extended family were lawyers, partly because she never expressed pride or pleasure about it—she too left practice early. For a few years, she worked in her father's business, and then she stayed home to raise me and to participate fiercely in school and community organizations.

So, my inclination to appreciate Freud's vision was established early on. Of course, as things have turned out, I am not a strict Freudian, and, in one particularly powerful way, I think Freud missed the boat. To explain why I think this, I have to skip 10 years or so—a decade in which my parents moved "up" and out of Brooklyn and in which the Dodgers, after finally winning a World Series, did the same—to my first therapy experience. This was immediately after college, and I was feeling adrift and aimless, with a lack of structure weighing heavily on me. Going into treatment, with a senior analyst at the Chicago Psychoanalytic Institute, was a difficult decision for me. I quickly found that talking about myself not only provided a welcome sense of relief from painful feelings but also opened up a sense of possibility and optimism about the future. It was transforming but not, as I think about it in retrospect, mainly because of what I learned about myself. Rather, what touched and moved me was that I had the chance to see my life through the eyes of a benign, fatherly man who seemed to be interested in my doing better than I was doing but who had no particular axe to grind about the direction my life might take.

There is more to say about my first experience as a patient that shaped my subsequent course as an analyst. Reflecting back on that time, I see that, though I was somewhat interested in myself—my mind and its workings—I was far more interested in my therapist. From my vantage point 35 years later, I recall, in a way that I couldn't quite be conscious of when it was happening, how attentive I was to his reactions and how his every response seemed to be a vote in a referendum on the way I was living my life. And, of course, I reacted to his reactions. When he seemed to be on my side—this didn't mean approving of my behavior, as I was pretty regularly screwing up—I was increasingly able to think about myself and to entertain the possibility of change. When he seemed more critical, I sometimes clammed up and became defensive. But consistently I watched him, and I went as far as I could, given the interpersonal atmosphere I was sensing.

To state the obvious, my attention to my therapist's attitude toward me was my transference, or at least an important facet of it. By my early 20s, I was quite convinced that things—interpersonal things, anyway—couldn't be taken at face value and that everything depended on the feelings beneath the surface. In turn, safety was possible only if you knew what was going on. But, as I suspect is more generally the case than most of us acknowledge, my transference, which reappeared in subsequent analyses and which I must admit was never very deeply engaged, shaped my analytic sensibility. I find my own needs in the needs of my analysands.

My early therapy ended, for a not atypical combination of clinical and logistical reasons, after about two years. During this time, and for the next year or so, I worked at a number of odd jobs and waited to be hit by some good idea that would point me in a professional direction. Eventually, the idea did hit, and I returned to New York to go to graduate school for clinical psychology. As I prepare this autobiographical statement, I find it interesting that, by the time I entered graduate school, with very little knowledge of the issues that psychoanalytically oriented psychologists were thinking about, I was already deeply committed to two lines of thought. My personal history, reinforced and to a considerable extent validated by my reading of Greek tragedy, had given me a powerful appreciation of the way that hidden conflicts and their attendant disappointments shape our everyday lives. Along those lines, I had developed a fair amount of skepticism about the trustworthiness of conscious experience, or at least about experience that can easily be shared with others. But at the time, as a result of my treatment, I had come to believe in the important role that the nuances of the analyst's behavior have in determining how effectively the patient is able to use treatment. These themes are central to my thinking today; I return to them regularly, and I find myself reworking them at various levels of abstraction.

Decades later, it is clear to me that, though these two sensibilities are held central by the two theoretical traditions that have attracted me, neither tradition fully values both. Freud's tragic vision draws me to him, but Freud never looked very deeply at the subtleties of the analyst's participation. He wrote, at least in his more formal discussions of the workings of the analytic process, that the analysand would be deeply affected only by the analyst's correct interpretations. Freud did not expect that the analysand would scrutinize everything that the analyst said; incorrect constructions, for example, would roll off the patient like water off a duck's back (Freud, 1937, p. 261). No patient who, like myself, had so carefully examined his analyst's every expression could feel at home with that perspective. In fact, it was bound to feel intimidating, implying as it did that "analyzable" patients need to be able to pay attention to themselves, not to their analysts.

In contrast to Freud and his followers within classical psychoanalysis, interpersonal and relational authors focus minutely on the nuances of the analyst's behavior and on the way that small things can either facilitate or inhibit the work. This legitimizes my experience as a patient in much the same way that Greek tragedy legitimized my experience within my family. At the same time, however, it is hard to find room for a tragic vision in contemporary relational views or in some of the more romantic branches of the American interpersonal tradition. There is a sense in these approaches that the analyst, provided he or she can muster enough sensitivity and flexibility, can get things right and thus create something that is more alive and more generative than the archaic experiences. There is an underlying assumption that time need not be quite linear, so that rectification and repair are possible. The romanticism, of course, doesn't sit well with me.

Despite my strongly (if preconsciously) held ideas about what mattered in psychoanalytic theory and practice, when I had to make my choices about graduate school I knew virtually nothing about what was actually going on in the field. Luckily and coincidentally (because my choice was dictated mainly by geography and serendipity), I wound up doing my graduate work in the clinical psychology program at New York University (NYU). At the time, the program was divided into two virtually independent factions, staffed by psychologists and psychoanalysts who represented the two intellectual perspectives that, unbeknownst to me at the time, reflected the themes that were important to me. On one hand, there was the Research Center for Mental Health, dominated before I got there by David Rapaport and now run by his students. Most of those students—George Klein, Robert Holt, and Donald Spence were full-time faculty, and Merton Gill was a visiting research fellow—were at work dismantling Rapaport's metapsychological edifice, but all of them were committed to a Freudian clinical sensibility.

On the other hand, linked fragilely to the research center through mutual ties with a two-person administrative faculty was a group of clinical adjuncts whose orientation was largely interpersonal with some influence from the early British object relations theorists. As things worked out, I took courses from the research center faculty while having supervision with the adjuncts. That experience, in retrospect, was less perplexing than it might have been. In fairness, I should probably say "in retrospect only" because at the time the multiplicity of voices was confusing to me, as it is to all newcomers. The theory stood as an impressive edifice within which clinical exploration could take place, safely and (at times) confidently. In most areas, Freud seemed to me to be asking more of the important questions than anybody else did. And, in an academic environment in which Freud's answers were being systematically deconstructed by the most powerful authority figures, it seemed possible (in a way that it probably was not anywhere else at the time) to think about what my own answers to those questions might be.

In supervision, I gained some understanding of the sensitivity to interpersonal nuance that I had felt in my own treatment. My supervisors were interested in exactly those areas in which Freud was least informative—the nature of the analyst's experience, the origin of the analyst's feelings and their impact on the patient, and so on. Over the course of a number of years, it began to make sense to me why I had been so involved in what my therapist had been thinking and in how he had been reacting to me. According to my supervisors, this was at least one central way of understanding the essence of an analytic process.

By the time I finished graduate school, I had any number of voices in my head—Freud's questions, his answers along with their deconstruction, my history of personal sensitivity to my analyst's feelings (reinforced now by similar reactions to a very different second analyst), supervisors' opinions to the effect that analysts do in fact have consequential reactions to their analysands, and a still unarticulated personal relationship with a tragic vision of life.

With all this, I began my psychoanalytic training at the William Alanson White Institute, an institute committed to a pluralism organized around the centrality of the interpersonal approaches of Sullivan and Fromm. My supervision at the White institute developed, for the most part, the sensibilities that had been formed in my own treatment and that had grown through my work at NYU. At White, though, I was more exposed to the conceptual grounding of interpersonal theory, which added another voice to my musings.

In a supervision group during my third year of graduate school, I met and became friendly with Steve Mitchell. Steve had graduated from NYU two years before I had. When he graduated from White, a year before I did, he began teaching a course in interpersonal and object relations theory at the National Institute for the Psychotherapies (NIP). The year I graduated, the instructor for NIP's course on Freud and the ego psychologists left New York, Steve recommended me for the position, and I was hired. From then on, our ideas about teaching our respective courses became a frequent topic of conversation. Steve found that it made no sense to teach interpersonal thinking in isolation from the classical theory to which it was in many ways a reaction. Similarly, I felt that the evolution of Freud's thinking, and certainly of the thinking of the ego psychologists, was to a significant extent a reaction to "outside" pressures—from Adler, Jung, and other dissenters (in Freud's case) and from the interpersonalists and the Kleinians (in the case of the ego psychologists).

One thing that emerged from our conversations about these issues was our book, *Object Relations in Psychoanalytic Theory* (1983). This book is, of course, an exercise in comparative psychoanalysis. When we conceived and wrote it, it represented a way of sorting out the voices that (as a result of our common training experience) clamored inside our heads. Our agenda was to clarify what seemed to us a confusing array of differing perspectives on a set of converging problems. Because of personal preferences, Steve gravitated to the thinking of theorists of what we called the *relational model*; similarly, my history led me to respect authors working within the tradition of Freudian drive theory.

As things turned out—and quite surprisingly to us—the book, along with contemporary events, was part of a dramatic shift in both the politics and the conceptual structure of psychoanalysis in the United States that began in the 1980s and that continues today. Remarkably, three other important radical books were published within a year of ours—Donald Spence's *Narrative Truth and Historical Truth* (1982), Merton Gill's *Analysis of Transference* (1982), and Roy Schafer's *The Analytic Attitude* (1983), a follow-up to Schafer's earlier plea for a "new language" for psychoanalysis. Each of these works critiques the epistemologic or metapsychological status of classical psychoanalysis, each immediately became popular, and each pushed us toward an increased appreciation of the role of the analyst's participation in the psychoanalytic process.

Probably not coincidentally, three of these four books were written by psychologists, though Mitchell and I were the only authors who were not members of the American Psychoanalytic Association. And at the same time these books were appearing, political attacks on medical hegemony were becoming more frequent and more effective. A lawsuit filed by psychologists against the International Psychoanalytic Association, the formation of the Division of Psychoanalysis (Division 39) within the American Psychological Association, and the creation of a group of autonomous training institutes for professionals excluded by American-affiliated institutes all helped open the field to new voices that were not socialized into traditional ways of thinking about psychoanalysis.

I never shared the outrage that many psychologists and psychoanalysts felt about either the dominance of the medical establishment or of the American Psychoanalytic Association. With my being from Brooklyn, or at least my corner of Brooklyn, exclusion from the mainstream had always been something of a badge of honor, an affirmation of a peculiar kind of specialness. I wanted recognition but was (and am) indifferent to membership. Let the Yankees be the Yankees, or let the American Psychoanalytic Association be the American, I thought—my own strivings seem more interesting than their successes.

Nevertheless, broad acceptance of our *Object Relations* book had an impact on the institutional climate. In 1991, Mitchell and I were invited to participate in separate panels at the American Psychoanalytic Association convention. During the floor discussion of Steve's panel, Merton Gill, who had befriended and generously encouraged us from the time when we were writing the *Object Relations* book, stood up to remark on the occasion. Psychologists had appeared on panels before, he said, but this year there were two on the program. And moreover, he noted, "this is the first year that we have invited *traif* psychologists!" As I look back on that, there could be nothing better than being both included and *traif*; neither would have been as satisfying without the other.

When Steve and I were writing our book, neither thought of it as serving political purposes. Our intention in undertaking a study in comparative psychoanalysis was to try to sort out (largely for ourselves) some of the themes that ran through the work of authors working in the different traditions to which we had been exposed— mainly ego-psychological and interpersonal, with occasional nods to Kleinian. Only fairly recently did I recognize the political impact of our book, and I take issue with some recent authors (notably Arnold Richards and John Gedo) who have characterized the work as political in its intent as well as its effect.

In retrospect, I have come to believe that, if history is written by the winners, comparative psychoanalysis is most likely to be written by the losers. In 1983, when our book appeared, the American psychoanalytic establishment was solidly controlled by the ego psychologists; interpersonal thinking was never acknowledged in their journals. Moreover, there was apparently tacit agreement between the ego psychologists and adherents of the most important dissident group, Kohut and his followers within self psychology, that both groups would be best served by developing their thinking in isolation from each other. Evidently, mainstream analysts believed that any psychoanalytic vision worth pursuing could be contained within the conceptual structure of classical thinking.

So comparative psychoanalysis, which sets itself the project of defining the scope of each model's approach and thus highlights their limits, by its nature makes room for previously marginalized points of view. This is why it is likely to be undertaken by the marginalized—that is, by those who believe that their own point of view adds something, something valuable and genuinely psychoanalytic, to what has already been said but has not been heard.

This was made clear to me in 1986, when Mitchell and I, surprised and gratified, were invited to appear at a "Meet the Author" session of the American Psychoanalytic Association. One discussant said of our book, "The question is not whether it is well done, because certainly it is. The question is whether it should have been done at all." Although I was initially taken aback by this stark comment, its meaning quickly came through: the very project of comparative psychoanalysis is based on the assumption that there are phenomena that cannot be adequately theorized within the structure of an evolving ego psychology. This assumption undermines the completeness and perhaps even the coherence of the received metapsychology and thus damages the psychoanalytic enterprise. Solving conceptual problems within the terms of the existing model strengthens the hegemony of that model; suggesting that there is a need to go outside the model inevitably weakens it. And we were pointing to legitimately psychoanalytic perspectives that had been developed outside the mainstream.

Now, two decades later, it would be jarring to hear anybody say that a psychoanalytic book shouldn't have been written. This is not, of course, to say that rancor has disappeared from our debates or that groups organized around particular ideas are not practicing exclusionary politics. Political integration is fragile, because it tends to create circumstances that fracture it. Broadly based organizations encourage the emergence of new voices and new ideas, but these voices and ideas are not always warmly received by the established membership, even when the organizations are reasonably open-minded. Ideas are criticized, feelings are hurt, and it often seems as if the path of least resistance is to break away, to start a new organization. Those who break away from organizations hope to create a structure within which new ideas can be expressed without the fear that their proponents will have to accommodate them to what comes to be thought of as "outside" criticism.

This was Freud's strategy early on. At his Tuesday evening meetings, papers were presented without discussants because Freud believed that the criticism inherent in the discussants' presentation would inhibit creativity. When he created a committee to decide which points of view were legitimately psychoanalytic, it was because he felt that it would be distracting to those who were developing psychoanalysis to have to respond to ideas that were too far afield.

So, political integration in psychoanalysis, which has been difficult to achieve, is perhaps even more difficult to sustain; centrifugal force is always at work. At the same time, another tendency—to believe that political integration should lead to conceptual integration or at least to some kind of convergence—works against the best interests of the field. Many analysts sympathetic to the goal of opening organizations to new voices also subscribe to one version or another of what Leo Rangell has called a "unitary psychoanalytic theory." I don't believe that a unitary theory, however general, can or ever will serve psychoanalysis well. There are, simply put, too many interesting ways to hear what our analysands have to say, and too many potentially facilitative ways to understand their experience, to force our listening or our understanding into the conceptual structure that any single theory has to offer.

Coincidentally, while writing this autobiographical fragment, I finished a draft of a paper that represents my first attempt to conceptualize a substantially new perspective on the origins and role of intrapsychic conflict. A few days earlier, I showed the draft to a friend and colleague who is identified with a classical version of contemporary conflict theory. In a brief phone message, he let me know that, to the surprise of neither of us, he disagreed with a great deal of what I had written—and he suggested we talk about it. I am, at this moment, waiting for his follow-up call. As I wait, I have two thoughts. First, I hope that my friend isn't too critical of the way I have represented the point of view he espouses. I don't mind if he feels a bit misunderstood—that is the inevitable and potentially generative result of an "outsider" commenting on a point of view that others know from "inside"—but if he feels I've missed the boat in some important way, I'll have to rethink my presentation.

My second and more important thought is that I won't be bothered if my friend is critical of the new ideas I'm developing. In fact, I would be a bit disappointed if he is not. Any disagreement that the two of us will have is likely to lead to an interesting conversation, as long as neither of us is too wounded by it. I have no hope of convincing him that the theory to which he has subscribed for decades has been languishing until my emendations of it came along. And I doubt that he has any hope of convincing me that I am wasting my creative energies trying to modify something that has long since been perfected. But, the conversation, if successful, will probe the dark corners of what each of us believes in a way that discussions with colleagues more in agreement never can, and it will enrich our thinking over the long haul, no matter how vehement each of us might become in the moment.

The hope that my work will stimulate and sustain this sort of conversation lies at the root of my participation in the institutional life of psychoanalysis. This hope itself is deeply rooted in my history of being excluded from what were certainly the most important conversations in my family. So, predictably, I want to participate. But I do not expect and would not welcome the kind of agreement that would lead to consensus about a unitary psychoanalytic theory. Consensus about anything interesting seems to me utopian at best; more deeply, I am afraid that consensus is usually the outcome of some sort of coercion. Therefore, I feel most myself and most creative when I can enjoy the generative tension that open disagreement offers. This is the best atmosphere for us as psychoanalytic thinkers and, ultimately, for our analysands.

Familiar tensions continue to haunt me when I think about psychoanalytic ideas. I remain impressed by the powerful ways in which our private lives shape (not only are shaped by) our social experience. I am drawn to a tragic vision of life and so to the Freudian emphasis on the ubiquity of conflict and on the inevitable elusiveness of full satisfaction. But I can never forget how attentive I was to the reactions of my first analyst or, for that matter, to those of my subsequent analysts right up to the memorable final minute of my last treatment. So, in my work I continue to search for a middle road. I used to think that, if I could find a middle road, the solution would have broad appeal (itself a romantic idea, based on a belief in or hope for particular kinds of happy endings). Now, I have come to see that middle-road solutions simply add one more voice to the cacophony—and that the middle road is as radical as any of the extremes.

But I am sure that a certain level of cacophony is for the best. I have traveled a road that began with a resigned sense of exclusion from the psychoanalytic establishment and that has led to inclusion in what I think of as its most interesting conversations. I'm still intrigued, however, by the idea of being a *traif* psychologist. Even though the meaning of being *traif* and the meaning of being a psychologist have changed dramatically over the years, I value the freedom that comes with the role. As I have always believed, being a Dodger fan is much more fun than rooting for the Yankees.

References

Freud, S. (1912). On the universal tendency to debasement in the sphere of love (Contributions to the psychology of love: II). *Standard Edition*, 11: 177–190. London: Hogarth Press, 1957.
Freud, S. (1937). Constructions in analysis. *Standard Edition*, 23: 255–269. London: Hogarth Press, 1964.
Gill, M. (1982), *Analysis of Transference*, Vol. 1. New York: International Universities Press.
Greenberg, J. & Mitchell, S. (1983), *Object Relations in Psychoanalytic Theory*. Cambridge, MA: Harvard University Press.
Schafer, R. (1976). *A New Language for Psychoanalysis*. New Haven, CT: Yale University Press.
Schafer, R. (1983). *The Analytic Attitude*. New York: Basic Books.
Spence, D. (1982). *Narrative Truth and Historical Truth*. New York: Norton.

Chapter 7

Credo: Psychoanalysis as a Wisdom Tradition

Nancy McWilliams

When I discovered psychoanalysis, I felt I had somehow come home. My decision to be a psychoanalytic therapist resulted from my sense that this vocation offered a perfect integration of my interests, talents, values, and core identifications. My interests included learning as widely as possible, especially in the arts and social sciences; as a child and adolescent I was immensely curious about myself, other people, and the world. My talents included a natural sympathy, an ear for music and emotional experiences in general, and some skill at teaching. My orienting ideals involved commitments to honesty and kindness.

Personal Background

Family Influences

These values came, respectively, from a father who was morally scrupulous almost to a fault and a mother who was unfailingly patient with others and compassionate about their suffering. My father venerated education, especially in the liberal arts, and my mother was memorably psychologically minded. Moral concerns infused our family discussions of both individual behavior and sociopolitical life; around the dinner table, we talked a lot about what would now be called social justice issues. (These conversations laid the groundwork for my eventual involvement in the movements of the mid-1960s.)

It was only well after my mother's death, when I was 9, that I realized she had almost certainly been influenced by psychoanalysis during her graduate years in the 1930s at Columbia Teachers College (before I was born, she had been a teacher of the deaf). She would frequently give voice to what I can see in retrospect as psychoanalytically influenced understandings of others. Such sensibilities were not prevalent, however, in the Republican, Protestant, upper-middle-class suburbs in which I grew up. Beyond a vague understanding that Freud had emphasized sexuality, I knew little about analytic theories until I was an undergraduate at Oberlin College, a school I had

DOI: 10.4324/9781003206248-7

chosen based on its having been the first to admit women on an equal basis with men and blacks on an equal basis with whites.

Educational Influences

Although I was fascinated by human psychology and specifically by individual differences, I did not take any courses in psychology at Oberlin. In 1963, the department had extensive requirements for its majors, the requirements that would limit my exposure to other areas of study. The yearlong, sophomore-level class in Learning, a demanding course involving lab work with rats—a feature I found unappealing—was a prerequisite to the junior- and senior-level seminars in which (as I saw it) students and professors could finally talk about human beings. In contrast, the courses offered by the Government (political science) department were centrally and immediately concerned with human psychology—not just voting behavior but also core human motivations. And the requirements for a Government major were less constraining.

I thus majored in Government, with an emphasis on political theory. I studied Plato, Aristotle, Aquinas, Augustine, Rousseau, Hobbes, Kant, Locke, Mill, and other political philosophers. I loved Alexis de Tocqueville's brilliant commentaries on the American mind. For my junior honors thesis, I had to examine and critique the political theory of an important thinker, and my faculty advisor (whom I later married, but that is another topic) commented that I seemed to be quite psychologically oriented. He suggested that I write on the political philosophy of Freud, and he handed me a copy of *Civilization and Its Discontents*.

From that point, I was off and running. My own psychology is very oedipally organized, and so reading Freud felt like finding words for things that on some level I had always known. I started devouring the writing of analysts whose work was then widely available in bookstores: Erich Fromm, Karen Horney, Norman O. Brown, Herbert Marcuse, Bruno Bettelheim, and, most influentially, Theodor Reik. What attracted me to Reik's work initially was that he wrote about female psychology as if it were interesting and valuable in its own right, rather than in the more usual tone of the day that implicitly construed femininity as a mystifying deviation from a male norm. To a girl who had idealized her dead mother and tried to emulate her feminine/maternal qualities, this perspective was an unexpected, priceless gift.

I was a highly moralistic adolescent, inspired by Freud's linking of truth with freedom. For numerous intersecting reasons (including, but not limited to, being a second child and hence inclined toward oppositionality, having lived in several different communities with different sensibilities, and identifying with a father who had radar for dissimulation), I was skeptical about surface appearances and conventions, and I loved reading the work of social critics such as Mark Twain, Sinclair Lewis, Jessica Mitford, John Steinbeck, James Baldwin, and Betty Friedan. By the time I began reading psychoanalytic writing, I was already attracted to certain ancient ideas, including the Delphic "Know thyself." The Freudian idea that knowing oneself could work in the service of a kind of personal liberation greatly inspired me. After Oberlin, now married, I moved to Brooklyn, where I took nonmatriculated courses in psychology at Brooklyn College.

In my early 20s, I contacted Theodor Reik, mostly out of curiosity to meet someone who had been close to Freud. My putative aim was to get Reik's advice about my career. Instead, he talked me into going into a personal analysis, which was then affordable via our insurance. Luckily, the clinic at the National Psychological Association for Psychoanalysis, to which he sent me (which he had founded when rejected by the medical institutes on the grounds that he was a psychologist), referred me to a psychoanalyst who was extremely well suited, by both temperament and values, for working with me (McWilliams, 2013). I entered treatment for what I saw as professional reasons, thinking that an experience on the analytic couch would prepare me to be whatever kind of psychotherapist I would eventually opt to become—much as learning classical music would be good preparation for a career in jazz or learning Latin would facilitate learning modern languages. Instead, I found that my time on the couch influenced my life in profound ways. Once that happened, there was no way I was going to be anything but an analyst.

Clinical Influences

I began to get clinical training after I had been in analysis for a few years. The fact that I had internalized a deeply therapeutic experience before being exposed to clinical literature was an asset to my evolution as a therapist. I had a feel for what each concept meant when applied, and I considered ideas skeptically when what I was taught did not match my own experience. My having read Freud and other analysts by this time was also critical. I knew what Freud had said (and not said), and I was familiar with the tone in which he wrote. When a mentor would insist that some procedure amounted to "the rules," or "Freudian technique," and that formulation did not fit with my prior reading or my experience as an analysand, I suspected that the teacher was sacrificing the breadth and depth of analytic ideas in the service of fundamentalism. I sought supervisors who were not only knowledgeable but also open-minded and nondogmatic.

I knew what elements in my analysis had felt helpful to me. They did not involve a rigid adherence to the rules of technique that at the time the medical institutes were calling classical psychoanalysis. Theodor Reik was "classical" enough to have been Freud's protégé, but he emphasized intuition, openness to being surprised, and what would later be considered an intersubjective sensibility. Although my analyst was highly disciplined and considered himself a Freudian, he was flexible, modest, and occasionally personally disclosing. He had a warm sense of humor. It was not his brilliant interpretations that powered our work; it was his presence, empathy, and confidence that I could face what I needed to face in myself if I would follow my associations all the way to their darkest destinations. I never felt he was pushing his understandings on me; instead, I was finding and giving voice myself to previously disowned personal feelings, fantasies, motives, and experiences.

An example of my analyst's flexibility is that after a couple of years of my seeing him individually three times a week, he suggested that we add one weekly double session with my spouse. Our marriage was in trouble, and I had failed to talk my husband into seeing an analyst of his own. I was able, however, to persuade him to join me in seeing mine, a known quantity about whom he was curious. That experience not only improved our relationship but also reduced my husband's resistance to going into treatment himself. After a year of combined individual and couple work, resulting in considerable progress, we both decided to end the joint meetings and to continue our individual analyses.

In our last marital session, as we reviewed our gains, my analyst commented in passing that some analysts disapproved of combining individual with couple therapy because seeing the patient with a partner would "dilute the transference." I remember my reaction: "They're thinking backwards. The transference isn't the *aim* of treatment, it's a *means* toward an end. Why would you put the goal of preserving the purity of the transference above the overall goal of improving a marriage?" Since then, I have seen similar conflations of means and ends, as when a supervisor praises a student for a therapeutic result but adds that it "was not really analysis," as if adherence to a particular analytic technique is more important than therapy outcome. It is one of my pet peeves, the idealization of a method at the expense of the purpose for which it was devised.

Credo

My core beliefs about psychoanalysis and psychoanalytic therapy reflect the earliest analytic influences on me, all of which were affected by Theodor Reik's legacy (Aragno, 2011; Nobus, 2006; Sherman, 1965). Reik was not invested in creating his own theory or "school" of psychoanalysis. Interestingly, although he was known for his oppositional streak and had had significant disagreements with Freud, he was never distanced as a heretic. This suggests me that the emotional tone in which he expressed divergent opinions somehow did not provoke hostility, a quality I have tried to emulate.

Psychoanalysis as a Wisdom Tradition

The term "psychoanalysis" has been used to describe (1) a specific therapeutic method (seeing the patient multiple times a week, using the couch, urging free association, addressing the transference as it emerges as a resistance); (2) a body of knowledge; and (3) an ethos (McWilliams, 2020). Some contemporary difficulties for our field derive from the fact that many people know only the first meaning of the term. I greatly appreciate the power of traditional analysis; I have fruitfully worked that way with many patients who have wanted to explore themselves deeply. But careful discriminations between "psychodynamic" and "psychoanalytic" may convey too rigid a boundary. When ex-patients talk about positive experiences in analytic treatment, they typically depict sensitive deviations from standard protocols rather than slavish adherence to a prescribed model. For this reason, I am grateful to theorists who have emphasized psychoanalytic spontaneity within an overall frame (Hoffman, 1998).

To me, the heart of our tradition is its accumulation of powerful ways to think about personality, subjectivity, and the meaning of many kinds of suffering. I have long been worried that a huge store of collective wisdom is being lost to ignorance and misunderstanding, abetted by the agendas of third-party payors, commercial interests such as drug companies, and some academics who have not seen a real patient for years. Clinical wisdom is hard to come by, and yet over more than a century, analysts have found metaphors and concepts that illuminate unconscious aspects of our complex human condition. This knowledge is valuable not only for treating mental health problems but also for exploring group dynamics, politics, art, literature, history, and other realms.

Emotional Immersion

My own experiences with therapy (and those of my patients, colleagues, and friends) attest that meaningful, lasting psychological change does not happen without turning oneself over to a deeply affective process characterized by intense vulnerability. Much of the healing in analytic treatment seems to me to be essentially a grieving process. Probably because of the consequences of the losses in my own history, my favorite paper by Freud (1917) is "Mourning and Melancholia," with its beautiful evocation of normal grief. I have also resonated to Loewald's (1960) haunting metaphor of turning ghosts into ancestors. Such formulations emphasize the fact that therapy involves not only behavioral and symptomatic change but also deep acceptance of what *cannot* be changed. This is the process that mourning accomplishes, and to mourn, we need a witness who can bear our pain.

I have been fascinated by the investigations of Rainer Krause and his colleagues in Germany (Anstadt, Merten, Ullrich, & Krause, 1997). On the basis of videotapes of seasoned therapists with complexly suffering patients, they have concluded that nonverbal emotional communications between patient and clinician have much more impact on outcome than the therapist's theoretical orientation, interpretations, or technical interventions. Their work supports the affective theories of Silvan Tomkins, one of my mentors, as well as the perspectives of analysts who have emphasized emotional relearning. Frieda Fromm-Reichmann, for example, was fond of noting that patients do not need interpretations; they need experience. I see the object relations theorists (Klein, Fairbairn, Winnicott, Bowlby, Guntrip, and others), with their focus on effectively infused relational patterns, as having accounted more comprehensively for human psychology and the change process than Freud did via the concept of drive. Even though I have not been at the center of that movement, I have admired the evolution of relational psychoanalysis.

My analysis left me with awe about unconscious processes. I take seriously that the unconscious is truly unconscious, and that it takes time and trust to access. I prefer to let an experiential therapeutic process unfold organically, and feel how it permeates the transference-countertransference matrix, over pursuing it as one might in emotion-focused therapy, Accelerated Experiential Dynamic Therapy or Intensive Short-Term Dynamic Psychotherapy. This preference probably expresses mostly a temperamental bias. I would feel impinged on and even manipulated by a clinician who was actively trying to elicit my emotions.

Intuition/Subjectivity/Empathy

In the 1930s, there was an argument (in my institute, it was referred to as the "Reik-Fenichel debate") about whether intuition or the systematic, deliberate dismantling of resistances constitutes the bedrock of psychoanalytic technique. Reik foregrounded what we might now call right-brained processes, supporting the intuitive position with stories (based on his having been Freud's long-time mentee and, briefly, his analysand) about Freud's actual style of clinical engagement. Despite some of the colder metaphors in his writing, Freud was often warm, playful, and influenced by his subjective impressions. NPAP's culture of course reflected Reik's view. When I read Fenichel, however, I found his more left-brained, abstract formulations convincing as well. That was perhaps the first time I realized I am more interested in integrating seemingly polarized perspectives, and in applying them selectively to specific clinical challenges, than I am in determining which theory or approach is superior *in general*.

Reik emphasized our natural empathy, something Kohut brought back to center stage after medicalized psychoanalysis had advocated a more sterile procedure. It distresses me that popularized notions of empathy confound it with sympathy—a feeling *for* rather than a feeling *with*—and (worse) sometimes equate empathy with being simply warm and supportive. Empathy cannot be formulaic, and genuine empathy is very hard to teach. If the behavior we intend to be received as empathic is not fully sincere, our patients will know. To approach the understanding of others, and to have a chance of helping them in a meaningful way, I believe we must be able to feel empathy with their uglier qualities: aggression, sadism, envy, terror, and craziness. This welcoming of their darkness requires our having deeply explored those territories in ourselves.

Respect

It is curious to me that there is so little psychoanalytic writing about the attitude of respect. Unlike empathy, which has been theorized extensively, respect is seldom mentioned as a core therapeutic value in analytic work, and yet it seems to me to be an irreducible component of emotional healing. Oren Blass, an Israeli analyst who studied at Rutgers, interviewed analysts on the topic of "respect for the patient." Several of his interviewees spontaneously noted that once they knew the details of a client's history, empathy came easily. But they opined that maintaining respect can be a difficult discipline, noting clinical categories (e.g., psychopathy or pedophilia) and problematic behaviors (e.g., compulsive gambling or infidelity) that typically required their having to struggle to find an attitude of respect toward the patient.

I have been sensitive all my life to how men construe women, especially the tone in which they depict us. My take on Freud's writing about women is that despite his misunderstandings, he was able to help many of his female patients because he respected them. My responsiveness to Theodor Reik's work, as well as my openness to my analyst's help, were centrally related to my feeling respected. I have come to understand respect as an attitude of *openness to learning* from someone else. It is not the same as admiration, but it is a kind of looking *up* at the other with the expectation that something valuable will come from him or her. Perhaps empathy can be framed as responsiveness to the hurt child within, whereas respect applies to the agentic adult. I see recognition of both self-states as critical to therapeutic progress.

In a diverse society, therapists cannot always have accurate empathy, but we can be respectfully open to learning from people who do not share our own assumptions and prejudices. I see respect as especially critical when we work with those who have been treated more as objects than as subjects, including most patients with psychosis, significant paranoia, borderline dynamics, trauma histories, dissociative problems, and substance use disorders, as well as those in groups negatively defined by gender, sexuality, race, ethnicity, belief system, ability, socioeconomic level, and other descriptors of subordinated status.

Honesty

Let me end by returning to the theme of honesty, to the assumption that self-delusion compromises our freedom to be our best selves and the conviction that trying to be honest is key to liberation from unconscious psychological demons (Thompson, 2003). A commitment to honesty about painful or embarrassing emotional realities fuels the self-disclosure in my writing style—part of that expresses my personality, part is my identification with Reik, an unusually confessional writer, and part is trying to be genuine (and genuinely modest) about what I think I have come to know.

Although I have never felt I understood Bion's (1962) concept of "O," Grotstein's (2004) explication of his notion of a "truth drive" feels right to me. One of the most welcome aspects of the relational movement has been its pursuit of greater frankness in case presentations and clinical discussions, especially about conscious aspects of countertransference. I witness each day how relieving it is to patients to find themselves able for the first time to speak hard truths. Not subscribing uncritically to Freud's Enlightenment-era positivism, I would not claim to be uncovering "the truth" in any psychoanalytic endeavor. But sometimes we can find *a* truth, and always we can hold our work up to the impossible but worthy ideal of representing our most honest efforts to understand.

References

Anstadt, T., Merten, J., Ullrich, B., & Krause, R. (1997). Affective dyadic behavior, core conflictual relationship themes and success of treatment. *Psychotherapy Research, 7,* 397–417.

Aragno, A. (2011). Listening with a third ear, a second heart, and a sixth sense: Standing on the shoulders of Theodor Reik. *Psychoanalytic Review, 98*(2), 183–204.

Bion, W. S. (1962). *Learning from experience.* London: Karnac.

Freud, S. (1917). Mourning and melancholia. *Standard Edition, 14,* 237–258.

Grotstein, J. S. (2004). The seventh servant: The implications of a truth drive in Bion's theory of "O". *International Journal of Psychoanalysis, 85,* 1081–1101.

Hoffman, I. Z. (1998). *Ritual and spontaneity in the psychoanalytic process: A dialectical constructivist view.* Hillsdale, NJ: Analytic Press.

Loewald, H. W. (1960). On the therapeutic action of psychoanalysis. *International Journal of Psychoanalysis, 41,* 16–33.

McWilliams, N. (2013). The impact of my own psychotherapy on my work as a therapist. *Psychoanalytic Psychology, 30*(4), 621–626.

McWilliams, N. (2020). The future of psychoanalysis: Preserving Jeremy Safran's integrative vision. *Psychoanalytic Psychology, 37*(2), 98–107.

Nobus, D. (2006). *Fluctuat nec mergitur,* or what happened to Reikian psychoanalysis? *Psychoanalytic Psychology, 23*(4), 684–700.

Sherman, M. H. (1965). Freud, Reik, and the problem of technique in psychoanalysis. *Psychoanalytic Review, 52*(3), 19–37.

Thompson, M. G. (2003). *The ethic of honesty: The fundamental rule of psychoanalysis.* New York, NY: Rodopi.

Chapter 8

Becoming the Analysts That We Turn Out to Be

Michael Parsons

What a psychoanalyst means by the concept of 'analytic identity' is bound to be autobiographical. It cannot be an abstract bit of theory; of necessity, it is rooted in an analyst's experience of how his or her own identity as an analyst has developed.

Analysts form their identities in all sorts of ways, and for each of them there is a trajectory by which they arrived at being the analyst that they are. They are mostly not aware of this in the moment, as it goes along. They are too busy doing what they have to do: coping with the demands of training, trying to develop their practice, working out how to teach and supervise. They discover in retrospect how they became the analysts they have turned out to be. There is no end-point to this. Throughout their working lives, analysts need to go on discovering how their analytic identities are developing. Maybe later in life, as their experience increases, the penny drops more quickly. What matters most, though, always happens at an unconscious level, and an analyst's awareness of how his or her identity took the shape it did surfaces only gradually.

Trying to describe one's analytic development will produce a series of vignettes: moments of realisation, when something surfaced in that unexpected way. Any straightforward, linear account would be suspect. The identity of an analyst progresses by looping continually back on itself, to find new meaning in experiences that have been worked on and understood, but which now, in the light of fresh experience, can be seen in richer, deeper ways. This kind of dynamic *après-coup* (Perelberg, 2006) is fundamental.

I did not know I wanted to be a psychoanalyst until I had already started becoming one. After qualifying as a doctor, I went on to psychiatric training. I was not sure what kind of psychiatrist I wanted to be, but among the various departments of my hospital I felt most at home in the psychotherapy unit. Eventually, I wondered about getting more training in this work that I enjoyed, and found myself being recommended to apply to something called the 'Institute of Psychoanalysis'. I did not know what this was—I had not, like some analysts-to-be, been reading Freud since the age of 15—but if it would help with the psychotherapy I was doing, so much the

DOI: 10.4324/9781003206248-8

better. I was accepted and, by the time I gathered anything about what being a psychoanalyst meant, I was on the way to becoming one.

My unconscious, however, was not so clueless. Much later, I realised that in the consultation where it was suggested I apply to the Institute, and in the interviews for admission to it, I was listened to in a way that resonated with something I had already discovered for myself. As a trainee psychiatrist, I was taught to conduct what was called an 'examination of the mental state'. This comprised the nature of the symptoms and the patient's current cognitive status; his or her previous personality, family history, social background; prevailing mood, signs of depressive ideation, suicidal thoughts, hallucinations or delusions, loosening of associations or flight of ideas, and so on. It was all very systematic: I began the task, I finished the task, I wrote my report. I soon realised that I got to know patients better and learnt much more about them if, instead of posing a sequence of questions, I simply asked them what they wanted to tell me about. As the conversation developed, I heard about everything the 'mental state examination' called for, and there was no problem in constructing the kind of presentation my teachers required. I was discovering, without knowing it, what it meant to invite someone to free associate. When I was listened to in the same way myself, I did not put two and two together but I think an unconscious sense of recognition must have told me I was in the right place.

Learning to carry out the mental state examination in this way involved unlearning some of my training as a doctor. Freud had to do the same. Doctors start by taking a patient's history. This gives them clues to what may be wrong, which they follow up selectively, using their medical knowledge to elicit from the patient whatever information they need to make a diagnosis. There is a footnote in *Studies on Hysteria* that shows Freud the doctor questioning a patient most forcefully in just this way (Breuer & Freud, 1893–1895, pp. 112–113fn). Elsewhere in *Studies on Hysteria* one can see him beginning to give up this stance, as when Frau Emmy 'said, in a definitely grumbling tone, that I was not to keep on asking her where this and that came from but to let her tell me what she had to say' (Breuer & Freud, 1893–1895, p. 56); or when, in his treatment of Katharina, 'I told her to go on and tell me whatever occurred to her, in the confident expectation that she would think of precisely what I needed in order to explain the case' (Breuer & Freud, 1893–1895, p. 129). Freud's method of pressing on a patient's forehead to provoke memories depended on the licence doctors have to handle their patient's bodies; giving up this technique was another shift away from his medical role. By the time Freud arrives at the need to practise evenly suspended attention so as to avoid any selectivity whatever, he is negating his own professional training (Freud, 1912, pp. 111–112). He had to discover that the way in which analysts attend to their patients is very different from how doctors attend to their medical patients. In this sense, to become a psychoanalyst Freud had to recover from being a doctor. All doctors who want to become analysts have the same unlearning to do about the nature of the relationship with their patients and the kind of attention they need to give them.

Analytic candidates also have to do a great deal of learning, about psychoanalytic theory in all its aspects and about the technique of clinical practice. At the same time in their analyses, they are discovering more about their own psychic make-up, about their personal values and what matters to them in life. Analytic identities, in all their variety, grow in the terrain between these two. There is a dynamic relation between the theoretical learning and the personal growth. Psychoanalytic training has both a didactic and a developmental perspective, and analysts will form their identities differently, according to which receives the greater emphasis.

Some analysts form their identities around a specific theoretical viewpoint. They find that a certain orientation offers a coherent, self-contained approach that feels right and speaks to them. Their identities as analysts then develop through an adherence to this particular view of psychoanalysis, and an ever-deepening immersion in it. For others, the primary consideration is not the coherence and correctness of a theoretical position. These analysts view analytic theory in relation to their personal struggle to know who they are and how they want to live their lives. This means exposing themselves to a variety of approaches. Of course, analysts in the first group explore how analysis can help them make sense of their own experience; but for others, the greater the diversity of ideas they interact with, the more fruitful the exploration is likely to be. Their analytic identities will be a tapestry, woven of threads from whatever sources help their understanding of themselves and of what being an analyst means to them (Parsons, 2009).

My own training, and subsequent development, as an analyst in the Independent tradition of the British Psychoanalytical Society, places me in the latter of these two groups; but for any analyst, there is no getting away from a tension between the freedom, on the one hand, of the individual, personal and subjective nature of psychoanalysis, and the rigorous need, on the other, for objectivity, theory-building and technical discipline. Both are essential, and the tension between them permeates the whole of psychoanalysis. It calls for ongoing work to live within this tension without trying to resolve it away, and to enjoy the creativity it can provoke.

How analysts manage the tension between rigour and freedom reveals something, not only about them as an analyst but also about the person that they are. Analysts, and people, are not abstractions. There is only whatever unique psychoanalyst, whatever unique person, someone arrives at being, through his or her own particular process of becoming. To be an analyst is a particular way of being a person, and an important part of developing one's analytic identity is to explore the way in which being an analyst is an expression of one's personal identity. In this sense, psychoanalysis is a vocation. With time, I began to understand why the French analyst Sacha Nacht wrote:

> I am speaking now of the person of the analyst in so far as he represents and *embodies* a certain deep inner attitude in the analytic situation. It is this deep inner attitude which, in my opinion, is a decisive factor, and that is why I have often maintained that it is what the analyst *is* rather than what he *says* that matters. (Nacht, 1962, p. 207)

Nacht emphasises that analysts cannot consciously decide on the quality of their presence at an unconscious level. It is a question of the truth of the analyst's being. In Edward Glover's words: 'A prerequisite of the efficiency of interpretation is the *attitude*, the true unconscious attitude, of the analyst to his patients' (Glover, 1937, p. 131).

If how analysts analyse is an expression of who they are, they have to listen to what goes on inside themselves in the same way as they listen to their patients. In my training, I learnt, of course, about monitoring the countertransference. The classical view of it was as an obstacle caused by unconscious factors in the analyst's psyche. The 1950s brought a new perception that countertransference could also function usefully to reveal unconscious aspects of the analytic relationship. As my analytic experience grew, I realised that there was yet more to it than this. My own interior situation was continually in resonance with that of the patient, and I saw that psychoanalytic listening needs always to be a double process, reaching outwards and inwards at the same time. Both directions are essential, continuously active and interdependent. What I hear stirred up in myself is not just useful countertransferentially; it is the medium through which I come to know the patient. An analyst's interior listening is not a matter of monitoring; it has to be just as continuous and free from preconceptions as the external listening to a patient's words.

Near the end of his paper on 'The elasticity of psycho-analytic technique', Ferenczi writes: 'The ideal result of a completed analysis is precisely that elasticity which analytic technique demands of the mental therapist' (Ferenczi, 1955 [1928], p. 99). This implies that the aim of analysis is to foster in the patient a quality which, for that development to happen, also needs to be present in the analyst. As Ferenczi implies, patients are enabled to discover something in themselves because they are in a particular kind of relationship with someone who is open to that same sort of discovery in his or her own self. This means that the analysis has to matter, in a significant way, to the analyst. The analyst must have 'skin in the game'. When Enid Balint wrote about her clinical technique as an independent analyst, she stressed two things: the importance of the imagination, and the analyst's capacity to wait. Although structure and training were necessary, she said, they were useless 'if the analyst's imagination, or the patient's, is imprisoned.

In order to release himself and the patient from prison, the analyst must exercise the ability to wait' (Balint, 1993, p. 129). This shows the same, typically independent, awareness as Ferenczi of a parallelism between the analyst's and patient's internal processes. However, Balint goes further. She sees the analyst's imagination needing to be liberated just as much as that of the patient. The analyst as well, that is to say, must have something at stake in the analysis. At some level, the patient will pick up whether or not this is true. Freud famously remarked that evenly suspended attention allows the analyst 'to catch the drift of the patient's unconscious with his own unconscious' (Freud, 1923, p. 239). The same applies in the opposite direction: the patient will unconsciously catch the drift of the analyst's unconscious. This is what Nacht and Glover were pointing to. Patients will only be able 'to hear from their own unconscious life' (Bollas, 2002, p. 10) or be open to taking themselves by surprise (Winnicott, 1971, p. 51), if they sense they are in a relationship with someone who is open to their own unconscious life, and to taking their own self by surprise.

To be an analyst, therefore, is to lay oneself continually on the line. For patients to free associate is a risk; they do not know where it will take them. For analysts, to enter into an analytic relationship is also a risk; they do not know where it will take them. As I grew more experienced, I sometimes found myself tempted half-consciously to dilute this: to let myself think I knew pretty well by now what I was doing, and that whatever happened, I could probably manage it. I did know pretty well what I was doing; that was true. I noticed, though, that if this was my working frame of mind, I might do adequate analysis but nothing transformative would happen. The risk for the analyst needs to be real. This is disturbing, but it brings rewards. An analytic relationship can only be enriching and enlivening for the patient, as of course the analyst hopes, if it also enriches and enlivens the analyst. This does not mean analysts parasitise the analysis for their benefit; to have their own psychic life at stake in an analysis is the only way the analysis can be transformative for the patient—and for themselves as well.

Analysts who teach and write express their analytic identity in how they do that, as well as in the way they work with patients. It occurred to me, as I was teaching on the British Society's training, that the standard way of doing clinical seminars was not very psychoanalytic. The leader invites someone beforehand to present a case. In the seminar, the presenter gives some background material and describes a session or two. Then the seminar considers what factors in the history may be relevant, the clinical material is discussed and the presenter is helped to reflect on their technique. All this is valuable. It is genuine teaching of psychoanalysis and the members of such a seminar will learn from it. As an experience for the participants, however, it is rather distant from the unpredictability of an analytic session. Members do not know the particular case (except the presenter, of course, and sometimes the sessions may even be precirculated), but everybody knows what form the seminar will take and what kind of experience to expect. The seminar leader is in charge, and on safe ground. Nobody has anything critical at stake, except perhaps the need to get a good report.

I found it was possible to do clinical seminars in a different way; one that could help participants, including the leader, to extend their vision of the analytic encounter and so enlarge the analytic identities they were developing. As a seminar leader, I did not ask anyone to prepare a presentation in advance, but began the seminar by simply asking whether anyone had a patient they wanted to talk about. There was an assumption, at first, that I must be asking for the usual sort of presentation, but on the spur of the moment. However, I was not requesting someone to provide the seminar with material to discuss. I was asking whether anyone had a case which, for whatever reason, made them want to see what would happen if they talked about it in any way they felt moved to. An analyst tries to convey to a patient: 'You are free to say whatever you want, however you want. You can make use of this situation in any way that interests you'. I was saying the same thing, only in the context of a clinical seminar. This was so unexpected that it took time for a group to believe what I really meant: that they could talk about their work however they wanted, that whatever happened would be what happened, and we would try to think about it psychoanalytically. It was difficult for candidates to let go of trying to perform well in the seminar. When they could, though, they felt the same relief that patients do when they can give up thinking analytic sessions are about trying hard and making a good showing.

This way of working required me too to step out of my comfort zone. As with patients, I had to put myself at risk, and allow myself really to have no idea what would happen in a seminar. Sometimes it was a challenge to trust that my own and the group's unconscious processes could find creative meaning in whatever this curious kind of freedom would produce. Once a candidate gave a vivid account of his patient's history and background, which produced a lively discussion. New aspects of the story kept appearing, and the discussion went on and on. Several times I asked the candidate if there were sessions he wanted to present, and he said there were. Each time the moment passed, however, and the unstoppable discussion continued. It was genuinely interesting, but I could not understand why the analyst did not take the opportunities I offered to present the clinical material he apparently wanted to. This was in the early days of developing this method, and as we neared the end of the seminar time, I felt anxious. Could one possibly have a valid clinical seminar, especially for candidates in training, with no clinical work described? If we got to the end and I had still not helped the candidate introduce it, what kind of seminar would that be? Eventually, I asked him not to present his sessions but to imagine what would happen if he did so. He immediately replied: 'Chaos!'. All of us, including the analyst himself, were startled. We had been enjoying a fruitful and productive discussion. Now suddenly chaos? Then we saw that the real interest of the patient's story must be being used to fend off something that both group and analyst were unconsciously afraid of not being able to deal with. This helped the candidate with his case, but more generally it was a remarkable psychoanalytic lesson in how positive elements may be made use of for defensive purposes. I think the experience let the candidates in the seminar, and myself as well, take a step forward in the development of our analytic identities.

In another seminar for candidates, I have explored experientially the idea that analysts hear more sensitively what is going on in a patient by becoming more sensitive to the responses they find stirred up in themselves. This seminar starts by tracing the development of Freud's listening capacity, as shown above in the *Studies on Hysteria*. Then we read poems aloud in the group. We discuss how the external music of the poem arouses internal music in ourselves, and strong feelings can appear as we do so. This illuminates the clinical situation, where the internal music aroused in a listening analyst helps the analyst understand more of the external music that is the patient. Participants are disconcerted, then intrigued, by another idea. I invite them to go outside at night and stand alone in the darkness, keeping still and silent for at least half an hour, just listening. The object is to observe how much more they are hearing at the end of the hour than at the beginning. On a still night in open country, what seems at the beginning like silence becomes after half an hour an extraordinary polyphony of sound. Even in an urban setting, members of the group found subtle variability and unexpected combinations in familiar kinds of noise, and discovered new sounds, previously unheard, gradually revealing themselves. As with the poems, we would link this experience to a kind of listening in the clinical situation that is able to hear, over time, much more going on in a patient than was detectable to begin with. For the final seminar, by which time the group had developed a strong mutual trust and confidence, I invited members to bring something of their own that had personal meaning for them. They were only to talk about it, however, after the others had listened within themselves to whatever associations it stirred up in them. As the evening went on, we shared together the various meanings we had all found in these items. The conversation was often profoundly moving.

These exercises—I suggested other ones as well—could take the group emotionally into unexpected places. I joined in with whatever I asked the candidates to do, and the experiences we shared were sometimes powerful. I intended this seminar to help the candidates learn something about psychoanalytic listening, and it did that. I only discovered as it went on that there was another point to it at a deeper level. As with the clinical seminars, it challenged the candidates and me to risk exposing ourselves to something unknown and unpredictable; and to trust that, whatever might happen as we did so, our psychoanalytic awareness would let us find meaning in it. This seminar too turned out, for all of us, to be about the development of our analytic identities.[1]

Note

1 For a fuller discussion of the clinical seminars and the listening seminar, see Parsons (2014, pp. 51ff, 216–221).

References

Balint, E. (1993). *Before I was I: Psychoanalysis and the imagination. Collected papers of Enid Balint.* Eds. J. Mitchell & M. Parsons. London: Free Association Books and New York: Guilford Press.
Bollas, C. (2002). *Free association.* Cambridge: Icon Books (USA: Totem Books).
Breuer, J., & Freud, S. (1893–1895). Studies on hysteria. *Standard Edition, 2.*
Ferenczi, S. (1955). *Final contributions to the problems and methods of psycho-analysis.* London: Hogarth.
Freud, S. (1912). Recommendations to physicians practising psycho-analysis. *Standard Edition, 12,* 111–120.
Freud, S. (1923). Two encyclopaedia articles. *Standard Edition, 18,* 235–259.
Glover, E. (1937). Contribution to symposium on the theory of the therapeutic results of psycho-analysis. *The International Journal of Psychoanalysis, 18,* 125–132.
Nacht, S. (1962). Contribution to symposium on the curative factors in psycho-analysis. *The International Journal of Psychoanalysis, 43,* 206–211.
Parsons, M. (2009). Becoming and being an analyst in the British Psychoanalytical Society. *Psychoanalytic Inquiry, 29,* 236–246.
Parsons, M. (2014). *Living psychoanalysis: From theory to experience.* London: Routledge.
Perelberg, R. J. (2006). The controversial discussions and *après-coup. The International Journal of Psychoanalysis, 87,* 1199–1220.
Winnicott, D. W. (1971). *Playing and reality.* London: Tavistock.

Section III
1980s

Chapter 9

Credo: Mutuality and Asymmetry[*]

Lewis Aron

I was raised in a kind of liberal, conservative family. My grandfather lived with us and he wanted me to go to a yeshiva. By today's standards, you'd hardly call it a yeshiva. It was a "day school," a Jewish Modern Orthodox school. Now, I loved it. I had a wonderful experience there. I loved the rabbis, I loved what they were teaching, and so I kept getting more religious. My father was not particularly religious; he was more religious for my mother. Also, I kept pushing to be more religious, so my parents would get more religious to accommodate me. I was an only child and they figured, "Well, if you like it, then we'll do it," so they got more involved. So then I pushed and got more religious and they would get more religious, and I'd get more religious and they would get more religious until eventually I rebelled against being religious! So I rebelled against the religion that I had pushed them to be. I created something that I had to then rebel against.

Then when I started my training, I applied to NYU because they had the most rigorous Freudian supervisors. I would go from one supervisor to another. And I picked the people that had the reputation for being the most Orthodox Freudians. And I was always disappointed because they weren't rigorous enough. And so I would push them to be more rigorous and I'd find a supervisor that was more rigorous until eventually, I rebelled against picking Orthodox people. And then I had to rebel against the Orthodox thing. This is called the repetition compulsion.

I think the yeshiva background is very much one of chavruta[1] learning, very much one of study partners. And I had study partners for years. However, it's also hierarchical model and there are mentors.[2] So it's both—it's not just that it's all flat—it is equal and it's hierarchical. It's both,

---

[*] This is a transcribed edited down version of a Skype interview conducted by Orna Reuven, Ph.D.; Gadit Orian, MSW; Ofer Dobrecki, M.A.; and Gideon Levin, M.A. from TAICP, April 5, 2016. As part of their training at Tel-Aviv Institute for Contemporary Psychoanalysis (TAICP), they wrote a paper on the influence of personal life stories on the theory psychoanalysts have developed. Lew responded immediately to their request.

DOI: 10.4324/9781003206248-9

and you get experiences with both ways of learning, with mutuality and asymmetry, including in the imaginary relationship to God. Judaism really prides itself on that people argue with God, the whole idea of a fight with God, arguing with God going, going back to Abraham's challenging God and saying, you know, is the judge of all the world not going to behave justly? How can you wipe out a city if there are 10 good people in it? Right? On the one hand, Abraham can argue with God, on the other hand, there are limits. And at certain points you can't argue with God, there's a certain mutuality, but there's also an ultimate asymmetry. You can challenge God and say, "Why are you doing this to me?" But at a certain point, God says, "Where were you when I was creating the world?"

The other thing I would extend, it's not only that older students sit with younger students. For me, one of the most important things personally, I think really, this is very vivid for me. When I teach, I sit around with my books, which was what my/the rabbis did when I was in school. They didn't teach, just lecture. They were surrounded by books on the table. This is before computers. They would teach and pick up books, and that's the way I like to work. One of my teachers, Rabbi Soloveitchik from Yeshiva University, described how he would sit at his table and he would imagine an argument between the Rambam sitting on one side and another figure on the other side; they were arguing and these people lived in different centuries. They didn't know each other and they were arguing across hundreds and thousands of years, but he could picture them all sitting at a table and he would hear the arguments. And he was part of the conversation.

I know that my goal was never to be a leader. My goal was to be part of the conversation. I wanted to feel I was at the table having this conversation. I know when I teach, even when I'm talking about Jung and Adler, I can picture Jung arguing with Freud and Adler objecting. But then I can also hear Steve Mitchell coming in and saying, "Wait a minute, there is common ground here." And for me, it's a very vivid, live conversation. What's exciting to me is not winning the argument or losing the argument. It's that I'm at the table, having this incredible conversation with these people; it's a very powerful thing.

Family

Mutuality did not come easily to me. It still doesn't come easily to me. There's another side to it, which is that I was an only child. My relationships were with parents and grandfather. I had no peers in my family. It was always a challenge for me to really work. I'm very good at being a director of a program because I'm hierarchical. I work well with other people and I think people like that I work with them. But it tends to be that I'm working with people that are students or I'm working with people that are teachers or they're working for me. I tend to feel much easier in hierarchical relationships. So I knew mutuality was both very important, but something I struggle with. So I think people write about what they struggle with. It's not that I'm good at it or that I'm bad at it, it's what I struggle with. It's at the front of my mind because I know that it's a struggle.

My mother encouraged my questioning and challenging literally every morning when I left school in the morning as a kid, she would say, "Remember ..." cause she learned this from the rabbis who would teach her, "Remember, ask good questions." It's not remember you should know the answers ... it's ask good questions. By that she meant challenging questions. What you were supposed to do was to challenge, but only up to a very careful point because if you challenge that maybe I don't believe in God, that's not acceptable. That's not a kind of challenge that was tolerated. So the answer to the question is very delicate, challenge, challenge, but always from within, never breaking the boundaries. So it was a complicated message of challenge, but nowhere you're allowed to challenge.

Relational Community

Steve Mitchell was very important to me. I think he was really an exceptionally gifted, unique thinker. He learned from all the schools and had a brilliantly synthetic mind. Steve and I talked about this a good deal. I always told Steve that I thought of myself as a Freudian, and even when I was working very closely with him as a relationalist, and he'd say, "Why do you keep insisting that you're a Freudian when you're so relational?" I said, "Because, if I was on a deserted island and I only had one book to bring, it would be Freud." And he got it.

I think that Steve didn't talk that way, but it's very clear if you read everything he ever wrote, the main person he was dialoguing with his whole life was Freud. He never got over dialoguing with Freud. He understood that every other school stood in the shadow of Freud and, his main contribution or one way of thinking about his main contribution is that he said, "Listen, none of these people can stand up to Freud. Fairbairn, he's great, but he can't take on Freud by himself. Sullivan, he's great, but he can't take on Freud by himself. Kohut has terrific ideas, but he can't hold a candle to Freud. But if we put all of these people together, maybe all of them together can stand up to Freud." So you can see that in Steve's own mind, it's Freud that's the towering figure that has to be challenged. You can't do it alone, so you have to create a big tent of people from all the schools because maybe all together they can push back against Freud. But Freud is the person you're dialoguing with.

Steve pushed to be the revolutionary. And I was too conflicted about being a revolutionary because I have too much of a conservative side. And this was true for Jay Greenberg also. It's why Jay and Steve split. Jay likes to think of himself as the one who would put the brakes on Steve. Steve was going all the way fast. Jay kept holding him back a little bit. And I had a similar relation to him. Steve just wanted to keep plowing forward, forward, forward. And some of us said, "Wait a minute. You know, revolution is good, but so is continuity." So this was part of the challenge.

I think about it in relation to the Jewish tradition, I don't consider myself identified with any one group of jury. I don't consider myself Orthodox, Conservative, Reform. I don't consider myself pure Zionist or post-Zionist or anti-Zionist or Hasidic. I identify with the whole Jewish tradition. I think there are pieces of Ashkenaz and Sephard I identify with, but it is the whole thing of Judaism that's important and I feel that way about psychoanalysis. I can identify at moments, only at moments, but I can identify at moments with the Lacanians and I can identify at moments with the Kleinians and I don't feel I have to choose. I feel like it's a conversation that I want them all at the table.

Partially, I have to say, I've been running the NYU program now for 18 years. And part of it is that that job keeps me thinking this way. And part of it is that because I think this way, it allows me to do that job—because the job is being the rabbi of the community. It's the Rabbi of a shul and the shul has a group that wants an Orthodox minyan and also wants a Reform minyan, and I don't want them to split and form different shuls. So my job is to be able to talk to all of them and get them to see that we have something in common and we can keep it together. That's what you do as the director of a program, when a program always has tensions. So my job as director of the program is what I was raised to be. I'm the Rabbi.

Exploring the Subjectivity of the Patient and the Analyst Family

I think that children, and I know it was true for myself as a child, are very conflicted about knowing about their parents. You know, it's easy to kind of romanticize it and say, children really want to know their parents "insides" and there's a sort of romantic feeling about how we want to connect with our parents in a deep way. But I think that's only one side of the story. The other side is we're terrified of really knowing our parents. It's very frightening. It's something we're inhibited about. We stay away from knowing our parents. We sometimes are just disinterested because it's not about us. I think it's very complicated, and again, I'm very focused on conflict. For me, the main thing from Freud is that it's all about conflict, it's all about psychic conflict. Any explanation of anything that's one sided is not psychoanalytic. If it's psychoanalytic, it's got to have the tension. I think that children want to know their parents and they want to connect with their insides and also they don't want to.

I think that when it comes to the patient and the analyst, there's a similar thing. There's a way in which patients really do want to know what's going on and they're searching it out and they're scanning it. And there's another way in which they're avoiding it and they don't want to know, and they're avoiding it purposefully and not purposefully and there's lack of interest in there. It's not that it's one or the other, there's always both. Certainly, this was true for me and my family. I think that my parents could be at moments very open with me and sometimes too open and too exposing and that other times they didn't share enough and didn't tell me enough. I think that a lot of my analysis and a lot of my life was trying to put together that combination of what I knew and what I didn't know, and really at some point struggling with, do I even know who my mother is, you know and struggling with this question. And why didn't I know? Was it because I didn't want to know? Was it because she really didn't want me to know? Was it because there was nothing to know?

Being a Patient

My main analyst was the person that analyzed me from the time I was 20–31 years old. I was in a little more than 10-year analysis, four times a week with a classical analyst. And he worked in a very traditional way most of the time. I knew relatively little about him and I think that was also partially me. I think partially I was motivated not to push him too much and not to find out too much. I think in some ways I wasn't interested enough. I was too involved with myself, but in retrospect in the years later, I think a lot could have been gained if he had helped me see that I was not knowing, not just because he wasn't telling me, but because I was afraid to look or inhibited to look.

I think part of it was a kind of trying to correct for something I felt I missed out on in my analysis. Part of it was that as I got older, the culture had changed and things were different and I could explore more in a way that I couldn't do when I was younger. And part of it was that I met other analysts who worked in very different ways and exposed me to different possibilities including Harold Searles. I hadn't worked with him so intensively. I saw him live quite a few times and I read his stuff very carefully, but he did have a very powerful impact on me. His use of his own reactions in such a direct way was very freeing for me. It helped me get over a certain kind of discipline. You know, I always wanted to be a good boy. I had to do it the right way. And there was something about his freedom to use himself that helped free me up, to not be so cautious and careful. Especially his main point was that therapists all want to be liked and nice and good and benevolent, the benevolent physician who the patient appreciates and likes. And he said, this is the biggest thing getting in our way that we're afraid to be bad objects, we're afraid, to just let ourselves out.

There was something about that that challenged me and helped me to try to not do everything by the book, not do everything so correctly, which of course goes back to my orthodoxy and rebellion from orthodoxy. I have had other therapies since my analysis, I've gone back to other analysts at various times in my life around specific issues. And in one case, in particular, I went to an analyst who was a little bit older than me, and I wanted to talk about things where I thought they would really be open back and forth. And I worked out an arrangement with him from the first session that our agreement would be, that we would both feel free to openly talk about our own experiences with very personal things. This was sort of Ferenczi-like, but not quite as formal as Ferenczi who was doing it in a more formal experimental way. This was of course many years later. I was with somebody who was a very senior analyst and I was already older and we agreed to really just open up with each other about very delicate matters. And I found that to be extremely useful, extremely helpful with limits. It's not that I'm advocating it. I wouldn't do it with everyone. The main thing I would want to say is analysis is not one thing.

Analysis has many different processes, depending on where the person is in their life and who they are and who the analyst is. And it's silly for us to think there's one right way to do an analysis. Two people can both have good analyses, but they do it very differently. They look very different from each other. At the same time, I think we need to really have a certain kind of discipline. We also need to respect that the process takes on a life of its own and it's not going to look the way we expect it to look. If it looks the way you expect it to look, that already is a certain kind of problem.

Self-disclosure

So when you deal with self-disclosure and talk about yourself, you have to know that both people in the room are conflicted about it. You want to be known and you don't want to be known. And the patient wants to know you and they don't want to know you. And so anything you do is hitting a grid of conflict, always.

The only thing I feel a little awkward about is because I'm in the midst of this cancer treatment and I've just had major surgery and I'm starting the chemotherapy. And of course, I'm in the middle. I had told all of my patients and my groups, then my students, that I was going to have the surgery and I expected to then come back, not knowing that they were going to find that cancer spread and it was worse than they thought. So now the patients have now heard that I'm going to be out longer.

So I have a lot of thoughts in my mind about self-disclosure and dealing with patients who are following the details of my life and the impact on different patients. There's a lot of overlap with what we've talked about, but I'm in the middle of a whole other thing. And of course also just my own facing a serious illness and mortality. Really it's life and death. We live on a day-to-day basis, not knowing what we're going to hear the next day.

Notes

1 Editor's note: a traditional Jewish approach to study in which a pair of students (chavruta) analyze, discuss, and debate a shared text.
2 Rabbis might intervene in some discussions, citing more important texts or more highly valued opinions on points being debated.

Chapter 10

Credo: The Sufferings of the World

Jessica Benjamin

> You can hold yourself back from the sufferings of the world, that is something you are free to do and it accords with your nature, but perhaps this very holding back is the one suffering you could avoid.
>
> Franz Kafka

If psychoanalysis were a religion, I would be not only a practitioner but also a theologian. I would be trying to reconcile my faith with the empirical and clinical knowledge we've acquired especially in the last 40 years. Fortunately, despite its spiritual concerns, relational psychoanalysis as we think today is as much a home for doubt as for belief. But beginning with my first encounter some 50 years ago, psychoanalysis appeared to me as not only a system of ideas and a method of thinking but also as a way to view the world. For some of us young radical intellectuals, there was a compelling attraction to the mix of Hegelian Marxism and Freud offered by the Frankfurt School of critical theory. Having the opportunity to study in Frankfurt, I was able to appreciate psychoanalysis as an integration of theory with practice, in particular the unique pre-war Vienna combination of socialization, pedagogy, and child analysis. Critical theory also gave me the tools to examine Freud's ideas in light of their contradictions, especially regarding gender and authority, common to the patriarchal world of Vienna in his time. This deconstructive project undertaken by feminists was needed to make room for a version of psychoanalysis that my 20th-century generation could inhabit; that would serve both interpreting our history and change the world, our practice.

That fertile period of cultural revolution was part of a broader transformation of psychoanalysis, liberating it from the shackles of one-person theory, the patriarchal bias of the Oedipus complex, and the 19th-century thermodynamics of drive theory. The relational turn finally foregrounded the analyst's participation as a subject (Mitchell, 1988, 1993)—the practical, clinical match to the theory of intersubjectivity I had sought to develop. My point of departure, what psychic capacities enable recognition between two equal subjects, crucial to the feminist project? What if we formulated the core developmental issue as the self becoming able to recognize the separate but equivalent center of subjectivity of the other upon whom we depend? How else could desire be mutually known and realized? If recognition is a crucial matrix of development—the intersubjective action that gives meaning and ratifies the impact of what we feel and do—we must be able to *give* it as well as receive it.

I had found in Winnicott (1971) the crucial formulation of how we actually come to recognize the outside other, realize our intersubjective potential. His proposal was that the encounter with an other who cannot be destroyed breaks down omnipotence and makes recognition of the outside other possible; when the analyst is neither retaliatory nor collapsing, she can be loved as an equivalent center of being an outside other. This means that the real, responsive other can now be differentiated from the inner world of bad and good objects, defensively internalized alá Fairbairn. Contra Freud, Winnicott envisioned a safe confrontation with the other's externality as relieving and joyful. It was as if Winnicott had translated the Hegelian problematic of master and slave into a developmental crisis, identified a fault line leading either to collapse of intersubjectivity or to recognition of the other—including recognition of the mother. Thus, we can experience an intersubjective world of freedom, based on neither partner controlling or complying.

I perceived Winnicott's intervention to be the most radical new idea of psychoanalysis in the 20th century because it meant that we are not simply analyzing transference and countertransference. Instead, we are creating a transformational experience of what it is to be a self with an other who gives recognition and is altered by our actions. It initiates a two-person idea of how the other can make a difference even as the self can have an impact on the other. This two-way street opens the door to mutuality as well as differentiation.

At the societal level, I argued, when the other actually establishes an equal subjectivity that cannot be destroyed—that is controlled and demeaned—recognition can be achieved. This is the difference (only) the other can make. I believe this idea holds true as well for the overcoming of oppression. The oppressor cannot grant recognition; he can only admit in the face of the rebellion by the oppressed that he has previously denied it. This would mean that men acknowledge their dependency, relinquish omnipotence, at the same time as women liberate themselves from objectification and subordination. Revaluing what was derogated as feminine in the split complementarity, formerly devalued aspects projected onto women must be owned by all.

Still, I perceived that the capacity to recognize others remains an abstraction if it is not grounded in a powerful psychological motive, a desire. The work of Daniel Stern and other infancy researchers did provide a developmental basis for this capacity, and so more broadly for a revolution in metapsychology. Importantly, the dyadic relation is not only one of giver and receiver but also of interacting agents who reciprocally regulate and recognize one another. Stern also identified the differentiating moment of realizing that there are *other minds* out there who see and feel what I do. Thus, mutual recognition requires not only attunement but also realization of difference. In different ways, Winnicott and Stern showed how we become capable of recognizing the other and thus resolving the crisis of dependency (called rapprochement by Mahler, Pine, & Bergmann, 1975). Integrating the other's separate will (mother wants to leave, I want her to stay) integrates a positive early experience of difference. The outside mother is the one whom I can love: I do not control her, yet she returns to me.

The contrast between the positions of mutuality and complementarity became a useful axis that clarified clinical (or parental) experience. But relational practice—embracing the both/and of intrapsychic and intersubjective—first enabled us to outline a way of working on this axis, armed with specific clinical categories such as mutual regulation, trauma, dissociation, enactment, rupture, and repair. Relational thinking also demanded that we go beyond the one-person idea of resistance to inquire into the joint participation in stuckness, ruptures, and impasses reported by practitioners of all schools. These experiences led me to make clinical use of my original formulation of the split complementarity between doer and done to, where each feels done to by the other.

Pushing Winnicott's insight, I believed that both partners must survive destruction, indeed the dyad itself must survive moments of retaliation or collapse of difference. This being so, we must find some position "beyond" the doer and done to relation, one not fully described by the notion of mutual recognition. Lacan's idea of the Third—briefly, that speech, or dialogue, was the alternative to kill or be killed—appeared to fit. The intersubjective Third could be formulated as a process, not a thing: going beyond the "kill or be killed" opposition to a relational position in which different minds, different realities, can both live. The Third as an internal position means relating to the other as both like (equal) but different, analogous to the depressive position.

Initially, I imagined thirdness as the shared intersubjective space that allows both to contribute in co-creating the "We"—Ogden's (1994) analytic third. We establish patterns of interaction akin to an overarching movement—as in "the dance" or jazz improvisation, as both partners align in direction, without simply mimicking or reacting. The early procedural and implicit patterns form the rhythmic Third, manifesting as the shared dyadic consciousness of caregiver and infant (Tronick, 2007). They are built on the basis of mutual regulation and accommodation which is essential, and the scaffolding of caregiver recognition of distress and attachment responses (Beebe & Lachmann, 2013). These basic actions form the template for the essential therapeutic action of psychoanalysis—recognizing suffering and distress, feeling *with*, exploring together.

The differentiating Third designates our ability to know other minds, recognizes different realities, and holds one's own without denying the other. Asymmetrical parental recognition—the objective difference between us—makes possible the mutuality of play. But the creation of symmetry, the coordination of two minds, encompasses moments of both joining and separating, harmony and dissonance—with the possibility of "resolving the chord" after dissonance, if not here now, then in another movement or iteration. Thus, the Third moves between breakdown and reconstruction; it works through the constant tension between openness and resolution, difference and togetherness.

Essential to this continual movement between breakdown and reconstitution of the Third is the act of putting things right, or what I call the moral Third. This term refers to the domain of working through repetition and negation, acknowledging violations and failures of recognition, witnessing trauma and injury; it is based on that developmentally necessary movement of rupture and repair (Tronick, 1989). That movement generates the representation of the lawful world in which we either repair breakdowns in recognition or acknowledge the failure to do so. To restore the connection to the lawful world is simultaneously to restore safety and hence affect regulation. Clinically, the idea of the moral Third points to its opposite, the position of the "failed witness," in which unresponsiveness to or denial of traumatic injury and pain is elided with repeating the injury itself (Benjamin, 2018). This failure—often the result of both partners' dissociation—may first precipitate our clinical opportunity for the missing recognition of the injury to emerge.

Clinically, I first elaborated the idea of the Third with reference to Ghent's (1990) idea of surrender as opposed to submission. Ghent, my psychoanalytic ancestor, drew on both Buddhism and Winnicott to propose the idea of surrendering not *to* someone but letting go. I proposed we conceive of this as surrender to the Third (Benjamin, 2004): specifically, the intersubjective process of working through the obstacles to receiving the feeling, suffering, protest, separate viewpoint or desires of the other. This is not done by submitting, by erasing one's own feeling, but rather holding both in tension. I reformulated Ghent's notion of *the patient's* surrender as a two-person process involving the *analyst's* surrender to the Third. Here asymmetry governs: the analyst goes first in surrender, facilitating the dyad's movement out of the complementary mode of opposition between self and other—doer and done to (Benjamin, 2004).

An essential insight emerged from the relational practice of surrender: that it includes acknowledging our own vulnerability. What often limits the analyst's ability to move into thirdness is self-protection. Vulnerability might include fear of our own badness, weakness, dependence on the other's response, and need for recognition of our own efforts; also our dependency on some form of mutual understanding to allow us to regulate and more deeply recognize the other. Accepting the fact of mutual vulnerability helped to overcome the tendency to blame the patient (as unanalyzable) or oneself (bad technique), the reification of resistance or countertransference. We recognized that the analyst too must change (Slavin & Kriegman, 1998). This acceptance of the symmetrical aspect radically changed our understanding of transference and countertransference. In the deepest sense, we surrender to the "What Is" of ourselves and our others.

Although classical analysis had implicitly and unwittingly fostered an ideal of the analyst as perfect container, the relational view would instead prepare us to expect the reality of disruption, failure, conflict, collision as part of the dialectic of rupture and repair. The idea of therapeutic acknowledgment, already laid out by Ferenczi (1933) and highlighted by Aron (1996), appeared as a vital way to unlock repeated and seemingly unavoidable impasses, enactments that took the form of doer and done to, accusations and counteraccusations by patient and analyst (Benjamin, 2009). The analyst must survive failing the patient, or even injuring them, in a way that dramatizes their experience (Ferenczi, 1933); the one who fails can then also be the one who receives the communication, witnesses, and acknowledges.

The relational attention to the analyst's participation in enactments suggested a jointly shared process in which we become part of the solution because we are part of the problem (Mitchell, 1997). Collisions could be fruitfully regarded as precipitating the awareness of dissociation, that is of unconscious or disregarded material and so the shift into a different self states, allows the analyst to resume joining or both partners to join or share exploration of the enactment's content (Bromberg, 2006, 2011; Slochower, 2006). Both partners would survive for the other, shifting together from the hated and feared affects, the shameful and disorganized states of nonrecognition into states of shared recognition: understanding, attunement, and co-creating "our Third." This movement toward recognition allows emotions to be brought into the window of affect tolerance, articulating and organizing experience (Fosha et al., 2012). The therapeutic action of working through enactments thus consists of forming affective schemas of self and other in the position of the Third and constitutes structural change. These patterns integrate the previously dissociated affective content and the new rhythmic-procedural schemas can then be linked with symbolic, reflective representation. Representations of the lawful world are internalized, replacing previous patterns of negation (Stern, 1985). Where we once conceived of intrapsychic repair of the object we now think of an intersubjective process: this underscores the necessity of *therapeutic acknowledgment* as relational repair, the movement out of doer and done to.

I suppose it is necessary to add that enactment is not all there is to intersubjective repair: our continuous, ongoing process of attending to the unformulated and unknown thoughts and feelings, of holding both self and other in mind, is essential. We conceive the analyst's authentic responses, analogous to mother's subjectivity, not merely as reactive countertransference but as creative and healing, meeting the need for the live responsiveness of an other mind (McKay, 2019), and allowing patients to dramatize their desire (Atlas & Aron, 2018). The symmetrical experiences of play and collaboration are balanced with asymmetrical focus on and attunement to the patient that foster the coherence and complexity of interlocking dyadic states of consciousness (Tronick, 2007). These states help to build internal working models of rhythmic thirdness and attachment that further self-cohesion and verify the representation of the lawful world. Such representations are then made durable through acknowledging repair of enacted violations—the Third survives. This process is a vital part of lifting the patient's dissociation as it facilitates experiencing *together* the unrecognized suffering or desire.

Having described the evolution of my theory and some of its clinical implications, I should try now to express the beliefs that inspired and sustain it—my credo. Previously, I articulate something of my own experience of surrender, comparing moments of letting go in analysis (mine and others') to artistic and spiritual experiences and even being in nature. I considered the parallel between moments that open us to experience the other without judgment, with compassion or co-passion (shared feeling), and aesthetic contemplation, immersion in an object, nature, art, and immersion in otherness as in the romantic aesthetic (Benjamin, 2005). In both, we relinquish ordinary consciousness in favor of a transformational experience, that is, experience with the transformational object (Bollas, 1979). Experiencing this space for orientation inward to solitude and creativity can be life-giving. Thus when we focus attention on the other this act represents not only a gift to the other; it is a source of expansion (rather than depletion) for the giver.

However, the analogy between art and analysis fits less well insofar as the analyst must reach beyond subjective immersion and identification to the risk of interacting with the other in order to witnessing and offer them space for further self-expression. As participants, we cannot simply dwell in connection, but surrender to the disruptions of fear, shame, guilt, and self-hatred that frighten us or dysregulate us beyond our capacity to contain. There is a danger of romanticizing and idealizing oneness, of imagining mutual recognition as only joining and never confronting different, clashing realities; never having to confront dissociation in breakdown, when a familiar union or integration is disrupted by the unexpected. Some analysts advocate healing rupture solely by restoring the flow, avoiding the no doubt painful experience of our exposure in breakdowns—forfeiting the reflective repair through shared analysis of ruptures (Boston Change Process Study Group, 2013). Our method of reflecting on the analyst's own "miss" required a radical step. It takes systematic practice to create trust that the Third can survive collisions, accept our strangeness to ourselves, the intrusion of the painful past and the emergence of unformulated experience (Stern, 2009). Using the analyst's interpretation to restore the flow of associations (Ferro & Civitarese, 2013) without addressing a felt dissonance may foreclose the emergent process (Stern, 2009) of shared discovery as we dive into the wreck (see Atlas & Aron, 2018). Our patients have sought our help in bearing the bleakest, harshest, harmed, and harmful parts of self; in looking backward to uncover the impact of negating identifications and mystification (Davies, 2004). Of course, it is the safety and attunement of the current bond that makes exploration of the ruins bearable. But acknowledging ruptures that expose analogues of the past that live within, where injustice and violation have done their damage, strengthens the moral Third.

My attempt has been to bring the idea of the Third together with concrete therapeutic practice, in which we work through the granular, phenomenal interaction of our individual histories and the often unruly or confusing exchanges of multiple selves. In addition, I've tried to unite the developmental idea of repair with the understanding of social healing, to affirm the transformative power of witnessing, suffering, and admitting the truth of injustice or injury on a broader scale (Benjamin, 2018). In contrast to one-person theories of illuminating the unconscious, this perspective suggests that insight into one's own unconscious constitutes recognition of and thus responsibility for one's relational impact. Practicing relationally showed us that, as Ferenczi (1933) first advised, we have to actually admit to our part in injury in order to step out of the doer and done to cycle of blame where the victim becomes an accuser. The moral Third is one way to think about this process of acknowledging real injury.

The need to respond to the other's pain and set right our relationship to the earth and its life forms animate our collective will to embody and create the moral Third. We affirm our belief in our capacity to repair the broken world precisely by facing, not glossing over, the destructiveness that denial has protected, by mourning rather than defending against the knowledge of terrible things (Bragin, 2007). The idea of mutual recognition does not imply complete self-knowledge nor a happy ending resolving breakdown once and for all—rather it supposes that we facilitate the evolution of thirdness through a wide variety of reparative action in which acknowledgment of injuries and failures of self knowledge plays a critical role.

Increasingly, we recognize how our own vulnerability comes into play precisely when we are faced with the need to make acknowledgment. Can we translate this experience as analysts to our role as implicated citizens responsible for repairing our country's damage to those more vulnerable than ourselves, those who have been oppressed and othered? Can Winnicott's idea of surviving destruction be expanded to show how one side is transformed and dependent on the other for transformation? If our survival enables the other to love, do we accept that we may also depend on the other to render us loveable in this way? Can we tolerate that being "good" means accepting that we are or have been "bad?" We have agreed that to survive for the other unsettles and disrupts us, then changes us (Slavin & Kriegman, 1998).

As a collective, we may agree to face the challenges of the other and be destroyed—that is to be wrong, to be changed, to suffer the internal breakdown of the unbearable, unmetabolized elements churning within our social world (Swartz, 2019) in order to release us from the doer and done to relation. But we can only do this insofar as we develop our ability to negotiate repair with others—with different and sometimes conflicting subjectivities—believing that living through the turmoil of conflict and transformation will change us for the better, give us access to unacknowledged truths and the potential for lawfulness where once was injustice.

As I said at the outset, psychoanalysis is for me a world view, a theory, and a practice, pointing toward a way of facing hopelessness while maintaining faith in repair. Or, it is an evolving historical project in which we are working together to contain and develop dialectical tensions that present as binaries: between the known and the strange, repetition and transformation, breakdown and recognition. It is a method, imperfect to be sure, of using our intersubjective capacities to hold such tension, to recognize hitherto unrealized pain and desire, and to move between trauma and repair. Through our wholehearted engagement in this practice, we continually reaffirm how our knowing of common vulnerability and suffering can become the site of solace and growth.

References

Aron, L. (1996). *A meeting of minds: Mutuality in psychoanalysis*. Hillsdale, NJ: The Analytic Press.

Atlas, G., & Aron, L. (2018). *Dramatic dialogue: Contemporary clinical practice*. London and New York: Routledge.

Beebe, B., & Lachmann, F. (2013). *The origins of attachment: Infant research and adult treatment*. New York and London: Routledge.

Benjamin, J. (1988). *The bonds of love: Psychoanalysis, feminism and the problem of domination*. New York: Pantheon.

Benjamin, J. (1995). Recognition and destruction: An outline of intersubjectivity. In *Like subjects, love objects* (pp. 27–49). New Haven, CT: Yale University Press. (See Psychoanal. Psychology Supp 1990).

Benjamin, J. (2004). Beyond doer and done to: An intersubjective view of thirdness. *Psychoanalytic Quarterly*, 73, 5–46.

Benjamin, J. (2005). From many into one: Attention and the containing of multitudes. *Psychoanalytic Dialogues*, 15, 185–201.

Benjamin, J. (2009). A relational psychoanalysis perspective on the necessity of acknowledging failure etc. *International Journal of Psychoanalysis*, 90, 441–450.

Benjamin, J. (2018). *Beyond doer and done to: Recognition theory, intersubjectivity and the third*. London and New York: Routledge.

Bollas, C. (1979). The transformational object. *International Journal of Psychoanalysis, 60*, 97–107.
Boston Change Process Study Group (2013). Enactment and emergence of new relational organization. *Journal of the American Psychoanalytic Association, 61*, 727–749.
Bromberg, P. (2006). *Awakening the dreamer: Clinical journeys*. Hillsdale: The Analytic Press.
Bromberg, P. (2011). *The shadow of the tsunami and the growth of the relational mind*. New York and London: Routledge.
Davies, J. (2004). Whose bad objects are we anyway? Repetition and our elusive love affair with evil. *Psychoanalytic Dialogues, 14*, 711–732.
Ferenczi, S. (1933). Confusion of tongues between adults and the child. In *Final contributions to the problems and methods of psychoanalysis* (pp. 156–167). London: Karnac.
Ferro, A., & Civitarese, G. (2013). Analysts in search of an author. Commentary on D.B. Stern "field theory in psychoanalysis II". *Psychoanalytic Dialogues, 23*, 246–253.
Ghent, E. (1990). Masochism, submission, surrender: Masochism as a perversion of surrender. *Contemporary Psychoanalysis, 26*, 108–136.
Lacan, J. (1975). *The seminar of Jacques Lacan, book I*. New York: Norton.
Mahler, M., Pine, F., & Bergmann, A. (1975). *The psychological birth of the human infant*. New York: Basic Books.
McKay, R. K. (2019). Where objects were, subjects now may be: The work of Jessica Benjamin and reimagining maternal subjectivity in transitional space. *Psychoanalytic Inquiry, 39*(2), 163–173.
Mitchell, S. A. (1988). *Relational concepts in psychoanalysis*. Cambridge: Harvard University Press.
Mitchell, S. A. (1993). *Hope and dread in psychoanalysis*. New York: Basic Books.
Mitchell, S. A. (1997). *Influence and autonomy in psychoanalysis*. Hillsdale: The Analytic Press.
Safran, J. D. (1999). Faith, despair, will and the paradox of acceptance. *Contemporary Psychoanalysis, 35*, 5–23.
Slochower, J. (2006). *Psychoanalytic collisions*. New York: Routledge.
Stern, D. N. (1985). *The interpersonal world of the infant*. New York: Basic Books.
Stern, D. B. (2009). *Partners in thought: Working with unformulated experience, dissociation and enactments*. London and New York: Routledge.
Swartz, S. (2019). *Ruthless Winnicott: The role of ruthlessness in psychoanalysis and political protest*. London and New York: Routledge.
Tronick, E. Z. (1989). Emotions and emotional communication in infants. *American Psychology, 44*, 112–119.
Tronick, E. Z. (2007). *The neurobehavioral and social-emotional development of infants and children*. New York: W. W. Norton.
Winnicott, D. W. (1971). The use of an object and relating through identification. In *Playing and reality*. New York: Penguin.

Chapter 11

Credo: Playing and Becoming in Psychoanalysis

Steven H. Cooper

My approach to psychoanalysis today is different than it was even five years ago and the same was true for five years before that. The theorist who has gripped my imagination from the beginning that got me most interested in psychoanalysis, Donald Winnicott, continues to do so. In the last 10 years, I have found myself working with and developing his unique ideas through my own clinical work and writing. I am continually astounded by what he was able to understand about development and analytic process.

When I think about my work, there are a few dimensions of interpretation or perhaps better stated, responsiveness, that stand out. These generalizations come with a caveat that I am different with each patient. Generally, though, my comments are fairly informal and more aimed toward responsiveness than explanation. I aim for a responsiveness that is direct, respectful, and hopeful about the growth that could occur or has already occurred.

I try to approach interpretation from Winnicott's observation that he interprets to show his patients the limits of his understanding. Regarding interpretations, I try to let go of my darlings as writers like to say about their overattachment to a phrasing or word. My responsiveness is squiggle-game-"ish." Perhaps it could be said that I aim to convey something along these lines: "I have faith in your ability to grow even if I don't always know how to facilitate that. I believe that there is something unique about this setting and the two of us trying, that can be useful. I would like to become useful in helping you with the process of becoming who you are."

There are two basic ideas that inform my psychoanalytic work. First, play is the dominant metaphor for understanding all psychoanalytic work. I will elaborate what I mean by play in much of this credo but I mostly refer to forms of "elasticity" (Ferenczi, 1928) in relation to our inner life and living with others. Conflicts are rarely fully "resolved." We don't "get over" loss. We don't even ever entirely stop repeating some of our solutions to early developmental points of failed or confusing dependency, confusion about sexuality, or trauma. Psychoanalysis more than anything facilitates our ability to play with our psychic lot in new ways. As analysts, we are, as

DOI: 10.4324/9781003206248-11

Winnicott observed, both participants and supervisors of play. As supervisors, our responsibility is to create a setting that allows patient and analyst to work with and learn how to better find play with their inner life. It is the setting that holds patient and analyst so that play can be discovered.

A second and related matter of importance is that in general this means that my countertransference is crucial to understanding my patients. I agree with Parsons (2009) that unless the analyst treats him or herself in the way that he treats his patients, nothing psychoanalytic will happen.

Often our resistance to understanding our patients and our own minds is where the analyst's work is most important. Psychoanalysis is a "contentious" process (Cooper, 2010, 2018, 2019; Ogden, 2004; Parsons, 1999, 2006, 2007) for both patient and analyst. No matter how much we want as patients to change and, as analysts, to facilitate that process, we hold on to familiar modes of adaptation so that we can ensure that things stay the same (Bromberg, 1998). My aim, to be as patient and supportive with my patients as possible, issues from an understanding that finding new forms of play is immensely messy and challenging. In fact, the idea that both patient and analyst resist new forms of understanding and behavior allows for some of the highest forms of intimacy and empathy between patient and analyst (Cooper, in press a). Paradoxically, one of the most important forms of play in psychoanalytic process is the cultivation of new ways to play with the patient's and analyst's resistance to finding new forms of play.

As much as we wish for change to be dramatic and stretching toward "resolution," most often change is more subtle. Yet the development of the capacity for play is breathtaking when it is instituted in new ways.

What Do I Mean by Play and Finding Play?

I try to find a receptivity within myself to the ways that patients are often saying things that they don't know that they are saying. Sometimes though, they know long before I do. Mostly, I am trying to be receptive to the forms of play that my patients introduce through new metaphors, free association, slips of the tongue, and conscious forms of humor about what they are struggling with. Sometimes the words are the same but there is a change in the musicality with which the words are said. I hear a different tone in someone's sadness like an appreciation for the experience of sadness. Or, in another moment, I might hear the patient's attachment to sadness, even a reluctance to let it go. Or, for another patient with repetitive self-reproach, I might hear a subtle form of gratification in the feeling which provides an entry point for me or a new comparison for herself. At these moments, I can reflect on a new part of the patient's feeling.

More and more I agree with Winnicott's observation that he interprets mostly to indicate to the patient the limits of his understanding. This helps to institute a process in the setting so that a patient can discover himself and gather up his or her feelings or as Winnicott (1945, 1968) termed it, the "bits and pieces" of his self. I prefer this to the term "self states" because it's an everyday term that is more subjectively based. The term self-state implies more organization, even it is trying to describe fragmentation, which is why I prefer everyday terms like "feelings" or Winnicott's "bits and pieces."

I think about play in relation to the struggle going on between new and old self and object experiences; in the struggle between unrepresented experiences trying to find move into representation; in the play of mourning in which we are trying to find ways of changing our relationship to old objects; and in the way in which limit and possibility are each constitutive of play.

I also find play in a particular paradox between Arendt's (1953) definition of love, borrowed from Augustine: "I want you to be" and the understanding that the patient is always in the process of becoming (Cooper, under review). Play can be found in the wish to appreciate the patient as he or she is (I want you to be as you are) and the fact that sometimes we and the patient can hold possibilities about who we are becoming (or even who we have already become who we have not yet realized we have become). I love the phrase "I want you to be" because it steps back from the possession and ownership in the words, "I want," toward a devotion about the possibility of the other person becoming who they will become.

Some Forms of Playing in Psychoanalytic Work

Play may be found in all of the tensions that I have just enumerated because psychoanalysis is by definition a path into what stops patient and analyst from being. I'll try to say a bit more about each of these forms of play.

One common form of finding play involves arriving at the seam between areas of represented and unrepresented experience (Cooper, 2018, 2019). Metaphors and stories increasingly take on meaning inside the patient and analyst and sometimes there are shared meanings through intersubjectively created objects (Green, 1975; Ogden & Ogden, 2004). Sometimes a patient will hear his or her words or phrases in a completely different way. One patient heard herself say something in referring to dating an available man that she had said to me dozens of times with smiles and a kind of glibness: "What fun is that?" As her sense of suffering in her erotic masochism moved into greater representation, she heard that phrase in a serious, less joking way. She felt the waste of time in choosing only unavailable men. She also felt her comments in a painful way, a sense that the derision toward herself cut to the bone. She could also better feel her self-destructive attachment to forms of erotic masochism in her transference to me.

An area of play that is quite common relates to the patient's attachment to internal objects. I am often trying to find capacities for play in understanding the ways that patients hold on to bad, sometimes persecutory objects rather than feel alone or helpless. Treatments optimally involve the analyst becoming deeply familiar with parts of the patient that are rigidly influential, troubling, and refractory to insight. These parts of the patient become animated in treatment as a host of characters with whom we regularly visit and communicate. The patient's adaptation in response to internalized objects creates what the patient and analyst come to learn as a kind of atavistic feature that we (the patient and analyst) learn how to converse with. The patient's internalized world is my compass in analytic work, including reaching new ways for the patient to gain purchase on their often, oppressive attachments to old objects. My participation is always framed in the shadow of these forces including my most improvisational and creative activities as an analyst.

Another way to get at this kind of play is to say that I am aiming to establish a dialogue with these parts of the patient. I might be welcome, unwelcome; the patient might be angry that I am an unreliable visitor or a visitor who won't leave; I might be an intrusive and impolite visitor; a visitor who wants to set up residence; or an overly formal visitor who the patient would like to be more familiar with.

To get inside the darkest and most refractory elements of the patient's adaptation requires a dedicated attention to internal objects (Cooper, 2014). It requires that we be as sensitive as possible to our complex and subtle reactions to our patients in the countertransference. Differences, even small differences in how we feel about our patients really matter. I try to pay attention to how I feel with the patient, including when I am struggling to listen; when I care in ways that seem excessive; when I don't feel like I care as much as I wish; when I am or am not sexually stimulated; when I am needing affirmation from the patient and the like. This awareness allows me to understand my patient's inner life and how and where we interact with one another. It is from this place in the patient and these places in the analyst that the analyst's personal participation issues forward. These are the places where play is found (Cooper, 2018).

It is probably clear from what I've said that a form of play is also found between the patients and analyst's overlapping and different views of psychic reality. Usually, patients come to these forms of play on their own. For example, a patient who has maintained a very negative transference toward me, rarely sees anything useful or worthwhile about what I say. I have suggested to the patient that he might need to find nothing worthwhile as a way to titrate his longings. He agrees but cannot really acknowledge this directly to me. He knows that I know this about the way that his shame works in everyday life and analysis. One day, the patient says to me, "I'm instituting a new policy when I disagree with you. I'm not going to insult you as much because I'm wearing you down and you can't take it." I said, "And you need me to stay with you?" The patient says, "I recently began to realize that you are a person. That seemed more important to me than whether I agree with you or not."

The patient here has found a complex form of play. He has realized that he no longer needs to locate his sense of degradation in me. He knows that I know about his shame involved in needing me but he is asking that it not yet be discussed. He can hold the idea of me as a person with his sense of being a person. I have survived his rage and sadness enough to move into a new form of play. The new play goes something like this: "Your just as wrong as you ever were, but I know that you are a person who has feelings and I don't want to destroy you. I need you but we can't really talk about that yet very much." The patient has preserved his equilibrium by still maintaining that I offer nothing by way of understanding him, but I have become a person with him, an unstated holding presence.

Play occurs often at a moment of dawning awareness of transference-countertransference enactment within both patient and analyst. Often these moments especially involve the analyst's new awareness of his or her own resistance to understanding transference-countertransference enactments. Through play, the patient's attachment to an internal object and enacted in transference-countertransference engagement is now slowly replaced with parts of self that can observe the internal object in a different developmental context than that which originally gave rise to the internalization. The patient can observe this internalized object as a debilitating type of psychic forfeit in a new way within the transference-countertransference context of analysis. Through newly discovered forms of play, these processes are occurring now in real time and less through frozen memorialization of what never was.

An extremely important and common part of play involves "the play of mourning" (Cooper, under review). Over the course of my career, I have tried to emphasize that limit and mourning are just as constitutive of play as more frequently described forms of play involving humor and more benevolent forms of holding (Cooper, 2000, 2010). In fact, it is the concept of limit that really made Winnicott's genius so apparent in his consideration of the holding environment. Winnicott emphasized the importance of the analyst as facilitative and able to be used but he also emphasized how limit, including the analyst's hatred in the countertransference, was constitutive of play.

In fact, I think that mourning is really not possible without a capacity to use/find play. Frequently in psychoanalysis, we are asked to help patients to separate from the refractory hold that internal objects have on us. Mourning is required. The cost of doing business with these objects often involves a great deal of psychic forfeit. Play facilitates movement from forfeit of self-experience, from the chains binding the self to an internal object, toward new experiences with self and other. In this sense, play epitomizes the density of analytic experiences that elicits both regression to earlier states and psychic futurity (Cooper, 1997; Loewald, 1960) in the form of potentially new experience. Play introduces a kind of incremental experience of what will be given up in changing.

A common form of play related to the capacity for mourning involves finding and understanding old parts of self or bits and pieces of self and seeing how they can be in conversation with new states of being. The mourning process often relates to elements of fantasy, identity, internal objects, and actually lost objects. Mourning is aided by the holding, receptivity, caring, and containment of the analyst just as it catalyzes the experiences in the transference that often need to be mourned.

I translate Winnicott's notion of "discovering the self" as an ability to recognize and express various feelings in the transference for the first time. While much of transference involves the repetition of early object experience with the analyst, there are also newly recognized experiences in the transference that reside alongside their primary relationship to early objects. These new experiences with self and the analyst form the basis for play, a transition toward the capacity for mourning, and the patient's ability to live more creatively.

I want to emphasize that I try to "never take for granted how much the patient is integrated" (Winnicott, 1945). I try to relax with the disparate voices and listen to the music of the patient's internal objects, my associations. This listening also includes a receptivity to unconscious fantasy both in the patient and in myself. These voices also form my understanding of the patient's and my own sources of resistance. Some portions of those fantasies are psychotic and can be really helpful in understanding parts of the patient that had been unclear. I want to be curious about anything that I am thinking, even things that seem quite unrelated to what the patient is talking about. I don't try to make sense of it too quickly. It's much better to avoid assuming a level of integration in the patient when it is not there so that the patient experiences an invitation for many parts of the patient to join the conversation. Reverie is sometimes helpful in finding new ways to integrate and converse with these disparate parts of the patient's inner life.

The epistemological and ontological dimensions of psychoanalytic work that Ogden (2019) differentiates come together for me in the following way. I am always trying to say something that derives from what I experience as directly connected to the patient's experience. Sometimes though, when I say things *about* what is inside the patient, it is in order to help the patient to become something that neither of us yet know about or anticipate. It is because I cannot yet find a responsiveness to them that is more directly connected to what they are communicating about who they are and who they are becoming. So, while the epistemological approaches of Freud and Klein are quite different than the ontological approaches of Winnicott and Bion, I find myself "speaking" from influences from both traditions. So for me, I would say that nearly all of the analytic work that I do borrows from both the ontological and epistemological traditions.

Coda

My work as an analyst is to establish a dialogue with internalized parts of the patient. This helps to institute playing and partly defines playing. This is not done through interpretations that are constantly aimed at locating and delineating internal objects even though I am in an internal conversation with them. Instead, my responsiveness is aimed at trying to facilitate the patient's capacity to be with his or her own person. Mostly this is done through affective attunement, including an attunement to my own experience. I try to get different parts of the patient on better speaking terms with other parts. I also want to open myself up to my voices and internal objects.

I end as I began with this observation. If we give ourselves over to the metrics of psychoanalytic change, subtle shifts in how we experience others and our own inner life are significant, sometimes breathtaking. The analyst's modesty is intentional, not as a postured stance but as a form of respect for how it is the patient's work to find the way to say what they have to say. Since what we are trying to do in psychoanalysis is quite ambitious, difficult, and risks failure, this genuine and practiced modesty is a part of how we help people to better become themselves in analytic work and in life. Play incrementally helps patients to discover spaces with which to tolerate the existential terror of change. Incremental as it is, the results can be exhilarating.

References

Arendt, H. (1953). *The human condition*. Chicago: The University of Chicago Press.
Arendt, H. (1961). *Between past and future*. London: Faber and Faber Limited.
Arendt, H. (1996). *Love and Saint Augustine*. Eds. J. V. Scott & J. C. Stark. Chicago: The University of Chicago Press.
Bromberg, P. (1998). *Standing in the spaces: Essays on clinical process, trauma, and dissociation*. Hillsdale, NJ: Analytic Press.
Cooper, S. H. (1997). Interpretation and the psychic future. *The International Journal of Psychoanalysis*, 78, 667–681.
Cooper, S. H. (2000). *Objects of hope: Exploring possibility and limit in psychoanalysis*. Hillsdale: The Analytic Press.
Cooper, S. H. (2010). *A disturbance in the field: Essays on transference-countertransference*. New York/London: Routledge.
Cooper, S. H. (2014). The things we carry: Finding/creating the object and the analyst's self-reflective participation. *Psychoanalytic Dialogues*, 24, 621–636.
Cooper, S. H. (2018). Playing in the darkness: Use of the object and use of the subject. *The Journal of the American Psychoanalytic Association*, 66(4), 743–765.
Cooper, S. H. (2019). A theory of the setting: The transformation of unrepresented experience and play. *The International Journal of Psychoanalysis*, 100, 1439–1454.
Cooper, S. H. (in press a). The limit of intimacy and the intimacy. *Journal of the American Psychoanalytic Association*.
Cooper, S. H. (in press b). The play of mourning.

Cooper, S. H. (under review). "I want you to be:" Winnicott's unique view of interpretation and ontological psychoanalysis.

Ferenczi (1928/1955). The elasticity of psychoanalytic technique. In *Reprinted: Final contributions to the problems and methods of psychoanalysis* (pp. 87–101). London: Hogarth. (Original work published in 1928).

Green, A. (1975). The analyst, symbolization, and changes in the analytic setting (on changes in analytic practice and analytic experience). *The International Journal of Psychoanalysis, 56,* 1–22.

Ogden, T. (1989). On the concept of the autistic-contiguous position. *The International Journal of Psychoanalysis, 70,* 127–140.

Ogden, T. (2004). The analytic third: Implications for psychoanalytic theory and technique. *Psychoanalytic Quarterly, 73,* 167–196.

Ogden, T. (2016). Destruction reconceived. On Winnicott's 'the use of an object and relating through identifications'. *The International Journal of Psychoanalysis, 97*(5), 1243–1262.

Ogden, T. (2019). Ontological psychoanalysis or "what do you want to be when you grow up?" *The Psychoanalytic Quarterly, 88,* 661–684.

Parsons, M. (1999). The logic of play in psychoanalysis. *The International Journal of Psychoanalysis, 80*(5), 871–884.

Parsons, M. (2006). The analyst's countertransference to the analytic process. *The International Journal of Psychoanalysis, 87,* 1183–1198.

Parsons, M. (2007). Raiding the inarticulate: The internal analytic setting and listening to countertransference. *The International Journal of Psychoanalysis, 88,* 1441–1456.

Parsons, M. (2009). The independent theory of clinical technique. *Psychoanalytic Dialogues, 19,* 221–236.

Winnicott, D. W. (1945). Primitive emotional development. In *Through paediatrics in psychoanalysis* (pp. 145–156). New York: Basic Books.

Winnicott, D. W. (1949/1958). Hate in the countertransference. In *Through paediatrics in psychoanalysis*, 1958 (pp. 194–203). New York: Basic Books.

Winnicott, D. W. (1968a). The place where we live.

Winnicott, D. W. (1968b). Playing: Its theoretical status in the clinical situation. *The International Journal of Psychoanalysis, 49,* 591–599.

Winnicott, D. W. (1969). The use of an object. *The International Journal of Psychoanalysis, 50,* 711–716.

Chapter 12

Credo

Adrienne Harris

What I have always held in mind about first encountering Emmanuel Ghent's powerful project, which he called Credo (Ghent, 1989), was that he thought people should write a Credo at the beginning of their career and at the end. He imagined someone new to therapy and analysis outlining a hoped-for project and then, as a career and life wound down, there could be a reckoning, a summing up. But, as it turns out, there is another variable. Unexpectedly, but then, I come to realize that it is also so obvious: it matters when, in historical time, you write your Credo.

A year ago, I would have written an essay very much organized around my appreciation for finding such a capacious home in psychoanalysis, my sense of the lucky circumstances in my career. I found myself wanting to speak of the encounter with Mitchell, Ghent, Bromberg and the relational turn, as well as earlier passions, the sequence of political activism, feminism and liberatory movements, engaged in the 60s and 70s, with questions of gender, sexuality, race, and differences of many kinds.

Now, I write in the midst of two entangled crises: the COVID-19 pandemic and the necessary visibility and palpable presence of racism in our country, the United States. For me, at this moment, to write a Credo requires a promise in regard to the future as well as a judgement and assessment of what being a psychoanalyst has meant to me from the beginning of my career and training in the 1980s to the present. In the overdue demand to attend to systemic racism, made an imperative in our current environmental and social crises, there is mourning and accountability, as well as pleasure and devotion to psychoanalytic work and its communities.

The beginning of my life as a psychologist occurred in the intense environment of the 1960s, the anti-war movement, and the inauguration of feminism and movements of liberation around gender and sexuality. Now, as a person both aging and hopefully maturing, I am again trying to identify my work—as a psychoanalyst and as a citizen.

In thinking how I, and we, as members of professional and civic and personal communities, need to work and repair the wounds in our cultures and our professions, I feel the challenge and the question: Do we have the will to do this work on racism, on whiteness and on many kinds of privilege? What is still true in regard to deconstructing racism is that powerful work is coming from people of color. Drawing on psychoanalysis, I consider, most significantly, Sheldon George who has a most compelling and crucial analyses. George (2016), whose intellectual ancestor seems to me to be Fanon, draws on a Lacanian concept, *jouissance,* to insist that we notice the excitement, often produced in concert with sadism, that undergirds and produces acts of white racial violence. Just as, in an earlier era, Fanon spoke of the black man as a *phobogenic* object, desired and feared, George sees the mix of toxic envy, shame and excitement in many acts and experiences of racism. What makes his work important and challenging is its grounding in a clear commitment to the unconscious roots of these complex pleasures and hatreds and thus the demanding work of excavation and processing that lies ahead.

For a number of years, I have used the writing of Credos in teaching courses on ethics. We would begin the class with the exercise of writing a Credo. Then at the end of the class—a day, a weekend, a semester—we would write a second version. What if anything had changed? Several years ago I wrote:

> At the beginning of the course: Analysis is a dream. I had a dream to open myself. I believe in suffering, in hard work, in following the train of ancestors: those in my field like Ferenczi and Winnicott, and Mitchell and Ghent and Bromberg. And in my family, I would start with Agnes Laing, my Scotch nanny, a coalminer's daughter, coming to Canada after the first world war, because (she tells me this as an adult) There was no work and no one to marry. My grandfather, John Lyle, quiet in behavior and radical in imagination, created a particular national Canadian vocabulary for mid-century architecture. I walk through the Union station he envisioned and worked on in Toronto and I like the scale of his ambition.

Now, writing in 2020, I would add something about my adult life choices. In the family I made in adulthood, I need to name and thank Bob Sklar, who I married in 1980, and among other influential advising, who wonderfully insisted that there was just no need for writing blocks or hand wringing about literary composition. He started as a newspaper guy working for newspapers in LA and Newark and really writing was just working. You sat down at a desk, you wrote and in a timely fashion, you handed in your copy. I liked the idea of just being a guy writing and when we moved into our loft in downtown NYC, we were going to make two studies but ended up with just one, a long line of bookshelves and a curving long desk, where we sat at either end and wrote.

When I think back to the beginning of an intellectual and personal journey that led me into the career as a psychoanalyst, teacher and writer, the word that comes to mind is "lucky." I started graduate school in the intense atmosphere of civil rights movements, the anti-war movement in relation to the war in Vietnam and in many women's liberation projects, in particular work on abortion rights and sterilization abuse. The University of Michigan was an intense and very politicized space. I read, I was educated in new modes of thinking and participating in the world. I was influenced and inspired by many courageous persons. Courageous and sometimes self-injuring.

This reminder of danger and limit in political work and life brings me to the second lucky experience coinciding with the first. At the time of the intense political life on campuses across America, I was also a young wife and mother. The presence and demand of young children and the counsel of a careful and thoughtful husband meant that I had to think hard about risks and danger. Many peers at that time were moving into more extreme states of action and militance. Most painfully, for me, was the death in an explosion in a town house in New York City of Diana Oughton, a young woman, my age, whom I knew slightly in Ann Arbor. She had joined a group making bombs and planning a more violent level of political engagement. Some of my choices were genuinely me practicing self-care, but I think the presence of young family was clearly part of my decision-making.

The third moment of luck and opportunity came in the 1980s when Steven Mitchell, Emmanuel Ghent, Philip Bromberg, and some others (my peers, in particular, Lew Aron, Antony Bass, Neil Altman, Jody Davies, Ken Corbett, Jessica Benjamin, Muriel Dimen, and Virginia Goldner) were forming the relational communities and projects: Journals, Book Series, Conferences, Institutes, life-long friendships, and enough tasks for several lifetimes.

In the early 90s, Lew Aron and I organized the first Ferenczi Conference in New York City and the most significant influence and figure in my psychoanalytic life came into view. I am sure this was undertaken through Steven Mitchell's direction. I am sure Steve had set this task before us and it absolutely changed our professional trajectories and probably the contemporary Ferenczian revival.

I loved Ferenczi's politics, his radical interventions in technique, his understanding of trauma, his work with shell shock, his engagement with femininity and sexuality in Thalassa, his registration of the horror of early neglect, his vulnerability, his love and responsibility to Freud. I mean responsibility in the Levinasian sense. Reading Judith Butler on our responsibility to the other, I register the complexity of that task, given the penetration of otherness into our own subjectivities, given that we can never be fully transparent to ourselves, given the complexities of our ties to and with others, I am naming here Ferenczi's complex loving responsibility to Freud and to his imagining and wishing how Freud could and needed to grow.

In Ferenczi's struggles with Freud and with himself, I see the inevitable dilemma of psychoanalysis. Who speaks? Who is spoken to? Language is both crystalline and unstable. Even as we use pronouns "I" and "You," the boundaries of these terms are unstable. We are more aware of this when a person's identity is marked by new forms: "they," "them." And we stumble and misspeak. But, in a sense, Butler, following Foucault and others, argues that pronouns are always carrying indeterminacy. It is also not always clear where the indeterminacy lies, in the speaker or the listener.

For me, at this moment, Ogden captures this dilemma best in his account of epistemological versus ontogenetic theories (Ogden, 2019). I see him in the conversation with Civitarese, Stern and others, and historically with Levenson, currently with Grossmark. The speech acts in psychoanalysis are creative, mutative, and unstable. Meaning is, at best, emergent. Who is speaking to whom and why and for what are the productive undergirding of all that is said. For one analysand, when I speak as imagining I know or assert something, I have abandoned her.

I began my career in psychology as a student of psycholinguistics, not only mastering Chomsky but also Vygotsky, living in the complexity, the fixed abstraction, and the fluid semantics of speech. That interest came back to me in the work on Sabina Spielrein, caught, as I was and have been, between cognition/linguistics and psychoanalysis.

Spielrein appealed to me, as a woman to be rescued and reconstructed. All too often misconstructed as "little girl" in a newly developing psychoanalytic community around Freud, even as Spielrein was one of the first women to give a paper at the Wednesday meetings, a paper that Freud quoted from in thinking about the death instinct. Spielrein also had a deeply creative career in Geneva under Claparede and in collaboration with Piaget and later in the flowering of psychoanalysis in post-revolutionary Russia, where her students must have included Vygotsky and Luria. Clearly, I have some long-lasting project of rescue and repair.

I did not think of the reparative impulses within my involvement with feminism and in the study of gender development. Working on envy, on competition and its conflicts with femininity, on struggles for ambition women routinely face and on child development have been projects over 30 years. That work comes out of daily practice also over the same 30 years.

And certainly fueled by feminism studied and practiced for decades. Ann Snitow, a colleague from the 70s, used to say about feminism: for some women, it was a moment when you could stop being a woman and become a person. For others, it was an opportunity to become a woman. I followed the later path, giving up a tomboy childhood, for the pleasure of female identifications.

I think, in this line of influences, of my psychoanalytic family, and so of Lew Aron, of his calm and joyous determination to thrive in work, to lead, and to inspire. The relational family is an intergenerational one. Mitchell launches a theoretical advance and a movement. Ghent, Bromberg, and my cohort Dimen, Benjamin, Goldner, Bass, and Davies were given opportunities and professional tasks that created and transformed our professional lives and public analytic careers.

I had two important experiences in analysis. Valeria Juracsek, a displaced Hungarian arriving in the United States in the 1930s, who gave me such structure and guidance in the 1960s and 1970s, and Roy Lillescov, who beginning in the 1980s was a ground and an inspiring entry into analytic modes of thought and being. While I was in analysis, I was consistently amazed at his calm ability to tolerate my aggression. Then I believed it was his formation as a child analyst, but over the years I have understood and appreciated that it was his depth and character, always so quietly (not silently) present.

So for me to write a Credo, I want to think of people who authored me, authorized me, witnessed, and initiated. This is one of my most central Credos. I am remembering this message, now as a statement, which seems to date from the 12th century. "Standing on the shoulders of others," which is the first part of a phrase, assigned first to a religious man, Bernard of Chartres, then appearing in the writing of Sir Isaac Newton in 1665. It has a follow-up phrase, not always included, but crucial: "Standing on the shoulders of others, you can see further."

To me, what it means, and I hold to it firmly, is the following: cite your sources, find your lineage, honor the ancestors, move it forward. An early reader of this Credo asked me to think about why I had named names. I had made a study of other Credos, appearing in *Psychoanalytic Dialogues* and in *Psychoanalytic Inquiry*. There is great variation in how and whether a writer identifies an influence by name. Some speak of trends, ideas, programs, institutions. Others name names. For me, I discover that "standing on the shoulder of giants" is absolutely a credo, a commitment to citing sources and influences, setting oneself in a family of influences, a lineage. I do it, I think, for the ancestors and for myself.

I believe I must try to do this myself and inspire this path in others. But I also know that this inevitably opens us to danger, shame, envies and grief. Seeing and setting oneself in lineages can make for accelerated differences, antagonisms. The naming of names is selective, of course. Perusing what I have written in this credo and others undertaken whenever I taught an ethics course, I am aware how little, in this credo, that I am speaking of play, how serious I present my purpose and projects. Two of my dearest colleagues, Ken Corbett and Steven Cooper, are currently writing and working on play as a profound and creative part of doing analysis and being an analyst. We find the same deep intentions in Ogden's work on the ontogenetic, phenomenological turn in psychoanalysis. It also appears in the work of the Italian Bionians Giuseppe Civitarese and Nino Ferro, who stress the aesthetic, creative elements in Bion's clinical theory.

All these analyst writers revel and work and thrive in intense counters with deep play. I certainly find my way into such clinical moments with pleasure and intention. But writing now in mid-summer of 2020, I think that we are all, however we are managing and working and engaging, so deeply held in conscious and unconscious fears that a sense of mission, of serious tasks, is very potent. One hears everywhere serious demands to understand and undo structural racism. It is not that this will not involve creativity, artistry, and deep play. It is that these social and personal tasks will take every ounce of courage we can muster. In particular, this will require a much more creative engaged encounter with shame, more usually the affect and self-state that stop thought and intellectual movement.

I think that this Credo, at this moment, has forced me to look with such fear and uncertainty at our psychoanalytic world and to want to think how we survive, our values, our modes of practice, our ethics. I believe, particularly at this moment when we have grave injustices to repair by deep work on ourselves and others, that psychoanalysis as practice, theory and institution must try to promote survival, bear witness and promote justice.

I feel very rooted and proud of my work, in all its manifestations, clinical, educational, editorial, literary and administrative. But there is a task that I have not succeeded at. It is in fact something as a profession, we fail at quite routinely. I felt relieved when I read Shelly Bach's determination not to retire (sadly he died earlier this year). I got the same pleasure from comparable conversations with my friend Donnel Stern. But all of us, I fear, really as a profession, fail too often at self-care. Good at the care and attunement to others, we are more usually working too hard, for too long, under difficult circumstances. We live with deeply demanding problems which we are devoted to solving, and not always with appropriate help. I have had many ideas about this, not the least of which is that for many of us, the biographical story often reveals ego precocity and early caretaking. (Harris). As I work with colleagues in this time of quarantine and crises, I see how general this problem is in our field, how intractable self-care can seem.

A Credo is perhaps, inevitably a version of giving an account of oneself: flawed but serious, depending on systems of ethics which draw on conviction and unconscious counterforces, risky and necessary. It is this view of our tasks of responsibility that must now be directed to the understanding of racism and whiteness and what is being called "white fragility." That term, it seems, must carry the sting of contempt, the rage at weakness within the context of privilege.

My current effort has been to work on two such projects, one emerging from a conference in 2017 in Boston on race and one from a conference on the Pandemic. The conference, my preparation for it, the aftermath and the paper, now published in American Imago are significant in terms of the backsteps, missteps in my participation. I agree to present a paper at the Conference and tried to get out of it. I had some scheduling excuses. Paul Lynch, the conference organizer, was unimpressed by my account and said of course I would be attending. I did and the experience was, in the best sense of that term, shattering. I worked on a paper for several years, a follow-up to a paper I had written on Whiteness some years earlier. The current paper "The Perverse Pact" went through a number of revisions and at every one, I would discover places in the text when I had sidestepped my own racism, covered up with a variety of strategies, including humor, self-deprecation, and amnesia. If I have learned anything from that process, it is that the unconscious denial is fiercely strong. Our long, centuries long, history of genocides, slavery, Jim Crow, and institutional racism is met, in all of us, with fierce resistance to thinking and knowing.

From the Perverse Pact:

> The overarching concept with which I will be thinking about these matters is one developed by Ruth Stein (2005): the perverse pact. This pact can be observed in individuals, in couples, in social formations, and in intersubjective space. What is powerful in this concept is Stein's attention to social links that are both very close and intimate and simultaneously very violent and drenched in hostility. Both terms—"perverse" and "pact"—are necessary ingredients.
>
> What I am concerned to do is to examine in myself and in other white persons, singly or in groups, the combined force of dissociation and violence that keeps racism in place. Dissociation and violence are an odd combination. This is precisely where the notion of a perverse pact can be useful. There is continuous racial violence in the United States. White people both know and "blank out" knowing these indisputable truths. I am using this concept—the perverse pact—to examine some of the self-imposed limits in regard to reflection and action, along with the unconscious conditions in which white guilt, and white fragility inhibit our progress towards genuine civil rights (DiAngelo, 2018). We need to appreciate the power of dissociation and amnesia and be much more scrupulous and suspicious about certain common ideas about guilt.
>
> Guilt needs to be distinguished from "guiltiness." This was an important idea in the work of Stephen Mitchell (2000): "A contrived sense of guiltiness can serve as a psychological defense against a more genuine sense of pathos or sadness for oneself" (p. 730). Guiltiness is riddled with narcissism and anxiety rather than genuine reparative impulses. Guiltiness masquerading as guilt is actually a barrier to mourning and reparation.
>
> In the contemporary context of Black Lives Matter, there is a new level of demand on white power structures and white individuals to understand the difference between reparation, which would actually be an offering, not merely a symbol. Reparation is a process that acknowledges indebtedness and change that means a giving up, a losing of space and place and material conditions, for the entrenched dominating presence of whiteness and racism (Harris, 2009).

The second project, began with an analysis of clinical work in the pandemic and also moved into a consideration of how race, caste and gender mark one's passage through various dangers, economic, medical and psychological. While it is crucial not to underestimate the devastation of COVID-19, it is also true that as a culture we have been offered an opportunity to examine and dismantle the structural racism that threatens any hope of a genuine democracy (Harris, 2021). This is where I feel the imperatives in George's work on jouissance and the toxic presence of envy and fear in systemic racism.

I feel I have been offered an opportunity to return to the political struggles of my young adulthood. Hopefully, in old age, I/we can do better, can avoid the fall into extremism and violence that blighted the idealistic vision of the 1960s, both in America and in Europe. It is clear to me that in answer to the demand for a genuine transformation, a dismantling of structural racism, none of us can say we don't know how.

References

DiAngelo, R. (2018). *White fragility: Why it's so hard for white people to talk about racism.* Boston: Beacon Press.

George, S. (2016). *Trauma and race: A Lacanian study of African American racial identity.* Baylor University Press.

Ghent, E. (1989). Credo: The dialectics of one-person and two-person psychologies. *Contemporary Psychoanalysis, 25,* 169–211.

Harris, A. (2009). You must remember this. *Psychoanalytic Dialogues, 19*(1), 2–21.

Harris, A. (2021). Working in the shadow of COVID-19. *Psychoanalytic Psychology, 38*(2):99–100.

Mitchell, S.A. (2000). You've got to suffer if you want to sing the blues: Psychoanalytic reflections on guilt and self-pity. *Psychoanalytic Dialogues, 10*(5):713–733.

Ogden, T.H. (2019). Ontological psychoanalysis or "What Do You Want to Be When You Grow Up?". *Psychoanalytic Quarterly, 88*(4):661–684.

Stein, R. (2005). Why perversion? 'False love' and the perverse pact. *International Journal of Psychoanalysis, 86*(3):775–799.

Chapter 13

Reflections on the Way I Practice Psychoanalysis*

Thomas H. Ogden

Periodically, I try to find out who I have become, and am becoming, as a psychoanalyst, by writing about that process as best I can (see Ogden, 1994, 1997a, 1997b, 2004, 2009). It is difficult to know where to start in this endeavor, but a point of departure that feels right to me now is that I must invent psychoanalysis freshly with each patient. In what follows, I address different aspects of the way I work as an analyst, while knowing at the outset that these parts cannot possibly come together as an integrated whole that accurately reflects my experience. But, by the act of laying them out here for myself and the reader, I hope they may be of use to the reader in gaining an understanding of how he or she practices psychoanalysis and may provide the beginnings of lines of thought with which the reader may make something of his or her own.

I find myself talking with each patient in a different way, with different tones of voice, different ranges of pitch, volume, and cadences of speech, different syntax and word choice, and in doing so communicate what cannot be said in any other way to any other person. This is not surprising to me in that I do not talk with one of my two grown children in the way I talk to the other; I did not talk with my father, at any stage of my life, as I did with my mother; I do not talk to my wife in a way that I do with anyone else. Each person with whom I enter into intimate conversation draws on me, and I draw on him or her, in such a way that I become a different person to some degree, and speak differently with each of these people. The more intimate the conversation, the more this is true. The conversations I have with my patients are among the most intimate that I have in my life.

I believe that each of my patients would be surprised to overhear the way I talk with any other patient. The way I talk with one patient would feel foreign to any other; what I say to one patient, and the way I say it, would sound too fraternal, too maternal, too formal, too something, to another

---

* Reprinted with kind permission: This chapter was first printed as a longer article titled: *Some Thoughts on Practicing Psychoanalysis* in *fort da* 22 (1): 21–36.

patient. To put it another way, one of my patients would, I believe, feel that the way I talk to any other patient does not suit her, and she would be right, because it was not meant for her, it was not created *with* her and *for* her.

The rhythm of the verbal exchange in my analytic work is also unique to each patient. The rhythm is not that of extended periods of silence while the patient talks, punctuated now and again by a comment on my part. Neither is it the rhythm of ordinary conversation outside the consulting room. The rhythm of the analytic conversation is unlike the rhythm of any other type of conversation. There are several interrelated reasons for this.

First, the setting in which the analytic conversation takes place is designed to provide the patient and analyst the opportunity for dreaming in such forms as waking dreaming (reverie), "talking-as-dreaming" (Ogden, 2007), "dream thinking," and "transformative thinking" (see Ogden, 2010 for discussions of dream thinking and transformative thinking). In an effort to create a space for dreaming (other than in the initial consultation session or sessions), I sit behind the couch while the patient lies on the couch. I explain to each of my patients at the outset of an analysis that their use of the couch allows me the privacy I need to think in a way that differs from the way I think in face-to-face conversation. I add that the patient may find that this is true for him or her, too. I work with patients on the couch regardless of the frequency of our sessions.

Secondly, I do not adhere to Freud's (1912) "fundamental rule." I have found both in my own experience and in the work of analysts who consult with me that the injunction to "say everything that comes to mind" compromises the patient's right to privacy, which is necessary for the freedom to dream in the session. So, rather than asking the patient to say everything that comes to mind, I tell the patient (sometimes explicitly, sometimes implicitly) that she is free to say whatever she wants to say and to keep to herself what she chooses—and that I will do the same (Ogden, 1996).

The upshot of these aspects of containment in the session (management of the analytic frame) is a rhythm of conversation that differs from any other conversation. It is a rhythm in which I am always present (always listening, sometimes talking), as the patient and I move in and out of various forms of dreaming. Waking up from dreaming in the analytic session is as important as the inherent therapeutic value of dreaming itself. Put another way, talking *about* dreaming—understanding something about the meaning of our dreaming—is, to my mind, an essential part of the therapeutic process.

The combination of these and other features of the analytic endeavor—including the fact that it is primarily designed to serve the function of helping the patient achieve psychological growth—contribute to the unique rhythms of the analytic conversation. That rhythm differs with each patient, and within each hour, but by and large involves an active interchange in which the patient speaks more than I do, yet neither of us "dominates" the conversation. I do not limit myself to brief statements. Now and again, I find myself talking at considerable length, at times telling the patient a story (sometimes a story the patient already knows, but pretends not to know so he or she can hear me tell it to them). As is the case with virtually everything else in the analytic relationship, the flow of conversation is a creation that only *this* patient and *this* analyst (the analyst I am becoming in the analysis) could bring to life in *this* particular way.

When I am not creating psychoanalysis *with* and *for* a given patient, the analysis feels generic and impersonal, both to the patient and to me. I am often bored during such sessions and may even fall asleep. Falling asleep under those circumstances is a signal to me that I am not able to dream the session *with* the patient, and may be unconsciously evading that work by attempting to "dream the session" on my own.

I conceive of my work as a psychoanalyst as that of dreaming *with* the patient aspects of his experience that have been too painful for him to dream on his own (Ogden, 2004). I use the term *dreaming* to refer to unconscious thinking, which I believe to be the richest form of thinking that human beings are capable of because it simultaneously brings to bear on an emotional problem a multiplicity of types of thinking—primary and secondary process thinking, synchronic and diachronic senses of time, cause-and-effect thinking, and thinking that releases the two from a sequential relationship.

It is impossible to say "where an idea comes from." My principal psychoanalytic teachers have been Freud, Klein, Fairbairn, Winnicott, Bion, Loewald, and Searles, but I have learned as much about psychoanalysis from poets, novelists, and playwrights. From one perspective, every sentence that I write about "my" way of practicing psychoanalysis ought to have a string of references appended to it in order to give credit to the people who have contributed to the development of the ideas I am discussing. And yet, from another perspective, no references at all are called for because what I make with their work is uniquely my own.

In the course of my life, I have been fundamentally altered by my experiences with my parents and with the three analysts with whom I have worked. I am fortunate to be able to say that the ways I have been changed by these experiences have been predominantly enriching and growth-promoting. Nonetheless, I have come to feel that I have a responsibility to become a better analyst than they were able to be for me. I feel the same responsibility holds true of the succession of generations of parents and their children. Fulfilling the responsibility to do better than they (both one's analyst and one's parents) is not an act of protest or revolt, it is an effort to make full use of them. I know that my parents wished that they could have been better parents to me, and I imagine my analysts felt something similar. This felt desire on the part of my parents was terribly important in my developing a need to imagine ("dream up") a way of becoming a better parent to my children and a better analyst to my patients. When I am with my grandchildren, it is clear to me that that my son is a better father than I was to him. This does not cause me to feel rejected or vanquished by him; quite the contrary, what greater gift could a child give a parent?

When I speak of a child or patient becoming a "better parent" or a "better analyst" than his or her parents or analyst, I have in mind (along with a great many other qualities) the child's (or analysand's) developing an enhanced capacity to carry the pain of the child or patient until the child or analysand has sufficiently matured to be able to carry it for himself or herself. In the succession of generations, of equal importance to the parent's or analyst's ability to carry the pain of the child or patient, is their capacity, at each step of development, to return to the child or patient *his own* pain, because it is *his* (the child's or patient's) and is a vital part of his sense of self. This holds true even, or perhaps more accurately, *particularly*, for a person's traumatic experience. The individual is killed off to the degree that the experience of trauma is left "unlived." The parent's and analyst's act of returning to the child or patient the responsibility for his pain is as difficult as carrying it, for to return it is to surrender a source of the parent's or analyst's sense of being needed, a feeling that is incomparably gratifying and self-affirming, and incredibly difficult to give up.

I find that psychoanalytic theory is not a thing apart from my experience with patients in the consulting room. While working with patients, analytic ideas are always in the wings. Even when analytic theory is out of my conscious thoughts, it nonetheless constitutes a "matrix" (a psychic context, a metaphorical womb) that sculpts the way I hold an experience while working with a patient. How could such fundamental ideas as the unconscious (in an analytic sense that few people other than analysts genuinely comprehend), dreaming (again, in the sense that only analysts understand), reverie, transference, infantile and childhood sexuality, and fear of breakdown not be part of the very structure of my mind and of my thinking at this point in my life? Theory becomes an encumbrance to me only when I find that I am using it in a way that answers, as opposed to frames or poses, questions.

The idea that the human mind needs the truth as much as we need food and water (Bion, 1962, p. 32), and that our minds—the unconscious aspect of our minds, in particular—are continuously in search of the truth have become central to my current conception of the analytic process. Being in touch with (intuiting) the truth of what is occurring at any moment in an analytic session, to my mind, is closely connected with the phenomenon of aliveness of the session. When a session does not feel alive, it feels to me, and to the patient as well, that we are not engaged in an experience that feels truthful. It is not that we are "lying" or "resisting" (terms that feel moralistic, and consequently destructive to an effort to think); rather, we are fearful of the truth of what is occurring at that moment (Ogden, 1995).

The idea that human beings have a powerful need for truth has further implications for me. The need for the truth is not a policing function (keeping oneself honest); it is more an expression of a need for the "freedom to think" the reality of one's experience (Symington, 1983), which is essential to psychoanalysis as a therapeutic process. My role as an analyst is to help the patient mature in ways that allow him to better encompass the realities of his emotional life. Helping a patient face the truth of his experience need not be a confrontational experience. I do not point out the truth to the patient, I live it with the patient until he or she is able to experience it on his own and express it in verbal or nonverbal ways. Integral to facing the truth is the patient's trust in me, and my trustworthiness. "The sacred space of fully open listening, reading, and conversing requires the vulnerability of maximal trust, trust in the essential benevolence of the other, and trust in the resilience of one's self to be able to come apart and even be changed significantly without losing one's essential sense of self" (Warren Poland, personal communication, 2014).

I often ask myself what I think I am doing with patients with whom I am working in analysis. A response to this question that has become increasingly compelling to me in recent years is the idea that each patient brings to analysis—almost always without the words and ideas with which to state it—the feeling that he or she has, in an important sense, died in infancy or childhood, or perhaps at a later stage of life—and hopes that work with the analyst will help him or her to reclaim his live "unlived life" (Ogden, 2014). The source of the psychic death is very often a set of events in infancy and childhood that involved the experience of "primitive agonies" (Winnicott, [1971] 1974) that were more than the patient could bear. In the face of terrifying events, the patient absents himself from his life and, in so doing, protects himself from massive psychic breakdown and a state of chronic psychosis. The patient, under these circumstances, reflexively protects himself by generating a psychic state in which the unbearable events are not experienced, and instead, persist as "unlived life." The individual is forever attempting to develop a personality system capable of containing the unbearable experience he has not lived. In the analytic setting, such a personality system is generated by the conjunction of the unconscious mind of patient and analyst. The creation of such a personality system is, to my mind, one way of conceiving of a fundamental goal of psychoanalysis.

We all have unlived aspects of our lives derived from early life events that were too painful for us to experience. These unlived events remain with us in the form of limitations in our personalities. We can feel these limitations in many ways including the ways we feel constrained in the generosity and compassion and love we are capable of offering our spouse, our children, our parents, our friends, our patients, our students, as well as those whom we do not know, whom we have the power to help were we able to find it in ourselves to give it. I believe we are all the time engaged in unconscious psychological work in the act of dreaming—both while awake and asleep, both on our own and with others—that is of help to us in becoming better able to encompass formerly unlived aspects of our lives.

As I look at my life at present, as I write this paper, I feel very fortunate that it has not been necessary for me to choose among what have become the passions of my life: the experience of practicing psychoanalysis; writing works expressing how I conceive of psychoanalytic theory and practice; writing other pieces in which I try to capture how I read particular poems and stories that hold profound importance to me; writing fiction; and not by any means least of all, teaching both psychoanalysis and creative writing in seminars and consultation. To a significant degree, these forms of experience, taken together, are who I am, and therefore what I bring to patients, students, and colleagues.

I have grown up and grown old with my patients and students and perhaps have become a bit wiser in the process. As a consequence of the unusual intimacy that psychoanalysis, and often teaching, entails, I have many loves in my life. Most importantly, I have had the chance to live with patients their disturbing life events that they had not yet lived, and have marveled at the courage they have shown in attempting to do so.

Perhaps the pieces of this effort to say who I have become and am becoming as a psychoanalyst might be tied together by saying that I have found that what suits me best in my way of being a psychoanalyst is working at the frontier of yet to be known truths of human experience, a place that is constantly engendering wonder and humility.

References

Bion W. R. (1962). *Learning from experience*. In *Seven servants*. New York: Aronson, 1975.
Freud, S. (1912). Recommendations to physicians practising psychoanalysis. *S.E.* 12.
Ogden T. H. (1994). The analytic third: Working with intersubjective clinical facts. *International Journal of Psychoanalysis*, 75, 3–20.
Ogden, T. H. (1995). Analysing forms of aliveness and deadness of the transference-countertransference. *International Journal of Psychoanalysis*, 76, 695–710.
Ogden, T. H. (1996). Reconsidering three aspects of psychoanalytic technique. *International Journal of Psychoanalysis*, 77, 883–899.
Ogden T. H. (1997a). Reverie and interpretation. *Psychoanalytic Quarterly*, 66, 567–595.
Ogden, T. H. (1997b). Reverie and metaphor: Some thoughts on how I work as a psychoanalyst. *International Journal of Psychoanalysis*, 78, 719–732.
Ogden, T. H. (2004). This art of psychoanalysis: Dreaming undreamt dreams and interrupted cries. *International Journal of Psychoanalysis*, 85, 857–877.
Ogden, T. H. (2007). On talking-as-dreaming. *International Journal of Psychoanalysis*, 88, 575–589, 2007.
Ogden, T. H. (2009). Rediscovering psychoanalysis. In *Rediscovering psychoanalysis: Thinking and dreaming, learning and forgetting* (pp. 1–13). London: Routledge.
Ogden, T. H. (2010). On three types of thinking: Magical thinking, dream thinking and transformative thinking. *Psychoanalytic Quarterly* 79: 314–347.

Ogden, T. H. (2014). Fear of breakdown and the unlived life. *International Journal of Psychoanalysis*, 95, 205–224.
Symington, N. (1983). The analyst's freedom to think as agent of therapeutic change. *International review of psychoanalysis*, 10, 283–291.
Winnicott, D. W. (1971[1974]). Fear of breakdown. In C. Winnicott, R. Shepherd, & M. Davis (Eds.), *Psychoanalytic explorations* (pp. 87–95). Cambridge, MA: Harvard University Press.

Chapter 14

Toward a Humanistic Psychoanalysis

Donna Orange

For my first 35 years, I heard, studied, and sang Credos. Later, having studied philosophy and having absorbed American pragmatism, including a "contrite fallibilism," I have now avoided credos for more than 40 years, understanding them as destructive, claiming too much certainty, and tending toward authoritarianism. Ironic that I should now be asked to write one.

And yet, we all live by something, explicitly or implicitly, directly or indirectly, thoughtfully or reactively. Becoming a psychoanalyst invites, even requires us, to confront our former beliefs, rejecting, complexifying, or refining them. Our own lifelong psychoanalysis provides us the opportunity to understand, at least in part, the origins and emotional underpinnings of our beliefs. Exposed to a range of theories, each based on philosophical beliefs rarely made explicit, and guided by many teachers and supervisors, the young and midlife clinician meets patients who seem to confirm or challenge these various points of view. Finally, it would seem, the senior clinician probably expects, and is expected, to possess a coherent and reliable point of view. Alternatively, might we rather resemble my mother-in-law who explained to me that she was learning how to be 98?

Coming to clinical psychology and psychoanalysis from studying American pragmatism and teaching philosophy, I thought of myself as a fallibilist, one who knows her understanding of anything is only partial and perspectival, and likely to be more than half wrong. Still, I brought too much certainty to my new studies. Having read the humanists of the 50s and 60s, Gordon Allport, Abraham Maslow, Rollo May, Viktor Frankl, Irvin Yalom, for example, I was sure that Freud had nothing to offer me, and that I could never be both philosopher and psychoanalyst. Studies of the feminists only confirmed my aversion. Freud, I believed, was just a scientific reductionist and misinterpreter of women's psychology. Much remained to be unlearned and undone.

In graduate school at Ferkauf/Yeshiva University, to my surprise, psychoanalysts, both Freudian and post-Freudian, were everywhere in the early 80s. Some were proto-relationalists; others introduced me to Heinz Kohut's self psychology. I began to realize that, at least by then, psychoanalysis included many variants, and began to imagine looking for psychoanalytic training. Before the lawsuit, of course, psychologists like me could not train in the institutes of the American or belong to the IPA, so my options were limited. Just as I graduated as a clinical psychologist, however, several independent analysts opened a new training institute (IPSS, the Institute for the Psychoanalytic Study of Subjectivity, New York). Founders George Atwood, Beatrice Beebe, Bernard Brandchaft, Jim Fosshage, Frank Lachmann, and Robert Stolorow all taught me there, and all have influenced me to varying extents. Early relational influences came from Stephen Mitchell, who taught the object relations course our first year at IPSS, and more traditional exposure included our Freud course with Martin Bergmann. So my psychoanalytic training was already complex, though shaped by self psychology in its intersubjective direction. A further, indispensable influence was my training analyst from NYU Postdoctoral Program's interpersonal-humanistic track, trained at a time when the relational track—to which I now belong—did not yet exist. My analyst believed in me long before I could believe in myself and taught me that a basic kindness was fully compatible with an analytic process.

So now, though retired from clinical practice but still supervising and teaching, what have I learned to believe about psychoanalysis? Why has it been worth my life, as it is for so many of my colleagues and their patients?

First, like most psychoanalysts, I believe much of our psychological life and motivation to be unconscious. In the oldest of Western philosophical traditions, we are bidden to "know thyself" continuously and fearlessly. But this will never be easy. In the words of my dear friend Warren Poland, "analysis by its very definition is the study of whatever it is that people do *not* want to know about themselves" (Poland, 2018, p. 5). This definition, without any jargon, places resistance in the middle of analysis. Not restricted to patients, it implicitly includes analysts, who share the same study, and the same desire not to know. As I understand it, unconsciousness includes not only the Freudian dynamic form, but even more powerful, the pre-reflective unconscious described and studied by phenomenologists like my earlier collaborators George Atwood, Robert Stolorow, and Bernard Brandchaft. Formed of tightly held emotional convictions about ourselves and others these thinkers call "organizing principles," this definition points into, and beyond, the consulting room, suggesting that analysis includes what people do not want to know about their ancestors, their children, and about the culture in which the individual comes seeking to study. It includes, in my view, the unformulated studied by Donnell Stern, and the normative unconsciousness brought to our attention by Lynne Layton. It points toward the other, whom we may not want to know as brothers and sisters, who may look different and speak other languages. Analysis, an ethical task as Socrates would have clearly understood, challenges us to acknowledge what we have not wanted, individually or collectively, to know about ourselves, including our unearned sense of privilege, our selfishness, our tendencies toward violence or toward submissiveness.

So psychoanalysis searches within a frame, whether rigid or more developmentally oriented. Over time, I have come to believe, with Anthony Bass (Bass, 2007), Robert Grossmark, and others, not only that fittedness matters but that continual adjustments to meet the patient are crucial. With some, the move will mean more structure and come to resemble traditional analysis. With many, the move will mean that while the analyst brings a preferred way of working, the patient will teach me about the meanings of various rules and teach me to experiment. I remember that Frieda Fromm-Reichman began every session with "how can I help you?" then found herself intuiting how to respond, sometimes sitting on the floor with a catatonic patient. At times we will be able to analyze together various meanings of the shifts we find together; other times these are so subtle that they simply become woven into the work. Taught by the infant researchers, we adapt to the rhythms of the patient. Taught by the cultural and contextualist colleagues, we find ourselves confronted by shared realities like extreme social injustice, climate emergency, and the pandemic that plagues us all. We can no longer analyze away questions about our own health or pretend we do not share the terror. Many of us, working in New York during and after the attacks of 9–11, began to learn these lessons years ago, though we still have barely begun. Sandor Ferenczi, beloved ancestor to so many of us, taught us the folly of discounting our participation and our shared humanity.

Thinking of Ferenczi reminds me of his "wise baby" or "little psychiatrist." As the eldest of 10 children born to parents seriously incapable and much inclined to violence, I attempted to support them so they could somehow be parents, and to protect my little siblings so that they could survive. Diapering and feeding babies, milking cows and goats, building fires, and maintaining the woodpile, I snatched every spare moment for reading. Still, no one expected or helped me to pursue higher education. I was simply useful and have always wanted to be. At 18, I escaped into a religious community and immediately began college, studying whatever I was told under obedience. After five years of teaching what today we would call middle school, I began, under obedience, to study philosophy, developing a critical mind and ultimately leading me away from authoritarian church and community. A first psychotherapy, engaging me in the search for what I had not wanted to know of family and its destruction of any self-confidence, led me to wander onto the path into psychoanalysis I ultimately walked. And yet, I oscillated, pathological accommodation style, between attachments to dictatorial others or dominating theories, and moments of rebellion. My current claim to independent status inherits these struggles.

My recent work has brought me from psychoanalytic theories, including the intersubjective, back to philosophy and ethics. Schooled from birth to be a caregiver, I have been drawn to an ethics of non-indifference, an ethical/ humanistic attitude that recognizes the priority of the other. Notice that I do not say that I place the other first. Instead, the face and voice of the vulnerable requires me to respond to a demand that precedes me. I am a first responder who always arrives late on the scene, after the traveler—the widow, the orphan, the stranger—is already beaten down at the side of the road. My status as subject (not ego) arrives when I respond: *Hineni*, me here. Ethical subjectivity results from a turn away from ego, the ego that Pascal believed began the destruction of everything. The suffering other befalls me, as Knud Løgstrup, Emmanuel Levinas, or Bernhard Waldenfels might say. My response must be non-indifference, even to the point of substitution. Substitution, not empathy or sympathy, shows up when a French policeman offers his life for a hostage, or a dying death camp prisoner forces his last piece of bread on a child who may have the chance to live.

When asked if my radical ethics amounts to masochism, I answer that the masochist wants to suffer for the forbidden sexual desires of childhood. The ethical person is willing to suffer to relieve the suffering of others, to accompany the other in pain and loss. The medical people in the wards with COVID-19 do not seek out suffering, but understand that they may not avoid it, that they may not leave the other to die alone, as Emmanuel Levinas would have said. As psychoanalysts, we accompany the other in their suffering, even when the process inflicts misery on us. This attitude and conviction has become the central organizing principle of my life, I hope.

Missing from my account here is an articulate psychoanalytic theory. My work has been shaped by encounters with humanistic psychology, self psychology, various intersubjectivities—especially including what both Lew Aron and I liked to call "intersubjective vulnerability," object relations theories, and of course, Freud, who has become ever more important to me. But I do not belong to any psychoanalytic school or denomination, and consider myself an independent, always trying to learn. This attitude has not resulted in a well-formed theory.

More than a credo or list of beliefs, I think our work is shaped by attitudes. Among mine are phenomenology, compassion, and the priority of the other. Putting aside for the moment all the recent talk of relationalists and intersubjectivists, levels of discourse, language games, and even of Descartes, let us consider what it might mean to think and practice psychoanalysis in a phenomenological spirit. I think it means at least three important things: (1) a focus on lived experience that leaves aside, "brackets," or suspends our interest in categories, dualisms, and in the "facts" studied by the natural sciences; (2) viewing relatedness as our primary human situation, and specifically I-You relatedness as the condition for the possibility of personal subjectivity; (3) embracing the indispensable asymmetry of our work that leads phenomenological psychoanalysts and therapists to live out the quiet discipline of placing ourselves in the background.

Rigid adherence to rules and theories seems to me incompatible with a humanistic psychoanalysis responsive to this irreplaceable, precarious other.

The primacy of lived experience means that, as psychoanalysts, we concern ourselves with what our patients are suffering. We attempt to understand this suffering—including their ways of coping with it until now—through our own situated and limited lived experience. We try to notice when our patient feels that we make him, her, or them into an It—reducing, observing, diagnosing, judging, knowing better, controlling, distancing—and when we seem to connect as a We, the I, and You of genuine dialogue, of communion. Instead of "treating" depression or psychosis, we undergo the situation with the other. Carrying our preconceptions—personal, cultural, and theoretical—as lightly as possible, we attempt together to make sense of, to understand the patient's suffering within the always-already living relation in which we find ourselves and which we continue to develop together. It is written that we should rejoice with those who rejoice and weep with those who weep. Unfortunately, in our work with devastated human beings, we weep more often.

Working phenomenologically also means to me seeing relatedness as our primary human situation. This means that we are born into relatedness, and that our coping capacities and our tangles develop, maintain, and transform relationally. Both agency and suffering are always situated, emotionally and temporally. Aging and dying means we are gradually losing our grip. Our work becomes a surrender to the loss of a sense of agency in the relational worlds that have enlivened, sustained, and troubled us. At every moment, the phenomenologist will meet the patient within complexly nested lifeworlds more or less shared. We share a common humanity—with all its potential for good and evil—and are the Other to each other, the You that meets the I in mutual dignity and reverence. I am human, said Terentius, and nothing human is alien to me. This means, of course, that the evil and cruelty I abhor in others may also belong to me.

But the psychoanalytic phenomenologist has a special vocational burden—the requirement of asymmetry. Both Buber and Binswanger believed the teacher, the therapist, and the rabbi or pastor shared an obligation to treat the student, patient, or congregant as You without expecting, or even accepting, reciprocity. Emmanuel Levinas and Knud Løgstrup in turn defined the ethical relation—the infinite responsibility for the Other—as inherently asymmetrical. It is, therefore, no surprise that psychoanalytic phenomenologists seem drawn to theories and clinical attitudes that emphasize our responsibility to stretch empathically, to reach for contact, to understand, just as good enough parents do for many years, without expectation of any adequate recompense. The parent is primary support for the development of the child's personhood, and not vice versa, except in the situation of the parentified (It) child for whom the needed support does not exist. Psychoanalysts and psychotherapists, I believe, work in a similar ethical relation of this asymmetrical type.

So the phenomenologist accompanies the troubled, usually traumatized, patient patiently and unobtrusively, to borrow Robert Grossmark's term. With good-enough attunement to emotional life—both same and other—we join with the patient in the search for understanding, without too much knowing. When we guess it may support dialogic reflection, we self-disclose a little. We attempt a "minimally theoretical" psychoanalysis, working with experience-near concepts, and holding our judgments and diagnostic impulses as lightly as we can. We stay close to our patients, finding our way together, we learn what we can from everyone, and we seek comfort and support—always needed, sometimes desperately—primarily from fellow phenomenologists. We face our "infinitely demanding" work with "radical hope."

(I am grateful for this opportunity to make a personal statement. My thanks also go to Dilthey, Husserl, Merleau-Ponty, Gadamer, Buber, Binswanger, Levinas, and many living colleagues whose gifts to me I cannot further acknowledge because of space considerations. A few paragraphs are adapted from Orange, D. (2009). "Psychoanalysis in a Phenomenological Spirit." *Int. J. Psychoanal. Self Psychol.* **4**(1): 119–121.)

References

Bass, A. (2007). When the frame doesn't fit the picture. *Psychoanalytic Dialogues*, *17*(1), 1–27.

Poland, W. S. (2018). *Intimacy and separateness in psychoanalysis*. New York: Routledge.

Chapter 15

Becoming and Being a Psychoanalyst: Credo as Ongoing Journey

Jill Salberg

I entered therapy as an 18-year-old sophomore in college and was very fortunate to begin my work with an experienced psychologist/psychoanalyst. I hadn't known to ask for that at the time. I was feeling depressed and a bit lost, and I had tried through my University Health Center to speak to someone. Despite an abysmal interview with a psychiatry resident, I still felt that talking to someone could be helpful. That belief was answered with a therapist, recommended by a family member, with whom I began psychotherapy with; and eventually years later would become my training analyst. Within the first few sessions, I felt understood in some profound way that has stayed with me. My analyst was able to put into language and name what had been a confused set of feelings. In those early months, I found a place I could open up inside of myself and have help making sense of what I was experiencing as well as validation for those feelings. This finding of what I would call my emotional truth and moments of clarity was very powerful. It is at the core of what I aspire to do when working with patients, students and supervisees.

I have learned to appreciate that things take time, listening carefully is crucial, waiting is invaluable, and you never quite know how something will unfold in the work. At the end of my first analysis, I asked my analyst if he had known who I would develop into, my lingering wish for an omniscient father figure. He kindly but definitively told me he couldn't possibly have known since it had really been up to me to grow into who I became. That continues to guide my work as well. I believe in two intertwining processes: one restarts an interrupted, delayed, thwarted, or traumatized developmental process; the second is witness to someone coming "to know" what they have needed "not to know." We accompany our patients providing a feeling of safety till they are able of knowing the emotional truth of their lives.

I entered a second analysis in my late 40s with a female Relational analyst. I believe we deal with things at different times in our life, and the experience of living one's life can equally open up old wounds as well as new possibilities. Having a second analyst and a woman has been invaluable in allowing

DOI: 10.4324/9781003206248-15

me to deepen what I already had known and open up more fully dynamics involving early maternal loss and abandonment and issues of deprivation and envy that was transmitted across generations in my family. I came to understand that I had been carrying traumas from prior generations (Apprey, 1996, 2014; Faimberg, 1988, 2005; Grand, 2000; Harris, 2007; Salberg, 2015), undigested bits from my grandparents' lives surrounding an early maternal death that was then transmitted from grandmother through to my mother and re-enacted in her complex attachment issues to myself and my sibling. These unlinked and unknowable feelings, nonetheless, exerted great influence over my life. The hardest journey in our work with patients can sometimes be to help someone see that the very person they complain about, rail against and can hate is also partly who they have identified with and become. Further, these traumas and complex relationships, actual and internalized, continue to be re-enacted and lived out.

Knowing about generational transmissions carries weight and is the closest to a lightning bolt moment in terms of theoretical awareness for me. Many things came into alignment in terms of touchstones for me: Freud's early topographical model and work on mourning and the creation of an internal work of objects, British object relations theory and Mitchell's (1988) relational matrix. Coming to understand that ancestor generations have transmitted their internalized worlds of selves and others, conveyed their unmourned traumas, losses, and grievances into subsequent generations increases intelligibility for me in the work. I have come to believe that many generations must be listened for with patients.[1] The echoes and hauntings can take many forms as different voices, self-states, and self-other dynamics.

When I teach and think about major paradigm shifts in psychoanalysis, the first begins with Freud's ideas creating a revolution in mind (Makari, 2008). The next large change happened for me with what has been referred to as the Relational Turn; it ushered in new perspectives, further elaborated undertheorized ideas in terms of the subjectivity of the analyst and enhanced the complexity of understanding in regard to mutuality and yet asymmetry of the analytic dyad. The translating of what had been worked on in trauma studies into theories of psychoanalytic trans-generational transmissions has been that kind of paradigm shift for me as well. It has expanded the field of exploration and what I listen for with patients as well as the selves that enter the consulting room and the minds of the dyad.

Further, I believe a large part of my analytic work is tuning in to what is said and not said, what is said idiosyncratically, much the way Ogden (1997a, 1997b) and Bollas (1989, 1992), respectively, suggest in their work and includes seeing in what way the patient makes use of me (Parsons, 2009). My first analyst had trained at NPAP during the era of Theodor Reik (1984) whose work, *Listening with the Third Ear,* had informed my analyst and consequently my felt sense of being listened to. In looking back, I realize that what often strikes my "third ear" is when something sounds just a bit off. It is important to hear it and not correct it inside my head. These are moments when I can ask my patients to join me in listening to themselves and the ways in which they both do and do not saying something, the covering up what they can't yet fully know. These are also inklings, while avoiding feelings, memories, or ideas, of how intimacy with themselves and with others is foreclosed. In allowing the patient's mixed telling's to enter my mind I hope to create a space of safety for them inside me and inside the analytic room, in Winnicott's terms, inviting the true self to come out of hiding and begin to be known.

My second analyst was more relationally oriented and interested in developmental and attachment research. I've come to also listen for the age that the voice of the patient feels to me and wonder with them how old they are in this feeling; to think about developmental interruptions and derailments. I believe in self-states formed during our lives. In response to chronic relational trauma and by larger traumatic events these states become more split apart and dissociative.[2] When this happens while growing up, it can often sideline and derail developmental progress. In asking what age a voiced complaint or grievance might be I am asking my patient and myself to listen for the child or adolescent who still needs to have their voice heard. There are disappointments and also there are traumatic interruptions, in Winnicott's sense of the "going-on-being," of the child. Some of these involve losses and abandonments both small and large. I am listening for how mourning has been aborted and internalized structures of self and other are locked in. I remain aware of the reliving of painful events and listen for the desperate solutions that children come up with to maintain some ongoing attachment to the important people in their life.[3] While each analysis deeply affected me, it is a continual process of how to take further what has been internalized, see how theory explains and expands what I know and create new ways of thinking and working, being and becoming the psychoanalyst I want to be. In this way, a major aspect of an analysis is learning to trust oneself, to be able to rely on one's intuitions, suspicions, and the unpredictable analytic process.

Training and Influences

I had first read Freud in a philosophy course that same sophomore year that I entered treatment and have continued to read him ever since. I feel deeply involved in a long relationship with Freud's enterprise, one in which I argue with him in my mind a great deal of the time concerning issues of gender, sexuality, race, and class. I am always in his debt for the gift of his conceptualization of the unconscious and appreciation of its overarching presence in our lives. The richness of his work on dreams is a portal, an opening that at times can baffle but is endlessly creative and imaginative. The keenness of Freud's observations never fails to astonish me, especially when teaching his work. Each time I am reminded anew of his attention to the small inflections in people, the careful precision of unpacking ideas, even when I may vehemently disagree with his conclusions. Reading his essay Mourning and Melancholia one sees a great mind at work, creating a place for an internal world born from loss.[4] Equally, I marvel reading his work on mastering loss through his observing his grandson and creative solution of his "Fort Da" game.

I entered psychoanalytic training at the NYU Postdoctoral Program in 1982. Among the supervisors I had during psychoanalytic training, two, in particular, left formative impressions on me. The first was Ruth-Jean Eisenbud (supervised 1985–1987) a maverick in her approach to treatment. While a Freudian in her training and theoretical orientation, she quite easily disagreed with Freud on aspects of masochism and feminine development seeing both as less drive determined and more growing out of early life experience be it feelings of persecution or pleasure (Eisenbud, 1967, 1982). She took an important political stand at that time in her paper on lesbian choice supporting it as a legitimate sexual object choice.

Ruth-Jean also spoke about psychologists getting training in an earlier era as "on the lam." She meant that there were a few psychiatrists who didn't agree with the discriminatory training practices of the American Psychoanalytic Association. These dissenting analysts would run private study groups or supervision, training psychologists who wanted the advanced education but without the confining aspects of the American rules.[5] Something about her suggestion that it was a good thing to be a "fugitive from the law" was appealing and fit in with my growing suspicion that the rules of this particular psychoanalytic old boys' club did not suit me, nor did I feel I could or would want to "fit in." I was beginning to journey down a path more eclectic than a singular theoretical system.

Toward the end of my training, I took a course on British Object Relations with Stephen Mitchell. It was the combination of exposure to the object relations theories of Fairbairn, Klein, Winnicott, Guntrip, Balint, and others and Stephen Mitchell's enormous capacity to analyze and synthesize these theoretical ideas that I felt I might have found a way toward a theoretical home. This was during when the Relational Track was established at NYU Postdoc. A paradigm shift was underway and as a new graduate from this institute it was an exciting time. In joining the Relational track at NYU Postdoc, I felt I would be able to develop my eclecticism with a broad group of thinkers. We formed groups to develop courses, colloquia and study groups. The faculty that had fought to develop this new orientation (Bromberg, Ghent, Friedlander, Mitchell and others) wanted to encourage us all to be writing, teaching and thinking into new ways of working with patients.

I always felt Stephen Mitchell never met an idea he didn't like, always creatively playing with theoretical ideas. He broadened the conversation believing in a "big tent" approach to theory and how the conversation in psychoanalysis should not become reified. I went into supervision with Stephen for a few years and, after ending regular supervision, I then joined one of his study groups. Stephen was someone who also listened carefully, always wanting to know how it felt for me to be in the room with the patient. He believed that I was the one who best knew this patient, authorizing me to trust my feelings and ideas (Mitchell, 1997, 1998). Stephen's breadth and openness allowed me to begin to see how my first analysis with a Freudian analyst and my affinity for British Object Relations theory could become integrated relationally and include awareness of the intersubjective nature of the analytic dyad. Mitchell's work on analytic authority along with the work of Greenberg (1999) who integrated Freud's work on analytic restraint with more interpersonal and relational ideas on co-creation, and the expansion of relational ideas on multiple self-states and dissociation (Bromberg, 1996; Davies, 1998; Harris, 1996; and others) further freed me up to think and more fully trust my feelings, associations, and reveries (Ogden, 1997a; Parsons, 2007). Working with Stephen always reminded me of the childhood game, *trust,* where a friend stands behind you and you fall backwards for them to catch you. If you don't fully trust, you don't fall fully nor can they catch you easily. With Stephen, I felt that I didn't need to edit myself or what happened with patients in sessions.

This trust in the process is crucial so that the "yet to be known" can emerge and be discovered. A decade after Stephen had died, I returned to supervision in a small group to work with Philip Bromberg, whose writings I had found valuable. Bromberg was known for his small supervision groups that often continued for years offering a safe and intimate way to learn from him and each other. He had a particular gift for listening as well, being able to hear immediately in process note material or by audio tape when a patient would switch self-states and the accompanying shifts in the intersubjective moment in a session. This expanded my listening repertoire and enabled me to more fully recognize when mis-attunement to self-states can lead to enactments.

Writing this credo during the COVID pandemic here in the United States has been complicated. Some patients and friends have had bouts of illness with COVID or had loved ones die. This may be the first time that I am living through a traumatic and extended period of life simultaneously as my patients, where we each have fears for our health and well-being.[6] It has put into bold relief the differences in which each of us: myself, my patients, my students, and supervisees have been raised in terms of race, class, caste, culture, and gender. While I have been able to continue working safely and remotely and that is true for many people I work with it is not true for everyone. Additionally, I see more and more how seeped we are and inculcated into historical, political, social, and cultural traumas of oppressor/oppressed.[7] These legacies have deeply embedded roots in trans-generational transmissions from the beginnings of the country we live in (early genocide and horrific slavery), from the hierarchical aspect of caste and class as seen in how immigrants acculturate here and the intractableness of racism, sexism, and other biases and hatreds. This has stirred me to also understand my embeddedness in my own social, class, ethnic, and gendered background and has added another layer to how I understand the influences on my subjectivity and my identity. If the historical and social-political-culture that any one of us grows up in is taken more fully into account, the cultural traumas of being *othered* can be understood as not originating within the individual but as a response to the toxic cultural environment. This too would and should profoundly shift/enlarge the psychoanalytic scope.

Becoming a psychoanalyst is a long journey, perhaps an unending process. Along the way there can be many people, ideas that influence you and hopefully keep you open to the cultural, political, and historical world. In looking back, I can see how too tight a grip on theory reifies it, becoming stale and rigid, keeping a theoretical set of blinders on. The Relational turn was a major paradigm shift that deconstructed analytic hierarchies, shifted the field to accept two-person theories of mind, grew intersubjective approaches to understanding therapeutic dynamics and yet, possibly, installed new ones.[8] There is a kind of excitement psychoanalysis has with new ideas and ossification can later happen to almost all theories. This is an important and unsettling time given the state of the world but one that I hope will unsettle psychoanalysis forcing it and us to grow and discover the next paradigm shift.

In recalling when I first wanted to be a psychoanalyst, I realized that what appeared to be a straight path has in fact been an evolving process. My sense of a credo is not so much a hard and fast stance but a clarifying and a returning to certain touchstones that center my work. Each of these, the development of my psychoanalytic identity and the evolution of a credo are deeply intertwined. It continues to be a life lived in a self-reflective examination, internal conversations with people and their theories that I've read as well as external dialogue with others.

Notes

1 Haydée Faimberg's (1998, 2005) work and friendship has been formative around the listening to the echo of other generations.
2 See Bollas, Bromberg, Davies, Harris, Mitchell, Stern, and others.
3 In my work on trans-generational attachment trauma, I've explored how children enter their parents minds and trauma scenes to maintain attachment during times that parents feel absent (Salberg, 2015, 2019).
4 It is important to remember and note that Freud was born into mourning and loss. Before his birth, his paternal grandfather, who he is named for, died and within a year his maternal uncle died, and baby brother also died quite young. Loss surrounded him (Gay, 1998).

5 Psychologists who wanted to be trained in the American Psychoanalytic Institute system had to sign a form agreeing that they were only going to be using their education for research purposes and not to treat patients.
6 Although working in NYC during the attacks on 9/11 had some of these features, it wasn't an ongoing month into at least a year-long siege affecting both myself and my patients.
7 Gump, Holmes, Leary, Stoute, Vaughans, and others have written about the cultural trauma of slavery and racism that psychoanalysis fails to fully take up.
8 See *De-Idealizing Relational Theory* (2018) edited by Lewis Aron, Sue Grand, and Joyce Slochower.

References

Apprey, M. (1996). *Phenomenology of transgenerational haunting: Subjects in apposition, subjects on urgent/voluntary errands*. Ann Arbor, MI: UMI Research Collections.

Apprey, M. (2014). A pluperfect errand: A turbulent return to beginnings in the transgenerational transmission of destructive aggression. *Free Association: Psychoanalysis, and Culture, Media, Groups, Politics, 66*, 15–28.

Aron, L., Grand, S., & Slochower, J. (2018). *De-idealizing relational theory*. Oxon, UK & New York: Routledge/Taylor & Francis Group.

Bollas, C. (1989). *The shadow of the object*. New York, UK: Columbia University Press.

Bollas, C. (1992). *Being a character*. New York, NY: Farrar, Straus & Giroux.

Bromberg, P. (1996). Standing in the spaces: The multiplicity of self and the psychoanalytic relationship. *Contemporary Psychoanalysis, 32*, 509–535.

Davies, J. (1998). Multiple perspectives on multiplicity. *Psychoanalytic Dialogues, 8*(2), 195–206.

Eisenbud, R. (1967). Masochism revisited. *The Psychoanalytic Review, 54*(4), 5–26.

Eisenbud, R. (1982). Early and later determinants of lesbian choice. *The Psychoanalytic Review, 69*(1), 85–109.

Faimberg, H. (1988). The telescoping of generations: Genealogy of certain identifications. *Contemporary Psychoanalysis, 24*, 99–117. doi:10.1080/00107530.1988.10746222

Faimberg, H. (2005). *The telescoping of generations: Listening to the narcissistic links between generations*. London, UK: Routledge, Taylor and Francis Group.

Gay, P. (1998). *Freud: A life for our time*. New York, NY: W.W. Norton & Company Inc.

Harris, A. (1996). The conceptual power of multiplicity. *Contemporary Psychoanalysis, 32*, 537–552.

Harris, A. (2007). Analytic work in the bridge world: Commentary on paper by Françoise Davoine. *Psychoanalytic Dialogues, 17*(5), 659–669. doi:10.1080/10481880701632442

Makari, G. (2008). *Revolution in mind: The creation of psychoanalysis*. New York: Harper Perennial.

Mitchell, S. (1988). *Relational concepts in psychoanalysis: An integration*. Cambridge, MA & London, England: Harvard University Press.

Mitchell, S. (1997). *Influence and autonomy in psychoanalysis*. Hillsdale, New Jersey and London: The Analytic Press.

Ogden, T. H. (1997a). Reverie and metaphor: Some thoughts on how I work as a psychoanalyst. *The International Journal of Psychoanalysis*, *78*, 719–732.

Ogden, T. H. (1997b). Some thoughts on the use of language in psychoanalysis. *Psychoanalytic Dialogues*, *7*(1), 1–21.

Parsons, M. (2007). Raiding the inarticulate: The internal analytic setting and listening beyond countertransference. *The International Journal of Psychoanalysis*, *88*(6), 1441–1456.

Parsons, M. (2009). An independent theory of clinical technique. *Psychoanalytic Dialogues*, *19*(3), 221–236.

Reik, T. (1984). *Listening with the third ear: The inner experience of a psychoanalyst*. New York, NY: Farrar, Straus & Giroux.

Salberg, J. (2015). The texture of traumatic attachment: Presence and ghostly absence in trans-generational transmissions. *The Psychoanalytic Quarterly*, *84*(1), 21–46.

Salberg, J. (2019). Old objects die hard: Generational ruptures. *Psychoanalytic Dialogues*, *29*(6), 637–652.

Winnicott, D. W. (1967). The location of cultural experience. *The International Journal of Psychoanalysis*, *48*, 368–372.

Winnicott, D. W. (1968). Playing: Its theoretical status in the clinical situation. *The International Journal of Psychoanalysis*, *49*, 591–599.

Chapter 16

Against the Grain: On Challenging Assumptions, Bridging Theories, Practicing Self-Critique, Exposing Underbellies, and Doing the Right Thing[1]

Joyce Slochower

Confession: I'm the child of two Freudian psychoanalysts; the stepchild of a third. Psychoanalysis was part of the fabric of my childhood. My parents' offices were in our apartment; patients came and went while I played in my room. I don't actually remember, but I'm sure I had plenty of fantasies about the mysterious things going on in those offices. What did people talk about? Did those secrets pull me toward what was off-limits? Did I long to join my parents' world? To get—and give—what I imagined their patients got by way of understanding and help? Likely so.

I entered analytic training immediately after graduate school, firmly identified with my parents' Freudian orientation. Classical theory provided a comforting sense of certainty; there were rules to follow, a right and wrong way to do things. But analytic certainty came at a price and over time its constricting effect began to outweigh its value. I didn't want to answer *every* question with a question. I wanted to be freer to "be" within the therapeutic setting. I chafed at my Freudian supervisor's insistence that I maintain rigid boundaries when my patient seemed to need something very different. Things came to a head for me when a boundary I imposed backfired, significantly undermining the treatment.[2]

I longed for a therapeutic alternative and sought out an interpersonal supervisor. But that way of working didn't feel right either—staying in the moment seemed too limiting; it skipped over my patient's early history. Pregnant with my first child, I received Winnicott's (1964) *The Child, the Family and the Outside World* from a family friend. Winnicott's work was inspiring; his belief in therapeutic regression's mutative potential offered a compelling alternative to the classical model. Here was the mother/analyst I wanted to become and also the one I wished I had had.

But my fantasy of becoming a female Winnicott was rapidly undermined by my work with some very difficult patients, newly discharged from the hospital. I couldn't sustain the calm, holding stance I had envisioned; my patients expressed more hostility and impulsivity than need. I sometimes felt anxious, defensive; even helpless.

Struggling to reconcile my very unideal feelings with my vision of a Winnicottian analyst, it was my good luck that the relational movement appeared on the scene. Mitchell (1984, 1988, 1993), Hoffman (1991, 1998), Stern (1992), Aron (1991, 1992), and others articulated a compelling critique of the Winnicottian maternal tilt (patient as baby/analyst as parent). They argued that the patient is an adult who can "see" the analyst. From this perspective, the holding metaphor is infantilizing, even gaslighting.

Feminist psychoanalysts (Bassin, Honey, & Kaplan, 1994; Benjamin, 1995; Harris, 1997) added to this critique by challenging the idealization of motherhood and its demand for maternal self-abnegation. The analyst cannot eradicate her subjectivity or hold patients with anything like Winnicott's vision of affective attunement.

I resonated with these critiques but continued to feel compelled by Winnicott's analytic vision. Could the collision between relational and Winnicottian thinking be resolved? I wanted to find a way to bridge the divide, to integrate aspects of the idea of holding within an overarching relational umbrella. By both revising and expanding the Winnicottian holding metaphor, I found a way to integrate it within relational theory (Slochower, 1991, 1992, 1993, 1994, 1996a, 1996b, 1996c). Steve Mitchell invited me to contribute to the Relational Series; *Holding and Psychoanalysis: A Relational Perspective* thus came to be under his extraordinary editorship.

My premise was this: while intersubjective exchange may be a central relational goal, it's not always a therapeutic reality. Some patients cannot tolerate the presence of an "other" with a separate perspective without becoming seriously derailed. These patients need "holding"—a therapeutic frame in which the analyst tries to buffer evidence of her separateness with the aim of maximizing the patient's experience of emotional resonance (Slochower, 2002, 2004). However, holding also embodies a core relational goal: a deepened capacity for intersubjective exchange.

When I hold, I try to remain within my patient's subjective frame while bracketing those aspects of my subjectivity that would disrupt her experience. I'm not referring to whether or not she accepts what I say: a loud "no damn way, you're wrong" can be the opener for rich and useful interchange. But when my patient consistently shuts down, is unable to accept and work with, *or* reject my perspective while sustaining her own, I pause, therapeutically speaking. I ask myself whether I'm "off base," whether we're involved in a potentially useful—or problematic—reenactment. Is my patient responding to my being too much like "old objects" or too different from them? It's when I can't usefully unpack the enactment and its dynamic meaning that I move toward holding. My aim here is to help her feel seen, not from the outside in, but from the inside out (Bromberg, 1991).

Holding and Analytic Bracketing

The idea of analytic bracketing captures the doubleness of a holding experience and is key to a relational take on holding. If our subjectivity is omnipresent, aspects of us will inevitably leak into therapeutic space even when we try to hold. We can't delete ourselves, but we can work to contain what would be disruptive while privately acknowledging and struggling with our feelings.

Relational holding, then, privileges the patient's experience without requiring that the analyst ignore her own subjectivity. Adding to this relational perspective is the idea that a holding process is coconstructed: patients also bracket, unconsciously or procedurally, those aspects of the analyst's otherness that could derail things. This joint bracketing process establishes an illusion of attunement and facilitates the elaboration of interior process. Thus, for example, my patient Jonathan managed literally not to "see" my pregnancy until well into my seventh month. He thereby protected our relationship from a threatening outside intrusion and sustained a sense of our intimate connection. Of course, eventually my pregnancy entered analytic space and we moved beyond holding as we dealt with what he hadn't wanted to know or see (Slochower, 2014e).

While all this may sound deliberate, even choreographed, shifts in and out of holding are anything but: they're multiply determined—conscious, intentional, and not. In part, I move toward holding based on my clinical/theoretical point of entrée. In part, this shift is procedural, my spontaneous reaction to what I don't quite know I'm perceiving. On another level, it's enacted, reflecting a mutual, dissociated dyadic "dance." To further complicate things, sometimes we fail when we try to hold because we think we know what's needed but don't, because we're in the throes of an enactment, self-object failure, or other kind of misattunement. Or because there's simply too much for us to hold (Slochower, 2013a, 2013b).

Here's another revision of the Winnicottian holding model: not only regressed patients need holding; sometimes hateful, ruthless, and narcissistic patients do as well. Indeed, nearly all of us have had moments when the affective experience of that "no longer baby" is palpable—for example, after a loss or other trauma. Like my very capable musician patient who woke from a dream frozen with terror until she called me. I became, briefly, a soothing maternal presence who received her distress without also becoming disregulated. I held her panic until she could explore what had terrified her. Much later, she told me that this brief moment of holding had created the hope that her baby needs could finally be met.

After elaborating on holding's clinical function in and outside the consulting room, I extended my ideas about what underlies holding's therapeutic power. Holding supports interior process and limits the experience of being scrutinized. It buffers shame states by minimizing the sense of exposure and maximizing the analyst's witnessing function. My patient feels me to see her as she sees herself, rather than as she fears she'll be seen. Over time, a scaffolding that protects against humiliation can coalesce and allow us to address the origin and nature of these shame-filled self-states together.

False Dichotomies

The holding-mutuality binary, characterized by non-disclosure on one end and full disclosure on the other, excludes the complexity of clinical process (Slochower, 2017a). Critiquing our tendency toward theoretical polarization, I also addressed the complex impact of our analytic ideal on our vulnerability to "relational excess" (Slochower, 2017a). Despite our best attempts at containment, holding and mutuality interpenetrate because aspects of our personhood inevitably leak into therapeutic space. Besides which, we show plenty of ourselves by virtue of how and when we hold and when we don't.

The obverse, however, is also true: there's an element of holding lurking beneath relational work organized around self-disclosure and reenactment. First, full disclosure is impossible (because we analysts have our own unconscious). Second, no matter how much we value mutuality, there are things we don't tell because of our wish for privacy and/or because it would be too disturbing to do otherwise. We choose (partially unconsciously) what we bracket and what we express based on a mixture of our and our patient's personalities, needs, wishes, and anxieties, guided (hopefully) by our idea of what's therapeutic. Our background awareness of a patient's vulnerability to derailment guides us on a procedural level with regard to when and how we enter the clinical dialogue, how directly and how deeply. And I'm convinced this is true no matter where we sit on the containment-expressivity continuum (Slochower, 2006a, 2006b, 2008, 2011a, 2011b, 2012, 2013a, 2013b, 2014a, 2014e, 2015, 2018a, 2018b, 2018c, 2018d). Can we address the intersubjective element embedded within moments of holding? Can we explore the holding element obscured—but not missing—when we focus on analyzing enactments? And, most important, can we integrate aspects of our theory and clinical approach across apparent theoretical divides (Loewald, 1989)?

The Ideal and the Actual

Implicit in every clinical model is an idealized vision (variously shaped) of the analyst's capacity. Our idealizations are necessary *and* problematic—necessary because they help sustain us across the vagaries of clinical process and problematic because they collide with the actuality of our very unideal humanity. A series of papers and a second book, *Psychoanalytic Collisions* (Slochower, 2006a, 2014d) explore both sides of the analytic ideal. On one hand, our ideal sustains us in and outside the consulting room; idealized illusions help us develop and maintain a professional identity; they support our work when the work seems hopeless; they help protect us from self-doubt and anxiety; they support a range of generative, creative illusions (for example, about the quality of our writing or our analytic skill).

But illusions also invite us to skip over the collision between the way we want/believe we should function and the imperfect way that we actually do. They can invite a collusion between patient and analyst based on a mutual, unarticulated idealization, invite problematic acting out and/or emotional withdrawal on the analyst's part.

A particularly troublesome consequence of disavowed idealizations is their contribution to small and large boundary breaches. When a rigid professional ideal collides with the analyst's need/wish to get something for herself, it may pull her to act out in minor and more egregious ways. Analytic delinquencies (Slochower, 2003, 2009) and more serious boundary violations erupt, in part, out of the space between the ideal and the actual. While at times these moments reflect a coconstructed enactment, at other times they don't. We need also to address the individual (intrapsychic) elements that are sometimes responsible for our failure.

Our difficulty meeting the analytic ideal is starkly evident in the sexual boundary violations that have plagued our field since its earliest beginnings. While we've addressed the behavior of the perpetrator-analyst, we haven't queried the impact of sexual breaches on the larger community of (indirect) witnesses. What happens when we learn that an esteemed teacher, supervisor, or our own analyst, had sex with a patient? Our confidence in the violator is, of course, disrupted. But disillusionment often extends to our institute or even to the field as a whole. How do we metabolize this rupture of our analytic ideal? I describe my response to discovering that my former analyst had become sexually engaged with a patient in Slochower (2017b, 2017c) and also address my professional community's response to learning about a boundary violation by one of its faculty.

More recently, I've written about the collision between the fantasy that analytic work is timeless (Hoffman, 1998) and the actuality of our own (and our patient's) aging (Slochower, 2019). Aging affects our relationship to our theory and often reshapes the clinical work we do. Do we really get better over time? Or is this another illusion?

My interest in intra- and inter-theoretical critique found expression in two books, coedited with Sue Grand and Lew Aron (Aron, Grand, & Slochower, 2018a; 2018b). In them, we invited psychoanalytic thinkers to engage in a loving self-critique (what's wrong/missing in my theory) and in comparative critiques (what other theories influenced my own?). My contribution to this project involved an exploration of what I call relational excess.

Delineating the underbelly of our theories and their collision with what doesn't fit found expression in an essay on resistance from a relational point of entrée. Rather than relegating the concept to our Freudian and Kleinian colleagues, I suggested that we can integrate resistance's individual and intersubjective dimensions within a relational frame (Slochower, 2020).

Credo: Personal Reflections

One's credo is as inherently personal as it is theoretical. At least in the field of psychoanalysis, our work inevitably has dynamic as well as intellectual origins. I'd like to end by thinking about the former.

In part, my work on holding emerged from a wish to articulate something deeply meaningful in my life—my wish both to hold and be held. It also reflects my connection to my analyst parents *and* an assertion of intellectual independence.

I very much resonate with Aron's (1999) suggestion that we sometimes choose our theory to counterbalance who we are. Despite my clinical and theoretical allegiance to the holding theme, I rarely work like a Winnicottian. I tend toward directness; I try hard to find a way to articulate what I'm thinking and why and turn to holding reluctantly. In fact, many of my patients have pointed out (often—but not always—affectionately), that I hardly seem like a holding analyst to them; I'm most often described as someone who calls a spade a spade, albeit nicely. And I must admit that this characterization rather pleases me. So in a way, I formulated a theory of holding to help me contain *me*, to counterbalance my own preference for unshaded honesty. Incidentally, my pleasure is itself suspect; it likely informs (and limits) what I hear and don't hear about my patients' experience of me.

Over time, I've moved beyond an idealization of both analytic holding and relational engagement toward a broader theoretical position. I've also come to use theory more loosely than I used to; I'm more expressive of my subjectivity, more relaxed in the clinical moment. Yet I'm convinced that nearly everything I do by way of interpretation, confrontation, and working with reenactments takes place within an envelope characterized by a background awareness of patients' potential need for holding. So in a way, I hold even when I push. This, of course, gets experienced in a range of ways (good and bad) by different patients.

I'm also aware that I often aim to explore the underbelly of a given theory and way of practicing. To bridge differences, rather than emphasizing what divides us. I enjoy turning things on their heads, considering both the up- and downside of a clinical intervention. I find evidence of these themes across most of my work—in my early efforts to bridge the gap between Winnicottian and relational thinking and exploring the role of holding outside the consulting room; in reformulating the classical concept of resistance and including it within relational theory. I also enjoy surfacing what's *not* talked about—for example, analytic delinquencies and our communal response to learning about sexual violations within our communities. Now I'm working on a paper that addresses the other side of boundary breaches by challenging our assumption that a complete termination is always the way to go (Slochower, 2021).

In addition to the intellectual sources of these interests, I recognize my identification with my father in all this: I've always admired the ways in which he was a bit of an "enfant terrible" who flouted authority and went his own way. As I have, in part.

I end by identifying the rather simple clinical credo that has guided me across time. It was articulated by my first psychoanalytic mentor, my mother. She was a rule-bound mother, and I was certain that she was a rule-bound analyst. Imagine my surprise when I, a young adolescent, heard her mention that she was helping her patient get a (then illegal) abortion. "But you're not allowed to do that, are you?" I asked. My mother's answer was simple and simply stunning: "Either we're in the business of helping people or we're not."[3] Although she was committed to a classical model, if, in her view, psychoanalytic rules failed the patient, she threw away the book.

This credo is, I believe, foundational to an ethical psychoanalytic identity; it privileges the "care" element of analytic practice, a willingness to address patient need over theory or clinical rules. To be in the business of helping people above all is my red thread, a credo that has guided and sustained me in the face of its—and my—limitations.

Yes, it's an overly simple credo. It evades complexity—the ways that the analyst's beliefs and personal investments can color, even shape, her definition of "help." It implies that our patient's needs are easily identified and are unconflicted. It ignores the intersubjective element that can skew an apparently "objective" determination of how to help. Thus, my mother's choice to get her patient an abortion may have been informed by her feminist beliefs; it may have minimized whatever conflicts her patient felt about that choice. Still. It's a profoundly ethical ideal that I'm prepared to struggle with and strive for.

At 14, I was far too young to appreciate my mother's wisdom or the complexity that lay beneath her simple statement of purpose. I certainly do now. And if I can pass her wisdom on to those I train, I'll be more than pleased: whatever the particulars of your psychoanalytic ideal, find and hold firm to the business you're in—one grounded in an ethic of care. Hold your theory lightly and do your best to remain open to its limitations. Study, question, doubt. Try to retain an ethical stance when expediency would invite you to close your eyes to something troubling or give in to desire. Above all, enact that ideal by aiming to offer yourself, your wisdom, and your care to your patients ahead of your beliefs, your rules, desires, and your theory, while simultaneously acknowledging the impossibility of this ideal.

Notes

1 I thank Margery Kalb for her very helpful comments on an earlier draft of this chapter.
2 My supervisor insisted that I not agree to a patient's wish for a long analytic break during the summer, saying "either she's in analysis or she's not." Feeling I had no choice, I complied. My rigid stance ruined the treatment.
3 For a far more sophisticated and nuanced look at psychoanalytic ethics, see Ackerman's (2020) excellent essay "impossible ethics."

References

Ackerman, S. (2020). Impossible ethics. *Journal of the American Psychoanalytic Association*, 68(4), 561–582.
Aron, L. (1991). The patient's experience of the analyst's subjectivity. *Psychoanalytic Dialogues*, 1, 29–51.
Aron, L. (1992). Interpretation as expression of the analyst's subjectivity. *Psychoanalytic Dialogues*, 2, 475–508.
Aron, L. (1999). Clinical choices and the relational matrix. *Psychoanalytic Dialogues*, 9(1), 1–29.
Aron, L. (2017). Beyond tolerance in psychoanalytic communities: Reflexive skepticism and critical pluralism. *Psychoanalytic Perspectives*, 14(3): 271–282.
Aron, L., Grand, S., & Slochower, J. (2018a). *Deidealizing relational theory: A critique from within.* London: Routledge.
Aron, L. Grand, S., & Slochower, J. (2018b). *Decentering relational theory: A comparative critique.* London: Routledge
Bassin, D., Honey, M. & Kaplan, M. (1994). *Representations of motherhood.* New Haven, CT: Yale University Press.
Benjamin, J. (1998). *The bonds of love.* New York: Pantheon.
Benjamin, J. (1995). *Like subjects, love objects.* New Haven: Yale University Press.
Bromberg, P. (1991). On knowing one's patient inside out: The aesthetics of unconscious communication. *Psychoanalytic Dialogues*, 1, 399–422.
Harris, A. (1997). Beyond/outside gender dichotomies. *Psychoanalytic Dialogues*, 7, 363–366.
Hoffman, I. Z. (1991). Discussion: Toward a social-constructivist view of the psychoanalytic situation. *Psychoanalytic Dialogues*, 1, 74–105.
Hoffman, I. Z. (1998). *Ritual and spontaneity in psychoanalysis.* Hillsdale, N.J.: The Analytic Press.
Loewald, H. W. (1989). *Papers on psychoanalysis.* New Haven: Yale University Press.
Mitchell, S. (1984). Object relations theories and the developmental tilt. *Contemporary Psychoanalysis*, 20, 473–499.
Mitchell, S. (1988). *Relational concepts in psychoanalysis.* Cambridge: Harvard University Press.
Mitchell, S. (1993). *Hope and dread in psychoanalysis.* New York: Basic Books.
Slochower, J. (1991). Variations in the analytic holding environment. *The International Journal of Psychoanalysis*, 72, 709–718.
Slochower, J. (1992). A hateful borderline patient and the holding environment. *Contemporary Psychoanalysis*, 28, 72–88.

Slochower, J. (1993). Mourning and the holding function of shiva. *Contemporary Psychoanalysis, 30*, 135–151.
Slochower, J. (1994). The evolution of object usage and the holding environment. *Contemporary Psychoanalysis, 30*, 135–151.
Slochower, J. (1996a & 2014c). *Holding and psychoanalysis: A relational perspective.* Hillsdale, NJ: The Analytic Press.
Slochower, J. (1996b). Holding and the evolving maternal metaphor. *Psychoanalytic Review, 83*, 195–218.
Slochower, J. (1996c). The holding environment and the fate of the analyst's subjectivity. *Psychoanalytic Dialogues, 6*, 323–353.
Slochower, J. (1998). Illusion and uncertainty in psychoanalytic writing. *The International Journal of Psychoanalysis, 79*, 333–347.
Slochower, J. (1999a). Erotic complications. *The International Journal of Psychoanalysis, 80*, 1119–1130.
Slochower, J. (1999b). Interior experience in analytic process. *Psychoanalytic Dialogues, 9*, 789–809.
Slochower, J. (2003). The analyst's secret delinquencies. *Psychoanalytic Dialogues, 13*, 451–469.
Slochower, J. (2004). But what do *you* want? The location of emotional experience. *Contemporary Psychoanalysis, 40*, 577–602.
Slochower, J. (2006a & 2014d). *Psychoanalytic collisions.* Hillsdale, NJ: Analytic Press.
Slochower, J. (2006b). Holding: Something old and something new. In L. Aron & A. Harris (Eds.), *Relational psychoanalysis: Innovation and expansion.* New York: Routledge (pp. 29–50).
Slochower, J. (2011a) Out of the analytic shadow: On the dynamics of commemorative ritual. *Psychoanalytic Dialogues, 21*, 676–690.
Slochower, J. (2011b). Holding, collaborating, colliding: A cross theoretical conversation. *Psychoanalysis Inquiry, 13*, 501–512.
Slochower, J. (2011c). Analytic idealizations and the disavowed: Winnicott, his patients, and us. *Psychoanalytic Dialogues, 21*, 3–21.
Slochower, J. (2013a). Using Winnicott today: A relational perspective. *Revue Roumaine de Psychanalyse, 2*, 13–41.
Slochower, J. (2013b). Analytic enclaves and analytic outcome: A clinical mystery. *Psychoanalytic Dialogues, 23*, 243–258.
Slochower, J. (2014a). Idéalizations analytiques et le disavoué: Winnicott, ses patients, et nous. *Revue Francaise de Psychanalyse, 78*: 1136–1149.
Slochower, J. (2014b). The professional idiom and the psychoanalytic other. In S. Kuchuck (Ed.), *Clinical implications of the psychoanalyst's experience* (pp. 36–48). New York: Routledge.
Slochower, J. (2014e). Psychoanalytic mommies and psychoanalytic babies: A long view. *Contemporary Psychoanalysis, 49*, 606–628.
Slochower, J. (2015). *Collisioni psicoanalitiche.* Milano: Ferrari Sinibaldi.
Slochower, J. (2017a). Going too far: Relational heroines and relational excess. *Psychoanalytic Dialogues, 27*, 282–299.
Slochower, J. (2017b). Introduction to panel: Ghosts that haunt: Sexual boundary violations in our communities. *Psychoanalytic Dialogues, 27*, 61–66.

Slochower, J. (2017c). Don't tell anyone. *Psychoanalytic Psychology*, *34*, 195–200.

Slochower, J. (2018a). *Deidealizing relational theory: A critique from within*. L. Aron, S. Grand, & J. Slochower (Eds.), London: Routledge.

Slochower, J. (2018b). *Decentering relational theory: A comparative critique*. L. Aron, S. Grand, & J. Slochower (Eds.), London: Routledge.

Slochower, J. (2018c). Going too far: Relational heroines and relational excess. In L. Aron, S. Grand, & J. Slochower (Eds.), *De-idealizing relational theory: A critique from within* (pp. 8–34). London: Routledge.

Slochower, J. (2018d). D.W. Winnicott: Holding, playing, and moving toward mutuality. In *Introduction to contemporary psychoanalysis: Defining terms and building bridges*. London: Routledge.

Slochower, J. (2019). Getting better all the time? *Psychoanalytic Dialogues*, *29*, 5–548.

Slochower, J. (2020). Resist this. *Psychoanalytic Dialogues*, *30*, 64–72.

Slochower, J. (2021). Sequel. *Journal of the American Psychoanalytic Association*, in press.

Stern, D. B. (1992). Commentary on constructivism in clinical psychoanalysis. *Psychoanalytic Dialogues*, *3*, 331–364.

Stern, D. B. (1997). *Unformulated experience: From dissociation to imagination in psychoanalysis*. Hillsdale, NJ: The Analytic Press.

Winnicott, D.W.W. (1964). *The child, the family, and the outside world*. NY: Penguin.

Section IV

1990s

Chapter 17

Learning to Surf: Analyzing Adolescents

Mary T. Brady

One of the deep satisfactions of being and becoming a psychoanalyst is discovering one's proclivities. I could not have told you before I undertook psychoanalytic training that adolescents would become a career-long preoccupation. Ogden (1992) describes our experience as human subjects as "de-centered." I did not plan, but discovered my interest in adolescents. Perhaps I could say adolescents chose me, rather than I chose them, but that wouldn't be quite right either.

It is true that I have a measure of tolerance for adolescents' frequently scurrilous behavior. I can't tell you how many times a teen has asked me a variant of: "(C)an I leave now?" during a session. At some remove, such a challenge can crack me up. Of course, in the moment it isn't always all that funny. Such a provocation often reflects an adolescents' own difficulties tolerating him or herself. Often I can't know if an adolescent will continue to engage with me, however edgily. I can't know if our relationship can gather up their difficulties or whether it will be insufficient to the dangers at hand. What amuses me when I think of such a moment though is the way the teen has thrown me a curve ball. What am I going to do with it? What will they do with how I toss it back? Adolescents act in and act out to get to know themselves, and as their analyst I am in on the experiment.

What are the unconscious pulls that animate my proclivity for adolescents? Certainly, the rebelliousness or subversiveness (Brady, 2018a) endemic to adolescence rings bells for me. My Irish heritage equips me with a strong identification with the oppressed. Like many Irish Americans, my ancestors came to the United States during the Great Hunger (commonly called "potato famine"), a period of mass starvation and disease in Ireland from 1845 to 1849. Though the potatoes did rot of blight in the fields, the crops and the cream and the butter and the beef all went on ships to London, Liverpool, or Glasgow. The problem in Ireland not being lack of food, but the price of it. During the famine (under British colonial rule) about one million in Ireland died and another million emigrated (Ross, 2002).

Growing up Irish Catholic and female in Massachusetts during the pedophilia crisis in the Catholic church also fostered my "question authority" point of view. I partook of a group unconscious that involved the Irish, the Catholic Church, and of course my family of origin's version of these larger cultural group unconsciouses. For some time I understood that these sources contributed to my resonance with adolescents' skepticism. Yet, I sensed that there was something I did not really understand.

Over time I came to feel that what fundamentally animated my interest in adolescents was that I had been in some danger of missing the adolescent process myself. And while I fortunately did not entirely miss adolescence at its due time, my near miss left me with a protective feeling for the adolescent process. Perhaps I can give you some sense of this.

Fragment

I endured my early adolescence at Holy Name of Jesus Grammar School—a bare, crucifixed edifice in Chicopee, Massachusetts. Irish Americans peopled our school, Polish Catholics and French Catholics in separate enclaves down the street. The glamour lay with the priests, the robes and the incense. The nuns inhabited an inferior realm. We were not the enfranchised children of the next generation. We took what we got.

At home, for a time I had been my mother's girl—read to, sung to and rocked to sleep. The familiarity of the at-home mother. Father goes to work and deals with the outside world-wearing suits and telling jokes. A paradise of Little Women at home. Girl and woman familiar to each other neither intended for a larger realm. But the pleasures of this. None of the frantic schedules of children intended for success. We baked buttery cakes, filled with custard and shimmering with dark chocolate icing. Betty Crocker was our muse.

Then, my female fellowship with my mother changed. Perhaps some unbidden hint of sexuality on my part. No longer the little girl dressed in white for First Communion. I could feel the change by the way my mother washed my hair. Showers were mysteriously viewed as profligate by my parents. My mother washed my hair in the kitchen sink. Somehow, shampooing my hair had lost all pleasure for her and for me. Tenderness evaporated—replaced by a rough scrubbing.

When I look back I see the impossibility of it all. I could not stay in my mother's world of daily mass. I had to fumble into the next phase—bell-bottoms and boys with braces. I can see she felt rejected by me. She complained that I did not attend daily mass, but it was she I was not visiting sufficiently, fatally and disloyally decamping to other worlds.

Did I become deformed to my mother when my body disloyally decamped towards breasts and hips? She cried the first day I went to the adult instead of the cozy children's section of the library. Her tears made me feel afraid of the adult library—something sinister must lurk there. There was no stopping a subversive flood of ideas—Feminism! Marxism! Buddhism! Franny and Zooey hidden in my closet. Sexual passages read and reread. Union with my mother was over irrevocably.

You can see that adolescence seemed dangerous to me. I could have used a guide that I did not have. Accompanying adolescents now speaks to that need. Guide is not exactly the right word, as the job is not exactly to show the adolescent a way, but perhaps to imagine with them the ways they will find.

The coin of the realm with adolescents is action and experimentation, as that with children is play and that for adults is primarily speech. Sometimes teens' actions have a playful quality and sometimes are dire or even suicidal. Sometimes adolescents can think in a breathtaking way as they face the challenge of so much that is new and unfamiliar.

Over my clinical years, I have gravitated theoretically towards Bionian and Field Theory. I value Bion's concepts of waking dreaming and container/contained, as well as his admonition that the only point of importance in any clinical hour is the unknown. The latter is a bracing idea, as I can yearn for the known in the tumult of the clinical process. Adolescents are all about the unknown. They are fundamentally faced with what they do not yet really know about themselves. When they are honest they often admit this. One late teen tells me that stepping out of his dorm room is an overwhelming challenge. He feels inundated by the multiplicity of responses he has to those around him, and knows these responses signal different and often contradictory aspects of himself. How do you even get out the door when you recognize how little you know yourself as a teenager? As we get older we may know ourselves a little better and be less frightened of the not yet encountered. Or worse, perhaps we become dulled and inured.

The concept of psychoanalytic field is based on the Barangers' idea that the neutrality of the analyst is impossible. In the analytic situation, there are two people "unfailingly bound and complementary while the situation lasts and involved in the same dynamic process" (Baranger & Baranger, 2008/1961). Any psychoanalysis involves two subjects in space and time. What underlies this process/structure is a shared unconscious fantasy that is the product of unconscious communication and of a joint creation process. Ferro (1999) cites the vitality of the bi-personal field concept in freeing us from the idea that unconscious fantasies are only pertinent to one person. The goal of analytic work from a Field Theory perspective is broadening the shared field through the dream work of each of the subjects.

Field Theory would tell you that it is not all that important to pin down the characters in the field. The confused adolescent is me and I am them. The prospect of care is a character that speaks to my adolescent self who is afraid of what she is setting in motion.

Winnicott calls adolescence one of the most exciting things there is. I think that's right, although I also agree with the Uncle Frank in the film "Little Miss Sunshine" who advises his nephew Dwayne (who will only communicate with his family via note pad) not to miss his "prime suffering years."

When I was in analytic training I had the excellent fortune to have three adolescents in analysis with accompanying weekly supervision for some part of the three analyses. I saw younger children and adults as well. Something about the work with the adolescents was particularly riveting. Each teen feels present with me to this day 20 years later. Certainly, they provided huge and compelling challenges. They spurred my interest in eating disorders (Brady, 2015a), adolescent substance abuse (2015b, 2015c) and in braving erotic feelings alive between adolescent and analyst (2018b). It feels hard even now though, to fully capture the compelling urgency and immediacy of this work. It would be true to say that it was a privilege to study adolescence in depth and in statu nascendi. It would be true to say that the capacity for self-destruction in those so young concentrates the mind. It would be true to say that the delicacy of immediate and nascent sexual feelings in the room with someone so young is sobering and enlivening. And of course, you could say all of the above are true.

Bion, whose metabolization of horrific battle experience in WWI (Brown, 2012) led to his theory of alpha function, described that the analyst's task is to be able to "think under fire." I could think of numerous instances where this is true. But with adolescents, surfing is a metaphor that comes to mind far more often than "thinking under fire," although the latter can also be true. For me, surfing catches the adolescent (or myself in their wake), potentially upended, injured, or even killed by waves too tumultuous. Yet surfing also captures the sensual beauty of finding a balance, of the thrill of the ride, of a moment of being fully alive. Adolescents in analysis teach me to surf, surfing with me, as I teach them to surf, surfing with them.

References

Baranger, M., & Baranger, W. (2008/1961). The analytic situation as a dynamic field. *International Journal of Psychoanalysis*, 89, 795–826.

Brady, M. T. (2015a). Invisibility and insubstantiality in an anorexic adolescent: Phenomenology and dynamics. In *The body in adolescence: Psychic isolation and physical symptoms*. New York, NY: Routledge.

Brady, M. T. (2015b). Substance abuse in an adolescent boy: Waking the object. In *The body in adolescence: Psychic isolation and physical symptoms*. New York, NY: Routledge.

Brady, M. T. (2015c). "High up on bar stools": Manic defenses and an oblivious object in a late adolescent. In *The body in adolescence: Psychic isolation and physical symptoms*. New York, NY: Routledge.

Brady, M. T. (2018a). Subversiveness in adolescence. In *Analytic engagements with adolescents: Sex, gender and subversion*. Abingdon & New York, NY: Routledge.

Brady, M. T. (2018b). Braving the erotic field in the treatment of adolescents. In *Analytic engagements with adolescents: Sex, gender and subversion*. Abingdon & New York, NY: Routledge.

Brown, L. J. (2012). Bion's discovery of alpha function: Thinking under fire on the battlefield and in the consulting room. *International Journal of Psychoanalysis, 93*, 1191–1214.

Ferro, A. (1999). The bi-personal field: Experiences in child analysis. London and New York: Routledge.

Ogden, T. H. (1992). The dialectically constituted/*decentred* subject of psychoanalysis. 1. The Freudian subject. *International Journal of Psychoanalysis, 73*, 517–526.

Ross, D. (2002). Ireland: History of a nation. New Lanark, UK: Geddes & Grosset.

Winnicott, D. (1965). *The maturational processes and the facilitating environment*. New York, NY: International Universities Press.

Chapter 18

Credo: So Our Lives Glide On*

Ken Corbett

As I set about to contemplate a set of psychoanalytic beliefs, I was reminded of one of my favorite passages in English literature, from George Eliot's (1866/1995) novel, *Felix Holt The Radical*, "So our lives glide on: the river ends we don't know where, and the sea begins, and then there is no more jumping ashore" (p. 219).

There are too many tributaries in a human life to jump ashore, and give an orderly psychoanalytic account. There is too much to hear. There are too many modes of exchange, conscious and unconscious. There are too many voices, too many objects, and states of being clamoring for an audience. Mental processes are emergent and nonlinear; so too, is any analysis. Analyst and patient emerge, spill over, and emerge again. Unique idioms flow and overflow every analysis.

The same can be said about psychoanalytic beliefs: They evolve, circulate, and flow. Psychoanalytic believing, therefore, must flow onto an open field that affords the necessary consideration of dependent, coexisting, and even contradictory facts. An ordered catalogue of beliefs would be a jumping ashore without dripping the surfeit of the psychoanalytic enterprise.

Hence, contemplating a set of psychoanalytic beliefs must be an act of ongoing revision, with an eye toward how our lives glide on. Or more to the point, how they do not glide on, and how psychoanalysis offers the creative potential for change.

The Social Frame

I believe in foregrounding the gliding/guiding social as it shapes our minds, and frames our practices. I begin with the social so that it does not become an afterthought, divorced from the psychological. Studying social theory and philosophy led me to psychoanalytic theory. Reading Foucault and

---

* Reprinted with kind permission: This chapter was first published with the same title in *Psychoanalytic Dialogues* 31 (3): 253–261.

Ricouer in my first semester of graduate school led me to Freud. Reading Chodorow in that same semester led me to Klein, which led me to Winnicott. Reading Butler in my second year of graduate school led me to Derrida, Lacan, Sedgwick, and back to Freud. Some might look upon my route as circuitous, but I enjoyed and continue to enjoy the circulation.

The social is not outside the door; it operates within, always within. I believe that we, the humans, are always and already socially and historically constituted (even before birth), and reconstituted through "normative regulatory anxiety" (Corbett, 2009, p. 111). Normative constitution is not, however, an unremitting prototype. Norms are configured through variance, and thereby open to discontinuity and mobility. Similarly, cultural orders are open to rupture and expansion; yes, we live in a here and now, but there is also a there and then. Reckoning with the social frame, to the extent that we have, has allowed us to look toward a wider arc of livable lives; ideality is not reserved for the more normative among us.

By foregrounding the social, we stay on our toes, revising our beliefs and expanding our borders. 21st century clinical psychoanalysis surely has as much to do with feminism, queer theory, critical race studies, and social philosophy as it does with Freudian tenets, British object-relations theory, American ego psychology, or Relational theory. Arguably, the most influential work undertaken in psychoanalysis in the last half-century has been in the spaces between psychoanalysis and social theory. The gray-haired guardians have had to listen to the "outsiders" rattling the gate, seeking to become speaking subjects in a discourse that too readily spoke for, or more to the point, *about* them.[1]

At stake here is nothing less than how we measure the wellbeing of our fellow citizens, and how that being is employed to confer a life that is seen to matter. Who counts as a citizen? Who counts as a patient? Who counts as an analyst? And how does that identity follow on conventions of membership that construct psychoanalytic institutions? How do we rethink our psychoanalytic beliefs and ethics as we begin to consider who has been left out of the frame? How do we rethink our modes of care, including the social configuration of the clinical setting? How do we rethink the curricula that undergird psychoanalytic educations, to include a social education that serves to perplex our psychoanalytic beliefs?

Mental Freedom

I believe in the useful potential of mental freedom, and establishing a therapeutic frame in which that freedom can be risked, lived, and named. I am guided by Freud's (1915) bipartite model of mental freedom: (1) *Freedom is the unconscious made conscious* through the organizing authority of the reality principle. In this frame, the unconscious is made manifest and given to the patient through an analyst's knowing interpretations. (2) *Freedom is the lifting of resistance to the unconscious.* In this frame the unconscious manifests, one might say breathes, through states of being and becoming. The pivot is no longer interpretation, but one of bringing patients to the creativity of playing, and experiencing a new set of objects.[2]

I derive great pleasure in joining patients in the mental freedom found in playing and dreaming, even when the water grows dark with the blood of ghosts and the bile of bad objects. But I do not immediately jump into these streams; I wait. Patients anxiously defend against the establishment of transitional spaces that foster the lifting of resistances to unconscious processes. There is a delicate balance between waiting for a patient to arrive, and helping them experience their fears in so doing.

I strive to stay one step behind and lean into what I think of as an instructive uncertainty, a mode of unknowing. The position of constructive uncertainty is not equivalent to withholding or holding back, as it has sometimes been construed; it is, rather, an active, if not quite affirmative *something*: a containing-searching, a potential, and a mode of mutuality that may or may not be simultaneous.

I am not so much concerned with the content of what is being thought per se, or the interpersonal conversation as pace. I am more concerned with ferreting out shifts between affects and thoughts as these shifts do or do not allow for constructing and sustaining transitional space. It is within these shifts or crevices that I can comment on the interference. I do so in order to push at the boundaries of what can be experienced, akin to that which Michael Parsons (1999) calls, "the *sudden* pleasure of discovering an unexpected freedom of exploration" (p. 871; emphasis added). I believe that the unforeseen discovery should be in the realm of the patient's experience, and not as a matter of my rushing forward with too much naming and knowing. I move into the crevices, and keep my observations brief. I often speak in the voice of hypothesis. Such observations are offered in an effort to help patients as they experience and come to name their own anxieties, histories of trauma, personality structures, fears of breakdown, primitive agonies, bad objects, and so on. It is equally important to listen for the structural social histories that interweave a patient's capacities to play and dream. How do race, gender, sexuality, disability, and class inform a patient's experience of mental freedom, along with their experiences of the setting? How does the despair and disrepair of the social imaginary thwart us all?

My first patients were two three-year-old boys. I worked with them daily for three years, within a therapeutic nursery. I learned that children are rarely (almost never) looking for someone with a lot to say. I find this also to be true with adults, with whom I now primarily work. Too much talking is akin to wind drag, and slows the patient down. In other words, I learned how to move into transitional spaces without talking such spaces out of their potential. The importance that I place on the work of transitional spaces follows on the potential mental freedom to be found therein: aliveness, illusion, states of being, and the creation of the other.

Famously, Winnicott (CW, 2017) proposed that mothers adapt to an infant's needs, and that mothers, "when good enough, give the infant the *illusion* that there is an external reality that corresponds to the infant's own capacity to create" (p. 275, emphasis in original). A mother is made, then, found. And the reality of such finding is not simply frustrating or limiting, but enriching as it provides relief. Part of that relief unfolds through holding the loving and hating that together makes a mother and a baby together.

I find enormous satisfaction in moving with patients between illusion and reality: being made, then found in an intermediate area of experiencing. I am often confused, both unwittingly and with intent. Hour by hour, I feel myself to be enveloped in a polyphonic field, and I struggle to get my mind into and around the excess. Adding to my confusion, I often court it, indulge it, and mine it to see where it may lead. In other words, I strive to keep transitional experiencing in play, as per Winnicott (CW 2017):

> The third part of the life of a human being, a part that we cannot ignore, is an intermediate area of *experiencing*, to which inner reality and external life both contribute. It is an area that is not challenged, because no claim is made on its behalf except that it shall exist as a resting-place for the individual engaged in the perpetual task of keeping inner and outer reality separate yet interrelated (p. 267).

The resting *"experiencing"* to which Winnicott (CW, 2017) refers is *"illusory experience"* (p. 267, emphasis in original). We rest, we might say repair, through illusion. We also grow through the interchange of illusion and reality, including our capacity to move from merged objects to separate others upon whom we still depend, as we move into our dense and intense social worlds.

Further, I believe that mental freedom comes to life through the eroticism of coming into existence. In this light, I am keen to track the Eros that brings transitional spaces to life. Much can be understood through the contemplation of the infantile sexual as it defends against or expands experiencing. Infantile sexuality, as I see it, does not instinctively drive forth as a pre-coded expression of the body's needs; rather, it is an emerging outcome as infants are summoned into existence by the intimate and primary penetrations of parental preoccupation and care. Parental devotion not only potentiates biological life, it also inflects, enlivens, and disrupts object-relational life through libidinal turbulence. [3]

Attending to this primordial undoing, and the ways in which libido overrides relations and the self, aids us in understanding the relational troubles that generally bring patients into treatment. Importantly, I think that it also keeps us aware, to the extent that we can stay aware, of the rogue character of unconscious processes. It humbles us and stumbles us (in just the right way) as we seek to learn how the infantile sexual colors and creates therapeutic exchange. To what degree is the exchange ego-syntonic, or is it freighted by resistant residue that awaits further experiencing and integration?

I struggle to capture the hue and cast of patients' experiencing. How does their aliveness or deadness carry the parenting, and parental unconscious transfers that brought them into being? How do they sustain and link associations, psychically-somatically-socially? How might those links be freighted by trauma and primitive agonies? How has their access to experiencing and capacities for illusion shaped their personalities and modes of defense? How are they thus formed or "unformed," as per Alvarez (1998)? How might dissociation or depersonalization leave a patient blank to that which happened, but has yet to be experienced? How do their unique idioms shape the setting, and the gradual construction of a transitional area in which we can work (Cf. Bollas, 1979)? How does their idiom join with mine to find the language of our exchange?

I believe it is best to be multilingual when helping a patient move into "an intermediate area of experiencing" (between inner reality and external life, between them and them, between them and me, between us and world). Sometimes I speak relational, sometimes I speak interpersonal, sometime I speak within the dream, but almost always I speak those languages within the frame of play.

Playing

I believe that therapeutic action rests on returning to the past not yet experienced, and the aliveness not yet found. I privilege playing as my preferred mode of transit and returning (Corbett, 2017). Consider Winnicott's (CW, 2017) deceptively simple dictum, offered in "Playing: A Theoretical Statement": "Psychotherapy has to do with two people playing together" (p. 44). Winnicott is not describing one person playing while another looks on. He is not describing one person playing while the other person comments on the action. The two people are proximal or combined in present progressive action: playing together.

Winnicott is privileging the transitive hospitality of playing – "the space in or through which anything can or does move" (OED Vol. 18, 1991 [1884] p. 1012) – as psychotherapeutic action that serves to build therapeutic space and potential. Following upon his dictum about playing, Winnicott (CW, 2017) drew a distinction between play, play content, and playing:

> In the total theory of the personality, the psychoanalyst has been too busy using play content to look at play content to look at the playing child, and to write about playing as a thing in itself. It is obvious that I am making a significant distinction between the meanings of the noun 'play' and the verbal noun 'playing' (p. x).

By repeating *play content* ("using play content to look at play content") Winnicott folded obsessive rumination into his critique of what he took to be psychoanalysts' obsessive focus on play content, driven by their diligent quest to find unconscious derivatives, and busily interpret. Game over.

Some *thing*, Winnicott tells us, is missing: "playing as a thing in itself." He does not elaborate on this point, beyond describing playing as a "verbal noun." Doing and being are coupled in an intermediate state, in which playing is noumenal, not phenomenal. Playing is inferred through experience and the self-evidence of sense and presence, time and space. Playing is transitory, and thereby open to transitions, potential, unknowing, and being. Game on.

Playing should not be mistaken for lightheartedness. Like fantasy, playing includes many kinds of activities. Play is the expansion of experiencing, along with the paradox of depth. As Parson's (1999) summarizes, "The play element is not just an occasional aspect of analysis, but functions continuously to sustain a paradoxical reality where things can be real and not real at the same time. This paradox is the framework of psychoanalysis" (p. 871).

Illuminating play's paradox are the ways in which it is as much blood as it is glitter. Grief comes onto the field, and rage brings it to its knees. Envy and competition elbow their way down the field. Paranoid flight runs for the corners, where it lingers and haunts. Sputtering schizoid drones fly overhead dropping cluster bombs. Playing includes long periods of waiting and stillness, spellbound moments that are ungrounded and unchanging. As well, the potential of potential space does not simply jump the shark of the social imaginary's disrepair; more often, it follows on the bereaved inability to imagine.

Finding one's way as the analyst onto the field, and into the action of playing, opens onto a range of languages and modes of exchange from the interpersonal to waking-dreaming. Yet, play is neither a dream nor predominately interpersonal. It is potential, the liminal space created between the material and the psychic. I often feel that my best efforts unfold when I am pulled into a network of fantasy and onto a field where I can speak and play with the objects that come to life therein (Cf. Cooper 2019; Corbett, 2017). I think of these exchanges as more liminal than interpersonal. We slip the knot of the interpersonal, and enter the transitional and potential strangeness of playing. We enter an in-between space, a place of arriving, failing, and arriving again.

It is within these spaces that patients undertake the hard work of translating and repairing formative archaic influences, and determinative relational configurations. I think of this hard work, that has traditionally been called working through, as a zone wherein patient and analyst find the not yet found: sabotaging objects, necrotic love, malignant relational configurations, failures of recognition, modes of psychic retreat, primitive agonies, sexual intromissions carrying abuse, pathways riven with neglect, to name but a few. Working through comes to life (finding and failing, over and over) as object relational patterns and affective states are transferred between patient and analyst, who Green (1997) describes as "a potential object inducing transformations" (p. 276). I look for transformational openings: perhaps melancholia moves toward mourning, leaving room for the rest of illusion; or the hate-driven grip of obsessional patterns loosen, affording the contradictions and chaos of loving; or the dogged drear of neglect cracks just enough to allow for some sustained care. In such moments, other possibilities for recognition emerge: repressive and oppressive hierarchies are questioned, re-significations and new modes of identity come out, more inclusive relational dispositions are found, and bit by bit more livable lives come to be.

In keeping with my faith in the work of playing, I am especially interested in my experience of transduction and transfiguration as potential sites for reclaiming that which has yet to be found and experienced. How do I come alive or fall into deadness? How does my own inner world and transference-counter-transference bring me forward or hold me back? How am I transduced, unaware until it arrives in the potential spaces of enactment? How do I stumble on the field, and why? How do I make room for the hate's constitution and destruction? How do I remain steady, even still, in the face of the unbearable grief that so often arrives? How do I sustain the stable attention that values the loss, while preserving that which is left of what was loved and hated? How do I hold a life as it comes undone, while working toward reformulating, reintegration, and repair?[4]

I pay particular heed to moments when my patients take a temporal turn from knowing toward an aesthetic experiment in living otherwise; improvisational opportunities to shake the chain of material reality and historical consequence. So too, the ongoing reconsideration of psychoanalytic believing rests on the probity and potential revealed in these aesthetic experiments. It is the analyst's job to listen for those moments of improvisation, and the noise they make on the threshold of the past and the present as they clatter toward the future. It is our job – one might say, our ethical charge – to hone in on those potential spaces as they reveal how life may be otherwise livable. In kind, it is our charge to rethink our psychoanalytic beliefs to include the potentials that are not in our consulting rooms, to include patients who remain outside the setting, and to reach toward modes of practice and care that we cannot yet imagine.

Notes

1 I fill this space between psychoanalysts and cultural theorists with a brimming chorus: Lewis Aron & Karen Starr, Lisa Baraister, Jessica Benjamin, Daniel Butler, Judith Butler, Anne Cheng, Ken Corbett, Francoise Davoine & Jean-Max

Gaudilliere, Muriel Dimen, Daivd Eng & Shinhee Han, Franz Fanon, Michel Foucault, Stephen Frosch, Virginia Goldner, Francisco Gonzales, Janice Gump, Orna Guralnik, Griffin Hansbury, Adrienne Harris, Stephen Hartman, Saidiya Hartman, Annie Lee Jones, AB Huber, Lynne Layton, Kimberly Leary, Julie Levitt, David Marriot, Jade Mc Gleughlin, Robert Mc Ruer, Fred Moten, Jose Munoz, Ann Pellegrini, Eyal Rozmarin, Jaqueline Rose, Avgi Saketopoulou, Andrew Samuels, Eve Sedgwick, Gayle Solomon, Warren Spielberg & Kirkland Vaughans, Gillian Straker, Melanie Suchet, and Eyal Rozmarin.
2 Cf. Ogden (2019).
3 See Anzieu, 1993; Bick, 1968, Bulter, 2019; Laplanche, 1997; Scarfone, 2012; Winnicott, 1956.
4 My thoughts about working through are so over-determined, (so long in the oven), and rest on reading and re-reading many psychoanalytic theorists. It is impossible to pay due heed to them all. I direct readers to the following writers, to whom I often return on those days (and they are many) when I feel stuck: Alvarez, 1998; Aron, 2001; Benjamin, 1998, 2017; Bollas, 1989; Butler, 2005, 2006; Cooper, 2011, 20018; Davies, 2018; Green, 1993, 1997; Grossmark, 2012; Harris, 2009; Levine, 2016; Loewald, 1989; Ogden, 1997, 2012, 2019; Parsons, 1999, Seligman, 2014, Stern, 2013a, 2013b, Winnicott, 2017.

References

Alvarez, A. (1998). Failures to link: Attacks or defects? Some questions concerning the thinkability of Oedipal and Pre=Oedipal thoughts. *Journal of Child Psychotherapy*, 24: 213–231.

Anzieu, D. (1993). Autistic phenomena and the skin ego. *Psychoanal. Inq.*, 13(1): 42–48.

Aron, L. (2001). *A Meeting of the Minds: Mutuality in Psychoanalysis*. New York: Routledge.

Benjamin, J. (1998), Like Subject, *Love Objects: Essays on Recognition and Sexual Difference*. New Haven: Yale Univ. Press.

Benjamin, J. (2017). Beyond Doer and Done To: Recognition Theory, *Intersubjectivity, and the Third*. New York: Routledge.

Bick, E. (1968). The experience of the skin in early object-relations. *Int. J. Pycho-Anal.*, 49: 484–486.

Bollas, C. (1989). *The Shadow of the Object: Psychoanalysis of the Unthought Known*. New York: Columbia Univ. Press.

Bulter, D. (2019). Riding instincts, even to die. *Studies in Gender and Sexuality*, 20(2): 106–118.

Butler, J. (2005). *Giving An Account of Oneself*. New York: Fordham Univ. Press.

Bulter, J. (2006). Precarious *Life: The Powers of Mourning and Violence*. London: Verso.

Cooper, S. (2011), *A Disturbance in the Field: Essays in Transference – Countertransference*. New York: Routledge.

Cooper, S. (2019), A theory of the setting: The transformation of unrepresented experience and play. *Int. J. Psycho-Anal.*, 100(6): 1439–1454.

Corbett, K. (2009). *Boyhoods: Rethinking Masculinities*. New Haven: Yale Univ. Press.

Corbett, K. (2016). *A Murder Over A Girl: Justice, Gender, Junior High*. New York: Holt.

Corbett, K. (2017). *Transit: Playing the Other*. Plenary address, Psychology and the Other, Cambridge, MA, November 2017.

Davies, J.M. (2018). The "Rituals" of the Relational Perspective: Theoretical Shifts and Clinical Implications. *Psychoanal. Dial.*, 28(6):651–669.

Elliot, G. (1995 [1886]). *Felix Holt the Radical*. New York: Penquin.

Freud, S. (1915). Observations on transference-love (further recommendations on the technique of psycho-analysis III). *The Standard Edition of the Complete Psychological Works of Sigmund Freud*, Volume XII (1911–1913): 157–171.

Green, A. (1993). *On Private Madness*. London: Karnac.

Green, A. (1997). The intuition of the negative in Playing in Reality. *Int. J. Pyscho-Anal.*, 1071–1084.

Grossmark, R. (2012). The unobtrusive relational analyst, *Psychoal. Dial.*, 22(6): 629–646.

Harris, A. (2009). *Gender as Soft Assembly*. New York: Routledge.

Laplanche, J. (1997). The theory of seduction and the problem of the other. *Int. J. Psycho-Anal.*, 78: 653–666.

Levine, L. (2016). Mutual Vulnerability: Intimacy, Psychic Collisions, and the Shards of Trauma. *Psychoanl. Dial.*, 26(5): 571–579.

Loewald, H. (1989). *Papers on Psychoanalysis*. New Haven: Yale Univ. Press

Mitchell, S. (1995). *Hope and Dread in Psychoanalysis*. New York: Basic Books.

Mitchell S. (2000) *Relationality: From Attachment to Intersubjectivity*. New York: The Analytic Press.

Ogden, T. (1997). *Reverie and Interpretation*. New York: Jason Aronson.

Ogden, T. (2012). *Creative Readings: Essays on Seminal Analytic Works*. London: Routledge.

Ogden, T. (2019). Ontological psychoanalysis or "What do you want to be when you grow up?" *Psychoa. Quart.*, LXXXVIII, 661–684.

Parsons, M. (1999). The logic of play in psychoanalysis, *Int. J. Psychoa-Anal.*, 80: 871–884.

Oxford English Dictionary (1991 [1884]). Oxford: Oxford University Press.

Scarfone, D. (2012). Winnicott: Early libido and the deep sexual. *Canadian J. Psychoanal.*, 20 (1): 3–16.

Seligman, S. (2014). Paying attention and feeling puzzled: The analytic mind as an agent of therapeutic change, *Psychoal. Dial.*, 24, 648–662.

Stern, DB, (2013a). Field theory in psychoanalysis, part 1: Harry Stack Sullivan and Madeleine and Willy Baranger, *Psychoanl. Dial.*, 23: 630–645

Stern, DB, (2013b). Field theory in psychoanalysis, part 2: Bionian field theory and contemporary interpersonal/relational theory. *Psychoanl. Dial.*, 23: 487–501.

Winnicott, D.W. (1956). Primary maternal preoccupation. In *Through Paediatrics to Psycho-Analysis. Int. Psycho-Anal. Lib.*, 100:1–325. London: The Hogarth Press and the Institute of Psycho-Analysis.

Winnicott, D.W. (1974). The fear of breakdown, *Int. Rev. Psychao-Anal.* 1, 103.

Winnicott, D.W. (2017). *The Collected Works of D.W. Winnicott*, Volume 9, 1969–1971, L. Caldwell & H. Taylor Robinson [Ed.]. Oxford: Oxford University Press.

Chapter 19

Peasants, Fields, and Expanding Horizons in Psychoanalysis

Elizabeth A. Corpt

My work as a psychoanalyst has been shaped by my life. Of course, this is true of every analyst, but because my trajectory has differed in some markable ways from that of many of my colleagues, I saw no way to authentically live *this* analytic life without some degree of openness about my personal experience; about how I made my way into *this* particular analyst's chair.

In his essay, *Cezanne's Doubt*, Maurice Merleau-Ponty (1964) says the following, "Although it is certain that a person's life does not explain his work, it is equally certain that the two are connected. The truth is that *that work to be done called for that life*" (p. 20). This essay was Merleau-Ponty's attempt to understand Cezanne's stance in the world—his constant restless doubt about his work—and to reconcile it with his remarkable contributions as an artist. Although I intend no comparison to the brilliance of Cezanne, something about Merleau-Ponty's statement, his noting of Cezanne's restlessness and constant doubt in relation to his work, resonates deeply with my own experience of becoming a psychoanalyst. This work, to be done, required this life.

Just as Cezanne appears to have labored to understand the geological underpinnings of his landscapes in order to give his paintings the foundational solidity they required, I choose to locate and write from my own psycho-social-cultural geology, so to speak, as a way to firmly affix my analytic identity to solid ground. There are most certainly many in this collection of credos who have amassed a far more impressive vitae than my own. I enter this volume, however, at the invitation of the editor because my paper, "Peasant in the Analyst's Chair: Reflections, Personal and Otherwise, on Class and the Forming of an Analytic Identity," seems to have secured some modest patch of ground in the psychoanalytic canon by virtue of its having emerged from a personal, embodied, deeply felt, and articulated social-class located position. I am grateful and humbled to be included here.

My paper, written about a decade after my graduation from analytic training, was first presented in 2011 at an independently organized conference in New York City called Bystanders No More. This conference, single-handedly pulled together by a dear friend and colleague, managed to bring together some 300 analytic practitioners to address the very issues that had been, for so long, split off from psychoanalysis as extra-analytic: social class, racism, sexism, homophobia, inequality, etc. Unlike most psychoanalytic conferences, this conference had a fresh and radical feel to it. Free of affiliation with any one institute or organization, and free from the continuing education economy, the energy of the speakers tapped into a kind of liberating freedom rarely felt in this field. I was inspired to take the risk of speaking personally about the complications and challenges of having come from a working-class background into this elite profession. In particular, I addressed the painful experience of passing that so marked my psychoanalytic training and my first decade-long analysis. In essence, I wrote and presented the paper I had only wished I could have read as part of my training experience; a paper that could also help me claim some sense of belonging in a field that had been, thus far, silent about social class. As I say in my paper,

> "I would venture to guess that, more often than not, even in the privacy of one's own personal analysis, the topic of sex will more easily be discussed than issues related to class, class shame, or relational anxieties having to do with class differences between analyst and analysand. When such issues do manage to surface, these concerns can easily be attributed to forms of neurosis or minimized as extra-analytic, that is, as life's givens, which lie outside the frame of the analysis—particularly once the analyst's bill is paid."
>
> (Corpt, 2013, pp. 53–54)

At the conference, the immediate response to my paper was rather stunning. Several people in the audience were inspired to rise up to share their own painful stories of class shame. Others came up to me afterwards to privately confess their class-related injuries. A few years later, my article was published.

Clearly, I was taking somewhat of a professional risk in being so open about my personal experience, aspects of my family history, my first analysis, and references to work I had done in my second analysis; an analysis I had entered in order to come to terms with the challenges and unanswered questions raised in my first. To personally locate myself in relation to social class seemed the only legitimate way to approach this subject and have the impact I wanted to have. In retrospect, I have no regrets about having written, presented, or published this paper. Over the last several years, as this paper has taken its place on the syllabi of various training institutes, I am pleased to say this paper has done what I intended it to do: encouraged analysts-in-training as well as graduated analysts to reflect upon their own social class experience as well as that of their patients, and to consider social class as a psychologically complex aspect of identity worthy of serious analytic reflection and exploration.

> "My intention in writing the paper is to make use of my lived experience of social class in order to evoke in you, the reader, your own lived social class experience and to consider its impact on the formation of your professional identity. With class in mind, I want you to consider your place in the professional community, your relations with colleagues who may or may not be like you, and, ultimately, your work with patients, be they from within or outside of the field. Lastly, I invite you to consider the overall impact of the disavowal of class on the field of psychoanalysis as a whole."
>
> (Corpt, 2013, p. 53)

Writing this paper also provided me a way to express my outrage, disappointment, and utter puzzlement regarding the overall silence of psychoanalysis on the topic of social class; a traumatizing silence that rendered both my first analyst and me mute with regard to the psychological injuries of class. Neither of us had a template or a language from within the field that could help us consider and approach the vulnerability of social class as a psychologically deep experience connected to shame, envy, loss, longing, and the desire to belong:

> "Despite the fact that I talked about the most intimate aspects of my life, four to five times a week, I managed to wall off the bulk of my class shame. How could I have spent so many years in a deep analysis without ever talking directly about my feeling as though—no—my certainty that I had hailed from a lower class than my analyst? I attempted to talk around it; about my experience of feeling like a *have-not*. That's what I called myself. My analyst was the *have*, and I the *have–not*. But, in retrospect, my talking about this was always with what I presumed was a shared sense of our thinking this was a distortion on my part; wasn't I, after all, in analysis and analytic training? How could I be a *have not*? By the looks of it, I was a *have*, but a *have* conflicted about being a *have*. I was functioning at a very high level and living a middle class life. Why, I wondered, was I persistently and defensively invested in this *have-not* identity?"
>
> (Corpt, 2013, p. 63)

My second analyst had written extensively on shame, and it is with him that I began to directly address class-related shame. I was particularly troubled by my inability to write. Shame, in all its permutations, is, of course, the very enemy of the ability to show oneself and to therefore gain a sense of belonging.

> "The price of maintaining a sense of belonging to one's analyst or analytic community may result in the candidate's needing to hide or disavow the importance of her class-related concerns. When brought to the analyst, if she is met by what Fowlkes (1991) refers to as "limited recognition or inadequate understanding of the meaning of the loss" (p. 544), this can set the stage for a form of class-related melancholia. I mean this in a way similar to Eng and Han's (2000) reference to racial melancholia. In the place of fruitful mourning of the actual injuries of class, and the working through of such existential dilemmas involved in the very human longings to belong and desire, there can be a silent foreclosing of analytic exploration and the relegating of class anxieties to various forms of pathology and/or intrapsychic conflicts having to do with narcissism, envy, and the like. Should this be the case, then yet another generation of analysts learns to form their identities built on the need to disavow aspects of self that fall outside an assumed shared ideal."
>
> (Corpt, 2013, pp. 58–59)

Over the last few decades, with the momentum of the culture at large and the dedicated work of many colleagues, psychoanalysis has begun to change. Psycho-social cultural concerns have clearly moved, if not charged, into the consulting room. More analytic institutes have begun to address the deep psychological impact of social, cultural, racial, sexual, and political factors on the forming and functioning of the human mind, and not just the minds and bodies of our patients, but our own. For several years, I had the pleasure of teaching Culture and Psychoanalysis with Lynne Layton at the Massachusetts Institute for Psychoanalysis. Our institute was one of the first to embed this course into its curriculum, but even so, early on, there was often resistance to the material. Anxious candidates perceived these topics as optional, irrelevant, and seemingly inconsequential to their practices. Clearly, the field of psychoanalysis had unconsciously relegated these topics to the back of the bus. It is my belief that these topics are simply too big and challenging for us to get our psychoanalytic arms around. We can so easily feel vulnerable, powerless, and ill-equipped to take them on. They remind us of our existential thrownness (Heidegger, 1962) into the world. We live our lives in the throes of them, just as our patients do; caught in a particular time in history and located in a particular place in the social order.

For quite some time, psychoanalysis has been welcoming a widening scope of analytic patients. This is all for the good, particularly the recent efforts by various training institutes to reach out to underserved communities. To my mind, however, this means we must embrace an ever-widening scope of analytic practitioners. We must actively encourage analysts of color, those with diverse social class backgrounds, and gender orientations. We must encourage those analytic practitioners already firmly in the fold to widen their perspectives on a diversity of lifeworlds (Orange, 2008). To establish a bridge between psychoanalysis, ethics, and philosophy, I have been focusing my writing on relational ethics in the consulting room (Corpt, 2016, 2017, 2018, 2020). Recently, I have begun to develop my ideas on ethical labor (Corpt, 2020):

> "Although I always want to know and stay close to my patient's reality, I simply don't think that's enough anymore. In fact, I think there are aspects of this position of waiting to learn from my patient that can be read as elitest, privileged, entitled, and even inhospitable. If we are to move beyond our ignorance when it comes to historical blind-spots, racism, sexism, classism, etc., then we must be willing to perform the ethical labor of educating ourselves about the lives and histories of those different from ourselves and to contemplate how those differences may be alive in us and between us in the consulting room. We need to be ready and willing to communicate or signal our openness, respect, and curiosity about the lived experience, histories, and cultures of those different from ourselves. Otherwise, our therapeutic passive receptiveness—our willingness to be taught- could be felt by our patients as disinterest, prejudice against, unspeakable superiority, or non-negotiable privilege. And should our patient's personal or historic trauma histories be ones in which dissociation, erasure, disavowal, and shame figure large, then all the more, we need to acquaint ourselves, as best we can, with what cannot yet be subjectively formulated or articulated. We need to actively consider the possible power relations and certain asymmetries involved."
>
> (Corpt, p. 228)

I realize that in embracing this perspective, I may run the risk of being perceived as going against the sacred notions of neutrality and/or evenly hovering attention or empathic inquiry. These notions, as important as they are, can, in and of themselves, sometimes assume a sameness of cultural contexts, a blindness to difference, or a silent accommodation to the analyst's cultural context. This, to my mind, goes against the very liberatory spirit of psychoanalysis. Can we not both educate ourselves and hold the complexity of what we learn, while simultaneously remaining close to the patient's experience? This is a challenge worth taking up.

Several years following the publishing of my paper, and well beyond a decade and a half since I finished my first analysis, I had the unique opportunity of returning to discuss my paper with my first analyst. This analyst had encountered my paper in a study group on shame and had some reflections and thoughts to share. What unfolded was a very moving meeting that included an apology for ignorance and blind spots. Reading my paper had led her to a reassess some aspects of her work with me, particularly a rethinking of the constraints of her overarching theory at that time which had led her to read my shame as envy. I came away from this meeting, deeply touched by her generosity and willingness to continue her deep reflections on our work so long after we had ended. To me, this is the heart of ethical labor.

In closing, this work to be done required this life. I have moved on to a successful psychoanalytic practice. Patients who have encountered my paper or references to my having written on this topic seem to have taken this as a sign that social class concerns and conflicts are welcome in my consulting room. Analytic supervisees treating analysands from working class or social class complicated backgrounds are eager to consider class as a vital aspect of deep work. I've had the pleasure of serving as President of the Massachusetts Institute for Psychoanalysis, and I continue to write, publish, teach, supervise, present, and of course, analyze. Currently, I serve as Co-Chief Editor of the journal *Psychoanalysis, Self and Context*.

Can I still claim to be a peasant in my analyst's chair? This identification continues to hold fertile meaning for me. I refer back to Berger (1992) and a passage initially quoted in my paper:

> "His ideals are located in the past, his obligations are to the future ... the peasant has a cyclic view of time. ... In the peasant's dream, work is still necessary. ... He may admire knowledge and the fruits of knowledge but he never supposes that the advance of knowledge reduces the extent of the unknown. ...The peasant is continually improvising. ... His observation does not allow the slightest sign of change to pass unnoticed."
>
> (Berger, 1992, pp. xi–xxvii)

The work we do in the field of psychoanalysis is, in many respects, not so unlike that of the peasant: vulnerable, uncertain, at the mercy of nature, including human nature, always in pursuit of growth as well as survival. Psychoanalysis can only be strengthened by preserving our connections to the earth.

References

Berger, J. (1992). *Pig earth*. New York: Random House.
Corpt, E. (2013). Peasant in the analyst's chair: Reflections, personal and otherwise, class and the forming of an analytic identity. *International Journal of Psychoanalytic Self Psychology, 8*, 52–67.
Corpt, E. (2016). The complications of caring and the ethical turn in psychoanalysis. In D. Goodman & E. Severson (Eds.), *The ethical turn: Otherness and subjectivity in contemporary psychoanalysis* (pp. 109–116). London: Routledge.
Corpt, E. (2017). Maternal ethics and the therapeutic work of protecting open futures. *Psychoanalysis Inquiry, 37*, 412–418.
Corpt, E. A. (2018). The ethics of listening in psychoanalytic conversations. *Psychoanalysis, Self, and Context, 13*(3), 220–228.
Corpt, E. (2020). Ethical labor: The ground between experience near and experience distant: Discussion of Phillip Cushman's two worlds or one. *Psychoanalysis, Self, and Context, 15*(3), 227–229.
(1962). *Being and time*. New York, NY: Harper and Row. (Original work published in 1927).
Heidegger, M. (1962). *Being and time*. New York, NY: Harper and Row. (Original work published in 1927).
Orange, D. M. (2008). Whose shame is it anyway?: Lifeworlds of humiliation and systems of restoration (or "The analyst's shame"). *Contemporary Psychoanalysis, 44*(1), 83–100.

Chapter 20

Analytic Eroticism

Dianne Elise

I believe that the practice of psychoanalysis is an erotic endeavor. My reader may feel taken aback. What do I mean by this statement? I realize that the word "erotic" with its specific connotation of sexuality elicits both excitement and uneasiness. In contrast, analysts seem to be comfortable with the term Eros, understood to mean a generalized life force even though bearing the name of the Greek god of sexual love. I favor an *explicit* retaining of the *erotic* in our developing view of how the analytic relationship works. I emphasize that an invitation is issued to an embodied experience of maternal eroticism (Kristeva, 2014), where an atmosphere of libidinal energy is a crucial aspect in enlivening—"vitalizing" (Alvarez, 2012)—the intersubjective field. When fully articulated as an energy potential in both participants, *analytic eroticism* can offer libidinal engagement within an ethical frame. As a clinical approach, analytic eroticism can provide a stimulus to emotionally engaged thinking—linking—that can lead to transformations in many dimensions including the erotic.

The Erotics of Development

I consider Kristeva's (2014) publication a landmark paper of profound significance for an understanding of development that then has implications for the clinical dyad. Her concept of maternal eroticism opens to a wider view of the mother's role as a sexual being. Parental libidinal energies are understood to fuel the child's erotic vitality and to facilitate mental growth. Throughout my writing, I have described the nursing couple (Winnicott, 1965, 1971) as libidinally engaged, their sensual interaction forming a primal template for developing sexuality as well as for the mind more generally. Thomson-Salo and Paul (2017) recently offered a compelling account of infant sexuality in reciprocal interaction with parents that provides support to my theorizing. Drawing from infant observation, neurophysiology research, and infant-parent clinical work, they exquisitely detail parent-infant erotic life. We can recognize that attachment and sexuality are intertwined beginning with the earliest object relations (Benjamin, 2017; Widlocher,

2002) rather than theorizing a pre-oedipal attachment that is then sequentially followed by a sexual development seen entirely as oedipal.

Kristeva (2014) builds upon both Freud and Laplanche, depicting with much specificity the erotic, bodily relationship of mother and infant in which the infant as a sexual being comes to life. I view Kristeva's concept of *maternal eroticism* as the theoretical and developmental counterpart to Freud's concept of *infantile sexuality*. Joining maternal eroticism and infantile sexuality, we can now theorize the potential space of the mother-infant erotic matrix.

I want to enlarge our scope beyond that of a traumatic overload of parental enigmatic signifiers as compromised or contaminated communications that disrupt (Laplanche, 1997) the mother-infant. Instead, I am concentrating on the stimulus to the development of the child's libidinal self by being enveloped in an embodied, erotic relation with each of the parents. I am bringing attention to the *healthy* contribution of parental eroticism to the child's development, with pathology resulting from *deficiencies* in the parental erotic matrix.

Although I am highlighting the vitality and creativity stimulated through parent-infant erotic interplay, much regularly can and does go awry in parenting, as the vast psychoanalytic literature attests. My attention is to the advantages of ample maternal eroticism and to the problems stemming from a deficit. Just as we regularly encounter failures in holding and containing, so too can maternal eroticism go awry in a number of directions. Similarly, analytic eroticism can be used productively or, alternatively, fall prey to destructive dynamics.

Certainly, providing a calm, secure atmosphere ("holding") and modulating distress ("containing") are crucial parental capacities, but in order to thrive, children also need stimulating engagements. Parental libidinal energy also is needed, as Kristeva (2014) delineated, in order that parents can hold up during the varying demands of caring for a child, maintaining their investment in the face of much that is not gratifying in any immediate sense. All this has a parallel in the analytic situation.

I suggest that Kristeva's concept of maternal eroticism is on a par in heuristic and clinical value with Winnicott's concept of maternal holding and with Bion's concept of maternal containment, both in understanding development in the early mother-infant relation and in the relevance that each of these formulations has for the technical approach of the analyst. Holding and containing are each highly developed metaphors conceptualizing the functioning of the analyst within the clinical process. I believe that similar theoretical work can be done in employing the concept of maternal eroticism to delineate an additional, equally salient capacity in the analyst within the analytic field. The analyst holds, contains, *and stimulates*; each of these capacities is mobilized in the service of the patient's growth.

While infantile sexuality stirred by maternal "seduction" was a core aspect of Freud's developmental theorizing, he had no corresponding agenda for the analyst's position; in fact his recommended (paternal) stance of abstinence, neutrality, often rendered the "non-gratifying" analyst an *antilibidinal* figure. Winnicott's and Bion's use of a maternal metaphor provided analysts with a very different conceptualization of our technical approach, but with libido drained away rather than subject to restraint. Maternal eroticism, as the libidinal vitality and investment that a mother brings to her fully embodied engagement with her child, offers a metaphor for technique that can incorporate an analytic eroticism. However, clinicians can fear encountering, let alone utilizing, the erotic in the clinical situation, especially when it escapes the bounds of the more familiar oedipal transferences (Brady, 2018; Vaughan, 2017). Understanding our role in terms of attachment has been much more palatable, allowing for distance from the enormity of passions experienced in undefended vulnerability to the maternal (Elise, 2015, 2017, 2019). I believe that a creative aesthetic can provide a clinical container for the engagement and exploration of erotic life within the analytic field of each treatment.

The Clinical Relationship as an Analytic Field

Analysts have for some time had a growing interest in psychoanalysis as a creative project. We are a profession that values creating a space for meaningful personal truths to be put into words, or into some sense of shared communication, in order that the experiencing that accompanies those communications can be accessed and elaborated. Foregoing the original professional aspiration to "scientific" objectivity, analysts recognize the unique unfolding of each treatment. Current conceptualizations of the analyst's role stress that an analyst is a co-participant in the creative unfolding of a dyadic conversation meant to further the development of the patient's capacities of mind toward increasing elaboration of personal meaning.

The analyst as well must engage in these acts of creativity. I believe our ability to do so is greatly served by a connection with our libidinal, embodied energies. This creative unfolding is each dyad's "work of art"—the aesthetic dimension (De Cortinas, 2009) of the therapeutic process—taking place within an analytic field. Being creatively alive is not solely excitement/pleasure, but the soil in which psychic pain can be metabolized. Winnicott (1971) underscored that access to this quality of experiencing is just as crucial for the analyst as it is for the patient. The analyst's emotionally alive presence offers to a patient an object relationship with potential, a potential space where the patient might risk coming to life rather than remaining frozen in psychic stasis. This psychic awakening will likely be painful and must be approached carefully by both analyst and patient as they evolve their pairing. A patient's encounter with an analyst as engaged presence and creative co-participant will bring a slow, yet shocking awareness of what has not been. Yet, new potentials emerge.

As Winnicott emphasized throughout his work, an analyst's capacity to relate within and through a personally creative modality provides a particular environment that supports the patient's contact with the true self. It is important to recognize that Winnicott's concept of the true self does not refer to a static entity—a fixed representation of self; it is a quality of experiencing, *being*, that involves spontaneity, vitality, imagination, and aliveness in contrast to the compliance of the false self. The primary creativity of the true self needs to be understood as distinct from talent; instead, it is a "talent" for living.

Clinicians are thus contending with significant changes in contemporary understandings of our analytic stance. Even the word "stance" to describe what we are attempting to do—within a given session and throughout the treatment arc—sounds outdated, rigid, fixed, and immobile, though likely representing an improvement over the inanimate "blank screen." I prefer to think in terms of an analytic *approach*; "approach" conveys an image of embodied activity—to move toward—that can include recognition of a need to be still or even to step back in the service of promoting greater contact. Clinicians aim to work with each patient in a manner that will be most helpful to *that* patient in ameliorating the difficulties that have brought him or her to seek treatment. In this effort, I, like many analysts, see analytic field theory as a particularly sophisticated and felicitous model presenting a fresh approach to clinical process as an intersubjective, co-created journey.

As Ogden, Ferro, and Civitarese each compellingly illustrate throughout their work, the creative capacities of the analytic pair to imaginatively co-construct an aesthetic form gives shape and meaning to personal experience. I emphasize that this analytic process is not solely to *contain*, as in the modulation and tolerance of affect, but to *elaborate* the symbolic capacities of the patient's mind that in the analytic setting will most often unfold in a narrative building process. Analytic process can transform painful affect not primarily by naming, but through *the enlivening experience of creating that, in itself, promotes healing* and is thus "an essential element" (Schore, 2012, p. 142) of therapeutic progress.

The understanding of an analytic field—larger than the sum of the parts—leads to a changed role for the analyst, not as objective observer of the patient's mental contents, but as an implicated subject who must also attempt to register and articulate the unfolding experiences within the field. This approach to technique—now not solely to follow the patient, but also *to initiate*—focuses on the analyst's imaginative agency rather than on an over-reliance on a technical expertise based in theoretical abstractions. The field is viewed as encompassing the subjectivities of both patient and analyst, where each is implicated in its formation *and formed by it*. I believe it is fruitful to integrate more fully the richness of Winnicott's contributions into a field theory of analytic process.

From within the perspective of an analytic field theory, one way of viewing the relationship of Winnicott's and Bion's respective contributions might be to see Bionian thinking as a complex articulation of the coercive pressures of the field and Winnicottian thinking as giving more voice to the creative potentials of the field. Both perspectives are essential in a field theory approach to technique: the first in order to comprehend the powerful manner in which an analyst will be drawn into dynamics of mutual projective identification that she cannot initially, but must retrospectively, identify; the second in order to understand that areas of relative freedom within the field allow for a creative effort by the dyad that is central to the analytic goals. Winnicott's style of thinking is particularly evocative in envisioning what we might give life to in the analytic conversation. As analyst and patient "play" with and within the metaphoric realm, they create an emotionally meaningful narrative that not only has the potential to contain and transform psychic pain but to vitalize the creative energy of the personality.

Bringing erotic life to the analytic field

In thinking of my own clinical approach as a Winnicottian field theory (Elise, 2017, 2018, 2019), I am including in this model my specific emphasis on the erotic dimension of the psyche. Winnicott's account most especially emphasizes the development of a *creative* sense of self. I add that personal creativity is located within a libidinal connection to the erotic body. One might say that I am adding a Freudian element to analytic field theory in my attention to the libidinal aspects of embodied psychic life. As I have been identifying, to recognize that psychoanalysis has an erotic nature—that patient and analyst are libidinally engaged—can be troubling. Passion can destabilize one's sense of self—both in a clinician as well as in a patient—yet, we hope for an opening of the self to aliveness, richness of experience, and meaning. Erotic energy is a source of creativity. Creativity is exciting. Can we play with sexuality; can we engage the erotics of play?

I feel that we are missing something in having so removed our theorizing from the libidinal physicality of excitement that infuses creative engagement. A corresponding limitation exists in a technical approach that bypasses the imaginative elaboration of erotic life in the dream that is the analytic field. I specifically underscore the erotic as an important ingredient of the clinical situation—a lively spontaneity that partakes of the analyst's as well as the patient's creative self.

I believe that it is the erotic that unites the container and the contained within a libidinal matrix that supports the creative vitality of the dyad. Thus, I have proposed two expansions of analytic field theory: (1) more explicit attention to the creative potentials of the analytic field, and (2) conceptualization of an erotic dimension as the motive force by which creative potential is vitalized (Elise, 2019).

In my 2019 book, *Creativity and the Erotic Dimensions of the Analytic Field,* I underscore that erotic vitality is a stimulus to creative expression that is itself further stimulating. This relationship can be understood as mutually reinforcing: *erotic* ⟵⟶ *creativity*. Both the erotic and the creative have a further reinforcing relation to the expansion of the overall personality, expressed as: *erotic* ⟵⟶ *creativity* ⟵⟶ *expansion of the personality*. Each of these three aspects of experience develops in reciprocal relation to one another. Expansion of the entire personality is facilitated by an analytic process that integrates bodily components of experience, rooted in erotic vitality, with creative elaborations of emotional truth. Along with the aim of enlarging the containing function, we might think, with Winnicott in mind, of an increasing "creative function" as leading toward greater psychic health and well-being—not solely through the transformation of psychic pain, but in the expansion of the creative expression of one's unique and, I add, erotic being.

Winnicott and Bion each drew a detailed picture of the mother-infant relationship as central to the development of the personality. Although Winnicott underlined the importance of embodied experience, neither he nor Bion theorized an erotic texturing as foundational to both the development of the psyche and the analytic process. I see primary maternal preoccupation, reverie, and containment as *resting within, and only made possible by*, a mother's deeply embodied connection to her libidinal self; her erotic sensibilities provide the "juice" for her complex emotional engagement with her infant. A full formulation of the analytic field must include awareness of the centrality of the erotic in both the maternal matrix and in that of the field. This erotic-aesthetic dimension potentiates the creative interplay of the analytic process. By moving into a potential space of poetic ambiguity, creative imagination, and erotic vitality, we play with, and within, time and space in our relationship with each patient. Each analyst hopefully attempts to embody in a personal analytic style an approach to analytic process that catalyzes the healing potential of shared creation.

Concluding reflections

In my view, psychoanalysis rests on an ability to take nothing at face value, to have a questioning mind, to seek deeper understandings hidden in, *by*, plain sight. We go against the grain, challenging the ingrained, seeking novel connections between disparate "facts." Psychoanalysis is a continuing practice of extricating ourselves from anything rote, or remote, in order to arrive at a place of spontaneous interchange, surprising truths, painful realizations, weaving all this into an understanding that can welcome the unwelcome and relish the emotional immediacy of one's experience.

Psychoanalysis is play in the sense that one can let one's mind play with possibilities; we engage metaphor where flexibility of mind forms images that capture emotional truth and that can stir the soul. Although interpretation can be very powerful, psychoanalysis is also about *invitation*—an invitation to a vital exchange and a meaningful narration of the self. Psychoanalysis involves a deep listening to what is being said, what is not being said. It involves flexibility and fluidity of both thought and affect in interaction. Psychoanalysis is more than ameliorating distress; it is an ongoing process of expansion of the personality in many respects toward greater sense of personal vitality. As is true for a patient, a clinician must be a fully embodied participant for this process to unfold.

Psychoanalysis involves perseverance, attention, and intention, a steadiness, steadfastness of purpose, courage, commitment, a passionate investing in the mobility of the self and the capacity for change, a being with, and a bringing together. It is pain, excitement, humility, and hope. Analytic practice requires patience—immense patience—and kindness and respect. The clinician needs to stay alive in the face of much that is deadening, that works toward stasis; this effort takes tremendous libidinal energy, stamina, fortitude, poised readiness, and, in addition to receptivity, the ability to come forward and to initiate when needed.

Psychoanalysis is a relationship that provides a context for a patient to locate an undefended sense of self—and to be more aware of the defensive strategies that hide this self—in a search for, and hopefully a revealing of, an experience of authenticity. We seek through compassionate and passionate curiosity to engage in a deep exploration into the development of the personality, how it has come to be shaped. In what ways does that shape express the unique and valuable individuality of the person? In what ways does it interfere with a rewarding unfolding of life? What is in the way; what other way might be found? We are searching for what is, what has been, and also for what can become. Each clinical pair both shape and are shaped by the analytic space.

Psychoanalysis requires a "hello"—which may take days or years—and a *good* goodbye, with a long time in between where we do not give up. We work to envision a future seeded in the present that will afford a space to look back. Psychoanalysis is a conversation that lasts well beyond termination and that rests in the capacity to be humble in the face of the sadnesses of living while not refusing the potentials for joy.

References

Alvarez, A. (2012). *The thinking heart: Three levels of psychoanalytic therapy with disturbed children.* London: Routledge.

Benjamin, J. (2017). *Beyond doer and done to: Recognition theory, intersubjectivity and the third.* London: Routledge.

Brady, M. (2018). Braving the erotic field in the treatment of adolescents. *Journal of Child Psychotherapy, 44,* 108–123.

De Cortinas, L. P. (2009). *The aesthetic dimension of the mind.* London: Karnac.

Elise, D. (2015). Reclaiming lost loves: Transcending unrequited desires. Discussion of Davies' "Oedipal Complexity". *Psychoanalytic Dialogues, 25,* 284–294.

Elise, D. (2017). Moving from within the maternal: The choreography of analytic eroticism. *Journal of the American Psychoanalytic Association, 65,* 33–60.

Elise, D. (2018). A Winnicottian field theory: Creativity and the erotic dimension of the analytic field. *fort da, 24*(1), 22–38.

Elise, D. (2019). *Creativity and the erotic dimensions of the analytic field.* New York: Routledge.

Kristeva, J. (2014). Reliance, or maternal eroticism. *Journal of the American Psychoanalytic Association, 62,* 69–85.

Laplanche, J. (1997). The theory of seduction and the problem of the other. *International Journal of Psychoanalysis, 78,* 653–666.

Schore, A. (2012). *The science of the art of psychotherapy.* New York: Norton.

Thomson-Salo, F., & Paul, C. (2017). Understanding the sexuality of infants within caregiving relationships in the first year. *Psychoanalytic Dialogues, 27,* 320–337.

Vaughan, S. (2017). In the night kitchen: What are the ingredients of infantile sexuality. *Psychoanalytic Dialogues, 27,* 344–348.

Widlocher, D. (Ed.) (2002). *Infantile sexuality and attachment.* New York: Other Press.

Winnicott, D. W. (1965). *The maturational processes and the facilitating environment: Studies in the theory of emotional development.* The International Psychoanalytical Library (Vol. 64, pp. 1–276). London: Hogarth Press.

Winnicott, D. W. (1971). *Playing and reality.* London: Tavistock Publications.

Chapter 21

Credo quia absurdum

Bruce Reis

I try to keep moving. Don't want to stay in one place too long. What I'm looking for is the vibrancy of psychoanalytic thinking, the crackling of sudden ideas in the analytic space that surprises or that describes an emotional truth, or innovation in a theory that is rich and complex and elegant. When these things are found, they are like revelations. Nothing in psychoanalysis is more compelling. As Emily Dickinson (1870, p. 265) famously wrote: "If I feel physically as if the top of my head were taken off, I know that is poetry"; well, I'm looking for that from psychoanalysis.

The need for coherent theory provides the analyst with a third, an intellectual community, that structures the dyad in important ways and provides avenues for thinking. I believe that psychoanalysis itself has an unconscious, and that vibrant ideas emerge from the collectivity of that unconscious. These ideas bring new perspectives and understandings, allowing us to appreciate areas of our work that had previously remained occluded. When they arrive, these new formulations feel as if they've been delivered from the heavens—they open things up and allow us to see anew. Yet, I believe that the "selected fact" and the "over valued idea" (Britton & Steiner, 1994) are some of the greatest dangers practicing analysts face both clinically and theoretically. Like all such discoveries, clinical facts and valued ideas do not maintain their original power. Over time the fresh insights necessarily become hackneyed versions of their original brilliance, and we return to a fallow period of psychoanalytic work during which time new ideas begin to germinate under the surface, in the collectivity of our psychoanalytic enterprise. During such periods it seems as if nothing is happening. Fallow periods, in treatments as in the intellectual life of the profession, can be difficult to tolerate. Supervisees and patients alike are often anxious about such times, seeking the reassurance of conscious "progress" and understanding of the process. Analysts know, however, that what is occurring unconsciously during these times is often the most creative expansion of the process. It is essential in these times that we keep assurance that in order to get to the far shore, one must often lose sight of the shore from which we launched. This is no less true, I think, in the clinical situation as it is in the theoretical life of the community of psychoanalysts.

Thus, the continual destruction and reconstitution of the analyst's internal community seems a necessary process that will result in his sustained ability to remain open to the varied phenomena of clinical practice. Not only is this dynamic process at work within the dyad, it is also operative in the field at large. New concepts can bring much needed illumination to the process, but they can also be granted too much explanatory power by analytic groups, and become used as a brand campaign, and before you know it, everything is attributable to that one idea (e.g., enactment, the field, etc.). Better to keep moving.

I believe the analyst's psychoanalytic identity must also always be a work in progress. To be a psychoanalyst means to never fix for very long on a single perch. One must keep moving, keep asking questions, thinking new thoughts, dreaming new realities, and opening new intellectual vistas in order to remain true to the spirit of inquiry that is psychoanalysis. I believe that once an analyst considers themselves a member of a school of psychoanalysis (e.g., a Kleinian, a Bionian, a Relational analyst, an Interpersonalist, etc.), they have made a commitment to limit their field of vision and thus need to be additionally cautious about what they have excluded. As Greenberg (2015, p. 88) put it: "A Kleinian who is aware of (and maybe even faintly nagged by) attachment theory will be a better Kleinian than one who is not. And vice versa."

During my analytic training I had the good fortune to be in a reading group for a while with Stephen Mitchell. It seemed to me that he kept moving intellectually. When we would discuss a piece, Mitchell would look at it from all of the different angles. He'd think aloud about how it worked from one angle, but not from another. He was interested in thinking about things—about theory and about clinical process. It seemed to me he took a great joy in thinking. Most importantly, his scope was expansive rather than constricting. I benefitted from Mitchell's openness and intellectual curiosity. When I published my first paper in *Psychoanalytic Dialogues*, he wrote (Mitchell, in Reis, 1999) a brief introduction to it that reflects what I've said about his interests:

> "Psychoanalysis, like most intellectual disciplines, has a tendency toward self-referential insularity. And psychoanalytic ideas are grounded in everyday clinical work, generated in efforts to understand patients and ourselves with patients, and texted for their utility in the analytic process. Hence, psychoanalytic theorists and clinicians are often unmindful of the ways in which the problems and concepts we struggle with are also being addressed in neighboring disciplines, like philosophy, literary theory, and social criticism. Very often ideas from these other areas have been either intentionally appropriated or,

sometimes, unconsciously absorbed into psychoanalytic discourse. What we rarely appreciate is the way in which these issues have life of their own in the conceptual worlds of our neighbors, who grapple with them, test them in the crucible of the own methodologies, and come up with new conceptual strategies ...".

It helped my development as an analyst to witness Mitchell's openness to other fields. It also helped that I saw him create straw man arguments to further his own thinking, and hold intellectual grudges. Like anyone he had his own limitations, and my seeing these was also formative.

I've felt myself to have been very fortunate to have worked with a handful of other psychoanalysts who I regard as having the spark of genius. There are a number of very intelligent analysts, but having spent time with singular voices such as Daniel Stern, as a colleague in the Boston Change Process Study Group and Christopher Bollas, as a clinical supervisor, I feel exposed to another order of thinking entirely. Their work has been representative of the great courage it takes to simultaneously stand outside the bounds of psychoanalytic parochialism while expanding the limits of what we can think with regard to the clinical encounter. I've witnessed how it is no easy task to occupy this position vis-à-vis the analytic community and have been grateful to them for the example they set.

***

I believe that the analytic enterprise is not primarily an epistemic one. To me, a psychoanalysis is not a linear process, like a road to follow, but similar to the way Alice Munro (2015) who years ago wrote that

> "I don't always, or even usually, read stories from beginning to end. I start anywhere and proceed in either direction. So it appears that I'm not reading—at least in an efficient way—to find out what happens. I do find out, and I'm interested in finding out, but there's much more to the experience. A story is not like a road to follow, I said, it's more like a house. You go inside and stay there for awhile, wandering back and forth and settling where you like and discovering how the room and corridors relate to each other, how the world outside is altered by being viewed from these windows. And you, the visitor, the reader, are altered as well be being in this enclosed space, whether it is ample and easy or full of crooked turns, or sparsely or opulently furnished. You can go back again and again, and the house, the story, always contains more than you saw the last time. It has also a sturdy sense of itself, of being built out of its own necessity, not just to shelter or beguile you. To deliver a story like that, durable and freestanding, is what I'm always hoping for."

Since I believe in a developmental model of treatment I, therefore, believe that the aim of psychoanalysis, broadly put, is to revisit and repair deficits so that the individual can mature into capacities and capabilities previously unavailable to them. My experience is that at the end of an analysis individuals evidence more of these capabilities and are better able to enjoy and make better use of others, themselves, their work, and the world around them (i.e., durable and freestanding). Too often the cognitive understandings of an individual's psychodynamics serve as mere obsessional defenses agreed upon by patient and analyst.

> "After all, how far can consciousness go in its effort to comprehend the unconscious? Not so very far after all, particularly when both analyst and patient so often find thrills of understanding destroyed by new material, which sends them both packing, the one to free associative breakage, the other to evenly suspended attentiveness." (Bollas, 1999, pp. 27–28)

I believe that understanding is different from finding the emotional truth of a session. Finding and connecting with these often painful truths is a very large part of what I believe psychoanalysis is about. The process has to do with contacting these truths and experiencing them as an analyst, which already is a sort of sharing of them with (and allowed by) the patient and facilitated by the analyst's analytic receptivity. Bion (1970) referred to this experience as "being-at-one with the psychic reality of the patient," which is an intimacy that is itself transformative, even prior to the delivery of observation or interpretation. Bion (1967) wrote,

> "I think that what the patient is saying and what the interpretation is (which you give), is in a sense relatively unimportant. Because by the time you are able to give a patient an interpretation which the patient understands, all the work has been done."

In my own work, I have attempted to concentrate on the experience of "being-with" patients in a way that follows from my understanding of some of the work of the authors I've mentioned above.

I believe that psychoanalysis traffics in the non-rational and that this space need to be protected from an approach that stresses the primacy of understanding such that analyst and analysand can be open to whatever arises within the session. Thus, rather than having a credo, the analyst should adopt an approach of *Credo quia absurdum* that stresses belief in the impossible, or the absurd so as to affirm their commitment to the non-rational. Unconscious involvement between patient and analyst leads in mysterious and unpredictable directions. Playing with this precarious situation, as Winnicott (1971, p. 47) noted, constitutes the proper environment of a psychoanalysis:

> "The thing about playing is always the precariousness of the interplay of personal psychic reality and the experience of control of actual objects. This is the precariousness of magic itself, magic that arises in intimacy, in a relationship that is being found to be reliable."

In a psychoanalytic world of magic, I have been inspired by analysts who have found and created objects of thought in the joint creation of inter-subjective monsters (De M'Uzan, 1989), hallucinatory spaces (Botella & Botella, 2005), dream spaces (Ogden, 2005) and by making space within themselves for the patient's madness (Bollas, 1987; Searles, 1979). In these ways, the psychoanalytic space is akin to a novel by Rushdie, for instance, as the most recent one has been so wonderfully described by Winterson (2019):

> "No explanation is given and none is needed. Rushdie has always written as though the impossible and the actual have the same right to exist. Fiction is clearer than what we call real life in this respect—and, in any case, the question of what is real is a question asked but not answered by the novel. That is, the answer is askew to the question, and we shall come to it by and by—because by and by is how the novel proceeds, story opening out from story, jumbles of past, present and future, with alternative histories and futures. And who is telling the story anyway?"

***

I believe that psychoanalysis has never been a culturally syntonic practice, and never should be. To the degree that an analysis supports rather than challenges prevailing views it is failing. As analysts we work in a present culture focused on the immediate, but we value long reflection. Patients, having been told they are "consumers" treat their therapies as if they are commodities choosing analysts by location, hours the patient is available, fee and insurance carrier options, sexual orientation, race, religious orientation, and political orientation.

Psychoanalysts should be attentive to the spread of primitive omnipotence and patient's demands (often expressed in terms of this commodities list) that their conscious ego wishes be met before gratifying these without thinking psychoanalytically. Giant corporations ration mental health "benefits" to their subscribers, and even very ill people cannot get the help they require. Having done away with the category of personality disorders (American insurance companies will not reimburse for the treatment of personality disorders, only the acute relief of the symptoms of such disorders, despite empirical evidence that long-term treatment of these disorders is efficacious) a kind of -K has been instantiated nationally. Together with this development has been the overwhelming fetishization of psychiatric medications by these same insurance companies in literal partnership with Pharma. It is striking how successful efforts by these corporate influences have been on the ways people have come to think about what's troubling them and what need be done about it.

We concentrate on the individual, which is a radical act in this environment. Often a piece of our work involves helping that individual out of a cultural mindset—having to do with ideas of progress and optimization that never involve impediment or loss. Sometimes we need to introduce the idea to the patient that fantasy is a complex issue involving unconscious forces that need reflection, that it is not something that they should actually wish to ever be realized. The paranoid-schizoid position takes on the contours of the age. Bollas (2018) has recently described the presence of "psychophobia," a fear of the mind, that has taken over Western culture and transformed the "selves" that present in analyst's consulting rooms. The anti-intellectualism that pervades the United States at the moment supports the manic use of evacuative wishes and impulsive actions. People are concerned that they are "over thinking" issues when they are not "thinking" at all. What we sell is the reality of trauma, aggression, existential limitation, the long search and struggle for what is creative and genuine, loss, mourning, and ambiguity; what Americans have been told they deserve is the immediate provision of anything they want and that they should feel happy. This is a key time for a practice that is focused on the ineffable and the irrational.

If I were to add to what it is that I believe, I think I would also need to add something about the importance of my colleagues. Like any other profession, psychoanalysis has its political battles, sometimes quite vicious ones because, as the old joke goes, the stakes are so small. Being able to enjoy the good company of like-minded analysts has been a pleasure that has sustained me in this profession. Whether it's going out to dinner with a group of colleagues or for drinks or coffee during which confidential discussions ensue about the field meets an affiliative need that our very insular and in many ways secretive profession makes even more important. That a trusted colleague will spend hours of their time reading a draft of something I've written and giving thoughtful feedback to help me clarify my own thoughts and move forward (as I will do for them) is a terrific gift amongst those who care about similar things and about each other. I value colleagues from around the country and around the world who have Zoomed with me during the pandemic, sharing our experiences of doing analyses in the midst of unprecedented crisis, lending humor and fellow feeling in the midst of great losses. Winnicott (1969, p. 712) said though, with relation to patients being in treatment forever, that "psychoanalysis is no way of life"—and it's true for psychoanalysts too. Those analysts who have made it their way of life have served as cautionary tales for me, bringing to mind Phillips' (1997) caution about bad things happening when psychoanalysts hang out with each other too much. Winnicott meant that you've got to live your life, and residing too much in psychoanalysis, I've seen, can attenuate that living. For me going to the ballet, riding fast motorbikes, or sipping a perfectly made cocktail in good company will contribute mightily to taking me out of the psychoanalytic space, and will keep me moving.

References

Bion, W. R. (1967). On arrogance. In *Second thoughts* (pp. 86–92). New York: Jason Aronson.
Bion, W. R. (1970). *Attention and interpretation*. London: Heinemann.
Bollas, C. (1987). Expressive uses of the countertransference. In *The shadow of the object* (pp. 200–235). New York: Columbia University Press.
Bollas, C. (1999). *The mystery of things*. New York: Routledge.
Bollas, C. (2018). *Meaning and melancholia*. Routledge: New York.
Botella, S., & Botella, C. (2005). *The work of psychic figurability: Mental states without representation*. New York: Routledge.
Britton, R., & Steiner, J. (1994). Interpretation: Selected fact or overvalued idea? *International Journal of Psychoanalysis*, *75*(Pt 5–6), 1069–1078.
De M'Uzan, M. (1989). During the session: Considerations on the analyst's mental functioning. In *Death and identity: Being and the psycho-sexual drama* (Vol. 2013, pp. 79–97). London: Karnac Books.
Dickinson, E. (1870). *Letter to Thomas Wentworth Higginson in the letters of Emily Dickinson*. M. Todd (Ed.). Mineola, New York: Dover Publications.
Greenberg, J. (2015). Response to commentaries. *Journal of the American Psychoanalytic Association*, *63*(1), 85–100.
Munro, A. (2015). *A wilderness station: Selected stories, 1968–1994*. New York: Vintage Books.
Ogden, T. H. (2005). On not being able to dream. In *This art of psychoanalysis: Dreaming undreamt dreams and interrupted cries* (pp. 45–60). New York: Routledge.
Phillips, A. (1997). *Terrors and experts*. Cambridge, MA: Harvard University Press.
Reis, B. E. (1999). Thomas Ogden's phenomenological turn. *Psychoanalytic Dialogues*, *9*(3), 371–393.
Searles, H. (1979). Transitional phenomena and therapeutic symbiosis. In *Countertransference* (pp. 503–576). New York: International Universities Press.
Winnicott, D. W. (1969). *The International Journal of Psychoanalysis*, *50*, 711–716.
Winnicott, D. W. (1971). Playing: A theoretical statement. In D. W. Winnicott (Ed.), *Playing and reality* (Vol. 1971, pp. 38–52). New York: Routledge.
Winterson, J. (September 8, 2019). *Anything can happen: Review of Quichotte by Salman Rushdie* (pp. 1 & 20). NYT Book Review.

Chapter 22

Working It Out: Development, Politics, Multidisciplinarity*

Stephen Seligman

Giving an account of my analytic identity seems like a Sisyphean task, much like practicing analysis. I suppose this declaration is a basic statement in itself. I love analysis because it is concerned with what is not usually said, with what cannot usually be put into words, and with the more elusive, elastic and fluid dimensions of what goes on within and between people. I think of analysis as a kind of playground of honesty, with its affirmation of interpersonal and intrapersonal stress as a way to some more freedom.

Also as in each personal analysis, I find myself in the midst of contradictions of all sorts. I feel fortunate to have more-than-decent working conditions in a job where I can be helpful, at the same time that I am concerned that those benefits are not accessible to so many of my fellow citizens, whether as workers or consumers. I'm fascinated by the rich imagination and multiplicity of the many analytic traditions, even as I am irritated by the sectarian politics that have so constrained it, with all-too-often hidebound small-mindedness and confounding of self-interests of all sorts with claims to superiority. I've gotten so much out of psychoanalytic organizations, even as I have never been satisfied with our efforts to reach out beyond our comfortably professional, White, comfortably bourgeois (and for most of its first century, straight male) confinement. Of course, there are exceptions on all sides.

As I've felt my way through this, my character style has found support in a kind of critical detachment and attitude of suspicion, in the analytic-epistemological sense, which has been generative for me, although at least intermittently problematic. I do think that this helped me think and learn beyond the usual boundaries of psychoanalytic discourse to get a broader perspective, looking to many other fields and experiences, trying to be both real and scholarly. Marxian inflected-critical social theory has always been a

---

* Reprinted with kind permission: This chapter was first printed as part of the introduction of Stephen Seligman's book, *Relationships in Development: Infancy, Intersubjectivity, and Attachment.* Routledge 2018, pp. 7–12.

bedrock for me (although I'm not sure how relevant all of that is as progressive politics are evolving today through so many generational and historical shifts). I enjoy theory a lot, and it's been important to me to treat theory with rigor and care, especially since many analysts seem to have implicit theories that guide their everyday practice, even when they declare that they are not interested in theory. Generally, much analytic theorizing has seemed a bit casual to me, and perhaps more problematically, self-referential and unconscious of its institutional, historical and personal contexts and motivations.

Instead, I've tried to take a multidisciplinary approach and an interest in historical contexts. This seems like a good way (though not the only way, of course), to think more clearly, to situate myself (and ourselves) in relation to our current and past institutional, political-cultural and historical situations, to bring together what is most useful and truest in our different perspectives. It's worth having the broadest understanding of where our ideas originated and how they evolved. Further, it's worth abandoning some ideas that don't work so well anymore, including some that are long-treasured. (Along with many, I think that the dual-instinct model, with its insistence on an innate destructiveness, does more harm than good in both theory and clinical practice. This is perhaps a rather tame example, at this point. I questioned the notion of infantile sexuality more recently—provoking an audience member to exclaim, *sotto voce,* "Heresy!)

Some of the related disciplines for me include infant and child development research, psychology and other social sciences, philosophy, critical social theories, including feminism and queer theories, and cognitive and affective neuroscience. The list of historical contexts is very long, in some sense almost infinite. In my own recent work, I've featured a few of these: World War I and II, the rise of fascism and anti-Semitism in interwar Europe, the migration of the psychoanalytic center to Britain and the United States, the rise and decline of psychoanalysis in the postwar United States, first in its ascendancy in the prosperous and optimistic 1950's and 1960's, and its fall from grace in the medicalizing momentums of neoliberalism, psychopharmacology, care management, neoliberal commodification of services and selves, and more, beginning in the last decades of the twentieth century.

The field with which I have been most familiar is the interdisciplinary research and clinical intervention with infants (under threes) and young children that began to emerge in the 1980's and has continued to be influential today. This is a wide-ranging domain. In one direction, it has expanded into developmental neuroscience and epigenetics (gene expression over the life span is affected by early stress, for example) and in another, supported a worldwide network of psychotherapy and other psychotherapeutically-inflected services to "under fives" and policy initiatives of all sorts (free child care or parenting support for women in prison who have had babies during their incarceration).

The most important lessons from all of this are that early development matters the most in determining the life course (all other things being equal), and that relationships are the most important dimensions and determinants of such early development. Recent research has also shown that economic and cultural factors are very important in determining such key developmental variables as health, longevity, work productivity, and that early intervention makes a big difference.

In appreciating research, I don't want to give the impression that I assign some kind of superior value to "science," especially for psychoanalysis. Many of the claims for descriptive psychiatry or psychiatric neuroscience or genetics seem quite overblown and, often, economically and ideologically motivated.[1] I do think, however, that empirical and observational research is one of that array of scholarly pursuits that be useful to analysis—refining our thinking, expanding our sense of what is happening, showing that some of our assumptions really don't hold up in the face of certain facts. This should be done with caution, but it's worth the risks. The explosion of research about trauma and its effects on the brain, the body, and individual *and* cultural development over time offers a recent example.

Again, there is something of a contradiction here for me. I am also sympathetic to critics of the applications of observational studies to analysis who argue that analysis is a special way of knowing that occupies an entirely distinctive epistemological ground. The strongest argument for this position that I have seen is from Andre Green (2000) in a published dialogue with Daniel Stern. While I am persuaded by this as an ideal, I also think that giving up some of it is worth the costs, especially outside of analytic practice itself. There are at least two core tensions here that are fundamental to what I see as crucial to the analytic sensibility: between ideals and what helps, and between the value and limitations of what can be observed. I approach analytic theory-building—including clinical theory—as improved when different knowledge and methods are included, while I think that what makes analytic practice distinctive, as much as anything, is the immersion at the frontier of the ordinary and orderly structures of thinking and feeling that are usually taken for granted and frequently useful in a number of regular social activities and discourses. Psychoanalysis thrives in the fields of contradiction.

This captures something of how I think about these matters: I think of these different approaches as strategies, or perhaps as sets of convictions and priorities, reflecting our individual and institutional characters, temperaments, aesthetics and experiences. Each presents its own costs and benefits, rather than being right or wrong. Since analysis is such a subjective matter, all sorts of ideas might work for some people, including becoming very helpful to both analyst and patient in a particular analysis. But this doesn't mean that they are universal, even among analytic patients. This can lead to any particular concept being asked to explain more than it can—to do too much conceptual or clinical work.

Many of these difficulties seem inevitable. Analysis is difficult work, especially because it is so isolated. We rely on our judgment to a much greater extent than other professionals (although this is not always acknowledged). This leaves us more reliant on like-minded colleagues, organizations, and the wider field, which means that problematic group dynamics can lead to an array of problematic pressures: conformity, competition, psychic and social companionship and affection—including within the analytic hours, the satisfactions of feeling correct" based on affiliation rather than critical thinking, external and internal supervision that becomes punitive and constricting, rather than creative (a socio-psychic process that is often rather disturbingly—if ironically—called "the analytic police'), and more. Many of us overlook how much our choices of analytic persuasion and more important, quite specific ways of conducting therapy are determined by our personal histories and perhaps most of all, by our analysts.

One particular interdisciplinary synthesis has captured my attention for much of my career—that between an overall intersubjective orientation and the emerging developmentally-oriented approaches that I described above. This hasn't been my only analytic commitment or aesthetic, as I am quite enthusiastic about the traditional interest in fantasy, unconscious and irrational mental and physiological life, primary process, defense, etc, along with the overall Freudian project of encountering what you don't know, what you don't let yourself know, and what you can't know. All of this has emerged in the context of my personality, personal history, and the emerging political-economic, cultural, and ideological circumstances, mostly in the larger world, but also within psychoanalysis. A bit of that appears below, and a much fuller account of what I call the "robust developmental perspective" that I have called "Relational-Developmental Psychoanalysis," is detailed in my 2018 book, *Relationships in Development: Infancy, Intersubjectivity, and Attachment.*

A Personal Backstory

I will begin here with a brief account of the evolution of my own interest in developmental psychoanalysis, which should also give some sense of the more general themes that—I'd like to think—have animated my analytic career. Writing this, I can imagine any number of other emphases, which I hope will also come through.

I finished graduate school in 1981, completing an innovative doctoral training program that included a strong introduction to life sciences, neurophysiology, and neuroanatomy, along with psychoanalysis and other psychologies and child development, followed by three years of hospital-based clinical training. I was impressed with the immediacy of the physically-present body and the methods and findings of the medical and natural sciences, even as I was aware of their limitations. At the same time, I remained engaged with political and philosophical themes and communities that had enlivened my own late adolescent and post-college years. I was a 1960s New Leftist in college, and afterwards a labor organizer and community mental health clinician, working for what I still regard as very just purposes, along with sorting out personal-developmental concerns. I had an intellectual interest in both social-political theories and psychoanalysis, along with wanting to include something of a social service/social action agenda in my everyday work.

There seemed to be a gap between analysis and the social theories that were influencing me: Marxism, the Frankfurt School (e.g., Benjamin, 1968; Marcuse, 1955), Structural-Functional sociology (Parsons, 1964), and emerging critical social theories like Foucault's (1978). By and large, these theories concerned themselves with power inequities, but they did not propose a strong psychological theory. On the other hand, psychoanalysis privileged asocial, individual motivations and personality structures at the expense of the social world, even as it offered a method suitable to the radical project of unearthing the hidden dynamics by which people collaborate with forces that frustrate, deprive, and even oppress them. But if the primitive instincts were driving the system, then how could one remain optimistic about the prospect for the basic changes that seemed so needed? And, as so many of my comrades in the New Left movements were returning to the more mundane challenges of personal and professional life as the movements waned, how could we think about these more private domains in a way that carried some of our earlier zeal for social justice (e.g., Benjamin, 1968; Marcuse, 1955), Structural-Functional sociology (Parsons, 1964), and emerging critical social theories like Foucault's (1978). The "Relational Revolution" was taking hold within psychoanalysis during these same years. Even as I began formal psychoanalytic training at a more established psychoanalytic institute affiliated with the American Psychoanalytic Association, I found the Relational turn best adapted to provide the overarching framework for an integrative and flexible analytic synthesis.[2] Its broad and inclusive approach drew on the more socially-oriented tradition of Interpersonal analysis, as well as insurgent feminism, critical social theory, and the new developmental research; it was critical of the Freudian psychoanalytic roots without rejecting them. The iconoclastic and flexible Relational approach to clinical work suited me well, both temperamentally and intellectually, offering a considered and serious alternative to the more traditional analytic clinical method in which I had been trained. Although many of my Ego Psychologically-oriented teachers were impressively dedicated, intelligent, and thoughtful, and some could be quite flexible (especially in practice), there still was a more or less uncritical acceptance of the established theoretical and technical conventions about drives, neutrality, and the like. Similarly, there was a surprising lack of cosmopolitan interchange with the various currents in the analytic world of which I was becoming aware, including Self Psychology, Lacanian and other French innovations, and of course, the British Object Relations groups (by which I had been most impressed for some time and which have recaptured my attention quite a bit lately, as I have been working my way through many of Winnicott's papers). The hegemonic North American Ego Psychoanalysis seemed to err on the side of asserting and exporting itself, without much self-critique or dialogue with other perspectives, within and outside of the analytic field.

My own enthusiasm for a broader view was further fueled by continuing work with children and especially by my special interest in work with infants and their parents. I have generally maintained an ongoing child psychotherapy practice along with seeing adults, but I have also worked throughout my career in the development of the infant-parent psychotherapy model proposed by Selma Fraiberg (1975, 1980), adapting its psychoanalytic attention to the "Ghosts in the Nursery" to work at the homes of the psychosocially and economically compromised, largely African-American and Latina families (Seligman, 1994, 2014b). There, straightforward and immediate responsiveness seemed as compelling with babies and their parents as it always has with children in psychotherapy. Earnest contact with babies washes away blocks to spontaneity and authenticity: Infants can communicate and respond directly and efficiently without the subtleties of language and are usually receptive to even small changes in the emotional and physical environment. Many of our infant-parent cases involved episodes of child abuse and neglect, recent immigration, and addiction amidst poverty and other sociocultural difficulties. As I was encountering this in the homes of such troubled families and in the midst of varied social service, governmental, and medical systems, I found that the core analytic ideas could be compelling in these unconventional circumstances, especially when put forward in clear and accessible language—and action. I also saw how much of the reserve that analytic therapists take for granted was overapplied, culturally crude, and often quite beside the point.

In my clinical work, I find value in all of the analytic orientations with which I am most familiar, as they are called forth by each emerging analytic situation, usually without much awareness of my particular sources at any particular moment. These include the classical Freudian, the structural model with its emphasis on defenses and psychic conflict, the Kleinian emphasis on phantasy and deep internal object relations, the deeply imaginative and developmentally-oriented Middle Group, and the contemporary Relational view, with its affirmative approach to the analyst's engagement and participation.

Psychoanalysis has always seemed to point toward this kind of intensity, but is too often distanced from these potentials by its own organizational, procedural, and epistemological hierarchies and rigidities, as well as its insistence on the primacy of the verbal. Beyond this, though, the Freudian illumination of ambiguity, conflict, fantasy, and the irrational, elusive nature of what can be said and known about oneself is indispensable—not just for our field but for the culture as a whole, especially as it seems bent on abandoning interiority for the worlds of commodities and prepackaged communication. But these core virtues are not fulfilled by the mystifications and orthodoxies that have stood in the way of a pragmatic, contemporary approach that could encompass what is most evocative *and* accurate and, I would dare to say, points us toward the truest experience.

Building Bridges: Strengthening Traditional Insights with New Knowledge

With all of this in mind, I take a synthesizing approach that discards outmoded ideas when necessary while retaining the most worthwhile insights available from whatever source. I believe that the vitality of psychoanalysis will emerge most deeply from the polyphonic transactions between adult analysis, developmental research, child psychoanalysis, and clinical infant work that are presented here. This integrative project calls for a balance of reconciliation and confrontation between differing conceptions of the analytic project, some of which may be contradictory. Although there are many ideas and attitudes that should be discarded, some contradictions should be entertained rather than resolved. Inconsistency is at the heart of psychoanalysis.

This evokes intellectual, cultural, and institutional tensions of all sorts. As I have said, I do not agree with the critique of the application of infancy research as overemphasizing what can be directly observed so as to dilute the core psychoanalytic method of learning about the dynamic unconscious: Embracing contemporary developmental perspectives does not mean that those core analytic conceptions need to be abandoned. Instead, they can be fortified as they are rendered more flexibly, made clearer and more accessible to colleagues in other disciplines and to our patients. At the same time, contemporary analytic communities who have been perceptively critical of the established traditions, such as the Relationalists and other intersubjectivists, can take advantage of the Freudian vision when it is updated with new findings and understandings in mind. (See Cooper, 2014; Corbett, 2014; Seligman, 2014a, for example.) My own view is that the applications of early development research to psychoanalysis have deepened it, exposed flaws in established orthodoxies, called attention to the observable details and patterns of dyadic interaction in psychotherapeutic process, and all in all, brought lived experience—especially of emotions and the actual body—into the analytic field. They offer support for the basic analytic strategy of making thoughtful, reflective contact with people in their distress, and open up space for us to think about the range of emotional and interpersonal stresses that we face every day.

Effective practical applications emerge, too: Programs to encourage parents to read to babies can be anchored in brain science; theories of internal representation and defense analysis support treatment of abused children and their parents; juvenile courts can be linked to relationship-based therapy programs, which are in turn illuminated by understandings about primitive countertransferences and the associated fantasies; fMRI-supported research about very rapid implicit emotional communication can help analysts in the grip of intense emotion with their analysands.

Psychoanalysis is a profound and generative enterprise, but we have been overconfident for too long. Twenty-first century theory, like other twenty-first century efforts, calls for a hybrid sensibility. Analysts have sometimes been too eager to tell others what we know, rather than letting ourselves be influenced by what they understand. If we can do a better job of importing, we can think more clearly and work more effectively.

Notes

1 Here is what NIMH Director Insel (2013) wrote about DSM-V when he announced that studies based on it would no longer be funded by NIMH, just after its release by the American Psychiatric Association:

> ... we cannot succeed if we use DSM categories as the "gold standard." The diagnostic system has to be based on the emerging research data, not on the current symptom-based categories .... We need to begin collecting the genetic, imaging, physiologic, and cognitive data to see how all the data – not just the symptoms – cluster and how these clusters relate to treatment response.

2 I sometimes use the term *Relational* to refer to the specific psychoanalytic movement, and at other times, to a more general perspective that stresses the centrality of relationships in development and personality. Although these often overlap, I've tried to capitalize the *R* for the first connotation, and use the lower case for the second.

References

Benjamin, W. (1968). *Illuminations: Essays and reflections*. New York, NY: Schocken Books.
Cooper, S. H. (2014). The things we carry: Finding/creating the object and the analyst's self-reflecting participation. *Psychoanalytic Dialogues, 25*, 615–620.
Corbett, K. (2014). The analyst's private space: Spontaneity, ritual, psychotherapeutic action, and self-care. *Psychoanalytic Dialogues, 25*, 637–647.
Foucault, M. (1978). *The history of sexuality, vol. 1: An introduction*. New York, NY: Vintage.

Fraiberg, S., Adelson, E., Shapiro, V. (1975). Ghosts in the nursery: A psychoanalytic approach to the problem of impaired infant-mother relationships. *Journal of American Academy of Child Psychiatry*, 14, 3:387–422.

Fraiberg, S. (Ed.). (1980). *Clinical studies in infant mental health: The first year of life*. New York: Basic Books.

Green, A. (2000). What kind of research for psychoanalysis? In: Sandler, J., Sandler, A-M., and Davies, R. (Eds.) *Clinical and observational psychoanalytic research: Roots of a controversy*. London & New York: Karnac Books.

Insel, T. (2013). Transforming diagnosis. https://www.nimh.nih.gov/about/directors/thomas-insel/blog/2013/transforming-diagnosis.shtml

Marcuse, H. (1955). *Eros and civilization*. New York, NY: Vintage.

Parsons, T. (1964). *Social structure and personality*. New York, NY: Free Press.

Seligman, S. (1994). Applying psychoanalysis in an unconventional context: Adapting "infant-parent psychotherapy" to a changing population. *Psychoanalytic Study of the Child*, 49:481–500.

Seligman, S. (2014). Paying attention and feeling puzzled: The analytic mindset as an agent of therapeutic change. *Psychoanalytic Dialogues*, 24:6,648–662.

Seligman, S. (2018a). *Relationships in development: Infancy, intersubjectivity, and attachment*. London and New York: Routledge.

Chapter 23

Credo: In Search of Transformation

Melanie Suchet

I was born 30 miles from the Cradle of Humankind, the paleoanthropological site near Johannesburg, where one of the earliest human fossils dating back 2.3 million years was found. I grew up living close to the earth, my toes digging in, sensing the pulses, the rhythms, and the connection to a stirring that lay beneath. I loved to watch how the sun moved across the sky and the sudden eruption of a storm without any warning. South Africa was a country of contrasts, a place of indescribable beauty beset by violence and hatred.

As a young girl one of my favorite fantasy games was to imagine being an explorer traveling down the Amazon in a small dugout, with all the travails and hardships I would have to encounter in what I believed was the wildest and most remote part of the world. Part of it was my tomboyishness, a refusal to be limited by my gender, but mostly it reflected my desire to traverse difficult terrain. I seemed to always be imagining the difficulties as well as the exhilaration and challenges of the life of one who steps outside the conventional path.

I did not come to the profession of psychology in any simple linear way. It was as if the work chose me. I was at the time, in my late teens, venturing into the exciting world of genetics. I imagined myself as a scientist, a lover of logic, and of rational, linear thinking. However, I started to pursue some undergraduate psychology classes, and serendipitously volunteered at a halfway house for schizophrenics, in the bustling neighborhood of Hillbrow, located in the midst of Johannesburg. I was assigned a patient with whom we were told to meet weekly for thirty minutes. We were promised supervision, which never materialized. There was something profound in this engagement with my patient, Marie, that I had not expected, nor could I fully understand. I was drawn in, and rather quickly, within the first few sessions. Sometimes she refused the visit. The next week she would berate me for having been gone for so long. The contradictions, the inconsistencies, the confused talk, and the incredible power of the intimacy and the vulnerability, both hers and mine, led me to pursue psychology further. Reflecting back, I think I had an experience of aliveness that I had not known. When she allowed herself to be revealed to me there was a sense of someone bearing their soul, and with that intensity, an awareness of how one could come closer to the truth of the self. I must have unconsciously sought that for myself too.

My initial training as a clinical psychologist, at the University of the Witwatersrand in South Africa, under the directorship of Gillian Straker, was an incredibly rich, diverse and dynamic experience. A carefully chosen group of 8, we were racially mixed, which living under Apartheid was the first time I was permitted to interact so intimately with Africans who were my equals. We had classes from 8 am until 5 pm, heavily influenced by the work at Tavistock. I remember reading Melanie Klein for the first time, and having to re-read her over and over, fascinated and perplexed simultaneously, as I worked to grasp the depth of her elaboration of psychic processes. Our training also included a weekly foray for three of us into the back wards of a black-only mental hospital. Our real mission was to document any torture or inhumane treatment blacks were receiving.

The theory of psychopathology had a political analysis deeply embedded in it. How unimaginable it would have been to think of them as separate. Depression in an African patient could never be seen simply as arising from within, but so closely linked to the repressive forces of Apartheid. Political consciousness raising was intertwined with psychological work, and many times we learned as much from our patients as they learned from us. It was clear to us all that race permeated every aspect of our lives. It informed who we were, not only by the edicts of the state, but by how the state's racism entered our beings. We had grown up with what Fahkry Davids calls an internal racist organization (Davids, 2011). Kleinian theory resonated, not only for its articulation of internal psychic processes, but for the understanding of the dynamics of a repressive regime.

It was in my early teens that my idealistic vision of my left-wing liberal Jewish family was ruptured by the dawning awareness that in having black servants, I was implicated in their suffering. Their struggles, their dispossession, and the inequities of their lives were a direct result of my life and that of all the lives of the whites I knew. Despite being against Apartheid, despite the rhetoric and our beliefs as Jews who did not want to be oppressors, we were implicated in a system we abhorred. Straker has referred to this as the melancholia of the beneficiary.

Apartheid impacted my psyche in more ways than I am even aware of, even now, some 35 years after leaving South Africa. There is no doubt that my wish to enter a profession in which ruptures can be healed, both of the internal and external varieties, was partly informed by the growing awareness of how I had harmed my beloved nannies, both directly and indirectly. The decision to leave South Africa and my family was guided as much by my wish to not remain complicit in a dehumanizing system as a wish to transform myself.

One of the surprising aspects of immigration to the United States was not the liberation from fear that emerges when moving from tyranny to freedom, I had expected that, but the inner liberation that arose when suddenly I had access to parts of myself I had not known were hidden. Political repression creates a parallel process psychologically. J.M. Coetzee, the South African author, wrote of something similar in his Jerusalem prize acceptance speech given in 1987.

> *"The deformed and stunted relations between human beings that were created under colonialism and exacerbated under what is loosely called Apartheid have their symbolic representation in a deformed and stunted inner life."*

My inner life, the part of me I valued the most, unbeknownst to me, was indeed stunted. There are no easy solutions in a corrupt society. Yet I was surprised at how much I had closed off, how many inner negotiations I had made unconsciously to justify living in South Africa. Immigration felt like a release. I wanted to venture deeper into psychic terrain. I knew that psychoanalysis was part of that journey.

My pursuit of analytic training, and my choice of the NYU Postdoctoral program, was informed by the cutting-edge gender work of the "Gang of Four" as they were referred to: Jessica Benjamin, Muriel Dimen, Virginia Goldner, and Adrienne Harris, all of whom were mentors to me at different times. Benjamin's book, *Bonds of Love* (1988), had a profound impact on me, integrating psychoanalysis with feminism and social theory. I came to understand the recapitulation of the master-slave dynamic, the appeal of domination and submission, and the deep search for recognition. It was also a study on power, something neglected in traditional theories, but one that has always seemed crucial to me.

Adrienne Harris' work, especially her book *Gender as Soft Assembly* (2009), spoke to my quest to explore the complexity of gender development, how gender is a magnet, a braiding together of intrapsychic life with the materiality of the body in the context of historical and social forces. My own explorations in my early tomboy and later queer identities has led me to a fascination with gender: the ways it binds us and frees us simultaneously. Venturing into transgender subjectivities was initially unnerving in the late 1990s. It forced me into territory that was unfamiliar and anxiety provoking. Psychoanalytic canon at the time did not support altering the body to match the sense of gender identity. Yet I came to an awareness, through my work with my patient that sometimes it is the container, the body, that must be changed, and what is contained will shift with it. The body, in its inseparability from the psyche, has its own power to transform: a revolutionary concept at that time. In my more recent work with gender variance I have come to understand how the diversity of gender possibilities allow for different expressions of self, gendered translations of who one is, and with it different ways of living as an embodied person. Gender is a way of becoming intelligible to the self, a way to create psychic expansion and fantasy expressions that transcend the material body. As I write this, I am aware of how much I seek ways to expand the self, not simply in the sense of Winnicott's (1960) true self, but in the many possibilities that exist for ways of being, and in awe of the avenues that allow for our many self states to be known.

Remnants of my childhood desire to enter wild and foreboding territories seems to still guide me. I am often drawn to what is often on the margins of traditional psychoanalysis. My exploration of race has been one of those journeys. I wanted to understand whiteness from the inside: its brittleness, its defensive posture, its narcissistic structure. In my paper "Unraveling Whiteness" (2007), I attempted to come to inhabit a different internal space, not one beset with guilt and shame, which we know only too well leads to dissociation and immobility. I wanted to find another way through. I came to understand the need to surrender to an acceptance of all that I did not want to own, to be, or to inhabit. If I could truly accept that I was the colonizer and the colonized, the oppressor and the oppressed, the racist and the antiracist, then I might find a less defensive space within which to live. Paradoxically, it was in creating this more internally receptive space, an unraveling of whiteness, that I was allowed to live more deeply in race. With this space of acceptance, I found I was able to move forward, to shift my focus to the other, to feel their pain and my implication in their suffering. My writing and my work are a form of self-to-self negotiation (Finkelstein, 2019), a deep interrogation of the self that holds the analyst accountable and responsible in the face of the Other. It is a search for ethical subjectivity.

My philosophy about transformation, about the essence of psychoanalytic change has shifted over the decades. It remains for me a journey of coming closer to the truth of self, of the self in relation to the other, the self in the other and the other in me. It is a weaving together of selves in the ways we create together new versions and visions of self as we inhabit each other. It is as if the transformation occurs in the space within us as well as in the space between us, in the co-created third. It is how you come to live inside me, a form of internalization of the other that is not a colonization or appropriation, but an embracing the other within. It involves the capacity to see that which has not yet come to fruition; a potential, a spark, and slowly allow for those sparks or newer self states to take shape and be enlivened.

Recently, at the Met Breuer, Oliver Beer created the Vessel Orchestra. He carefully chose 32 objects from the Met's vast collection for their acoustic quality. What he meant was that each vessel has its own hidden sound within, a note on which it resonates. He believes that every object carries its own "history of survival," its own individual narrative, which can be heard as a note, and translated into an orchestra.

Psychoanalysis is, for me, in part, the art of finding the hidden sound, a way of tuning into the essence, a way of capturing the ineffable, inexplicable quality of our humanness. Can I listen to the sounds of the bodies that carry their history of sorrows? How do I enter their space, and allow them to enter me? I work to find a way to rest in silence, not silence as a space without words, but silence as an evocative space of potential, a vibrating silence, in which and from which sound can emerge. It is a way of feeling resonances, of attunement, of sensing one's way through silence into a shape or sound that might come closer to capturing who we are.

I am drawn more and more, to mystical and contemplative traditions. It is from the mystics that I find a way to enter a state of sustained clarity, a wordless, thoughtless clarity. It is, paradoxically, in places of unknowing that I may come to know, a different kind of knowing, an enriched awareness, a knowing from the inside, an intuitive form of being. It feels like an immersion into the experiential, abandoning, even for a few minutes, the conceptual pull to understand, surrendering oneself to a communal consciousness.

To be still, open and vulnerable in the presence of the other, allows for an intimacy of presencing, an intimacy of coming to know beyond language. We are entering each other, joining in a vibrational field that might be called a third, a bi-personal field, a field of resonances, without words, or more aptly in a space beyond words. To be able to remain in a state of unknowing, a state of darkness, may grace us with the emergence of a different state of consciousness, a non-conceptual state of being, and with that an intuitive contemplative way of engaging. It is often elusive and mysterious, yet profoundly generative.

In some ways I have ventured far from my origins as a scientist, contained by numbers and the safety of logic to the relation between self and other, the alluring spaces of mystical contemplation. Yet I am still an explorer, a seeker and questioner, intrigued and drawn to the mysterious, my body is still connected to the soul of the earth, to the humanness that unites us all. This work is ultimately an attempt to embrace the unknown and the unknowability of each of us. I am driven to deeper ways of engaging and creating spaces for transformation, as I, venturing through new terrain, am moved and touched and open to change. Psychoanalysis remains one of the most powerful tools for liberating oneself from the constraints of the past, as we find ways to expand the self. We do this in and through the other, transforming what can be. I join my patients in my wish to enter realms of experience that challenge and simultaneously expand us immersed as we are in a socio-political world that informs us even as we attempt to resist its interpellation.

References

Benjamin, J. (1988). *Bonds of love*. New York: Random Books.
Davids, M. F. (2011). *Internal racism: A psychoanalytic approach to race and difference*. London: Red Globe Press.
Finkelstein, D. (2019). Personal communication.
Harris, A. (2009). *Gender as soft assembly*. New York: Taylor and Francis Group.
Suchet, M. (2007). Unraveling whiteness. *Psychoanalytic Dialogues, 17*(6), 867–886.
Winnicott, D. W. (1960). Ego distortion in terms of true and false self. In *The maturational process and the facilitating environment: Studies in the theory of emotional development*(pp. 140–157). New York: International Universities Press, Inc.

Section V

2000s

Chapter 24

On Truthlessness—Or, All in the Game

Stephen Hartman

I

Barack Obama and I share a hero and, in that hero's words if not his violent deeds, a credo. Omar Little—queer drug dealer, vigilante, and poet—was a much-beloved character on the HBO series *The Wire* (2006–2012). Played by Michael K. Williams and known to film and television critics as *Robin Hood*, Omar speaks the truth in aphorisms that are plain but not simple: "a man gotta have a code."[1] A psychoanalyst gotta have one too.

Omar doesn't see the world in black and white, good and evil, right and wrong. He operates according to a code of ethics that plumbs the chasm between kill and be killed. On the ruthless streets of Baltimore, survival is of the fittest, and so Omar's code is straight up if not round about: *don't harm anyone who isn't a player "in the game."* Omar steals and kills as to survive among thugs one must. But he only targets drug lords, their enablers, and their crew. Omar looks out for family and community: loyal, churchgoing, and, above all else, truthful. He takes account of the game and holds the game to account. He dons critique as armor and style as he trims the fatty untruth from what one must abide in order to keep the game playing as truthfully as it might.

Truth is, of course, contingent, perspectival, and raced. As Omar quips to a shifty white lawyer who represents his nemesis: "I got the shotgun, you got the briefcase. It's all in the game though, right?" Integrity rarely mirrors social rank; one must be reminded that they are a player from time to time. Omar's boys on the street and psychoanalysts sitting coach-side have at least this in common: the game can get the better of us. Lawyers, cops, drug dealers, psychoanalysts, most of us at some point or another sell who we are to maintain our position and stay in the game. We make compromises for convenience, rank or to keep the boat afloat. That's when the shooting begins. Patients see right through it. But their shout-out to the arrogance of power is easily neutralized as "transference." With colleagues, to justify position or rank, who hasn't at some point taken potshots at an adversary? Or, overlooked an inconvenient truth about the whiteness of our profession?

DOI: 10.4324/9781003206248-24

Omar chastens his minions lest they sell their virtue on the take: "Man, money ain't got no owners, only spenders."

2

Some truths take shape in the place where we are enjoined to make ourselves. Those truths become the scaffolding of a training analysis. They inform our "countertransference" as we strive to hear others' truths. They help us to query our foibles and focus on the task at hand. Play it neutral or play it disclosed, we become gamers in the service of relationality: technique is our ante and, after Omar, we do best to mind our opening bid.

In the eighth-grade woodshop, to simulate rustbelt economics in my working-class suburb of Cleveland, the sons of Italian and Polish immigrants were assigned the role of worker; white boys were made shop stewards and foremen; the "Orientals" and Jewish kids like me were assigned managerial tasks. There were no black or brown kids. Our teacher (of proletarian stock) encouraged roughhousing, in other words, class warfare. He looked the other way as spit flew and eyes blackened. This role-play was staged to contest the fixity of caste just as it affirmed caste and rendered hierarchy true (Wilkerson, 2020).

I escaped to the library to do "market research." The humiliation vested in jumping ship was infinitely preferable to being pummeled in the classroom, and so I learned about cultural capital and how to secure it. Somehow, though, I keep returning to the scene of the crime. I'm vulnerable to the interpellations of fraudulence that come with playing the game of scholar ruthlessly. I see jockeying for position all around me now that I'm once again perched at the top of the heap. These power dynamics are vulgar but necessary to intersubjective commerce and an intersectional point of view. And so play these games one do so as to cultivate intersubjectivity one might. But, not without scars that hide quietly under the couch during an attenuated game of hide and seek.

3

A person who rises to power beyond their station gotta have a code when rank is pulled. For me, entering my third decade as a psychoanalyst, clinician, teacher, and journal editor, I appreciate how risky this gambit is. A psychoanalyst gotta have a code, and for those of us who profit in the game of unformulated experience, that code demands truthfulness even as we become masters of dodging unconscious challenges to our legitimacy. Mutual but asymmetrical, we parry aggression as if by dint of a training analysis equipped to suss out truths from enactments that scramble the wounds of time. The ruthless quest for legitimacy is assigned to the patient—not the analyst whose investiture commands respect. We need to own that "the game" organizes the basic rules. The guild sculpts training requirements to standardize practice and protect the patient. In truth, these procedures secure brand and hierarchy to legitimize and rank practitioners of our wayward "vocation." What are the consequences of this imbroglio in "treatment" and for our profession's standing in the broader community?

Early in my career, I wrote about a newspaper photograph of a Palestinian teenager who surrendered at an Israeli border station. He was a would-be suicide bomber now and forever a terrified child. The essay was a book review of an edited volume that championed phenomenology and trashed postmodernism. The senior psychoanalysts who recruited me (in the role of ambitious queer postmodernist) encouraged me to spare no punches in my review. The stakes were tantalizing. I forgot the lessons learned in the eighth grade. I put on my boxing gloves. I used the photograph to query the political investiture of embodiment, and I believed every word I wrote. Naively, I slammed the authors for misrepresenting postmodern theory and ignoring the social in their phenomenological construction of the body. "Naïve" because I believed I would be met as an honest colleague with a challenging perspective—not as a boxer making a first appearance in the ring. In their published reply, one author suggested I were psychotic if not a suicide bomber who couldn't help but attack myself. It was a devastating if not a true interpellation of my class injury. I collapsed inward and didn't write for a year. I had yet to understand Omar's dictum spoken to players whose Achilles heel is upward mobility: "You come at the king, you best not miss."

4

A recent video, bound for festival release at South by Southwest but debuted as an Op-Doc in *The New York Times Online*,[2] depicts Freud and Dora side by side, then and now, time collapsed, his story and hers each overwriting the other's. It's a brilliant decoupage of live video, historical footage, and editorial montage. The filmmaker, Kate Novak, examines Freud's "truthfulness" through the lens of his female subject Dora. What is most striking about this short film is how *truthlessness* and ruthlessness are counterpoised allowing both the psychoanalyst and the filmmaker to find a *modus operandi* in hysteria. The upshot is (as we know): Freud played fast and loose with truth because a fungible truth served him well in a game that he was determined to master.

Freud was, after all, a man with a plan. However willing he was to prevaricate, hedge, revise, and resubmit his ideas for public consumption, public-facing psychoanalysis was intended to remain stalwart and true. Believers were scientists. Exiles were collateral damage(d). History more or less forgives Freud this trespass (and manages to dispense with the hyperbolic patriarchy that was Ego Psychology with a sigh) because the unconscious ranks among the great "discoveries" of modernity. We take

Freud's scatterplot of fickle alliances and theoretical contradictions to be the ruse of a shrewd founder who launched a discourse imprecise enough for circular reference back to Freud to map the expansiveness of a paradigm that, in Bion's reckoning, functions optimally when it sculpts truth from process rather than content. As Bion explains in his own solipsistic way: "the theory of functions makes it easier to match the realization with the deductive system that it represents" (Bion, 1962, p. 2). This structural functionalist, circular logic grounds truth in the same kind of self-reinforcing Borromean knot that prompted full-frontal attacks on Freud's metapsychology by critics who were hell-bent on proving that Freud's data were knackered in the first place (Crews, 2017; Grunbaum, 1984). Such is the game of History of Science.

Flash forward and, to a contemporary ear, Bion's circular epistemophilia exerts coloniality behind negative capability's elegant disguise (Hartman, 2018). Scholars who study the coloniality of knowledge (Quijano, 2007) examine how knowledge is systematized into epistemological frames that center truth in the very same social system that authorizes and administers truth. Like it or not, psychoanalytic approaches that champion a capacity of not-knowing end up centering knowledge in the person of an analyst who truthlessly knows. Likewise, the analyst who mystifies the position of "the subject who knows" so that the patient's presumed investment in the analyst's knowing may be demystified in the due course of treatment similarly centers truthlessness in the privileged position of the (typically white) analyst. Were Omar here, he might wryly opine: "all in the game, yo, all in the game."

Alas, I spare no punches once again and anticipate a black eye: a risk I bear as a player who abides by Omar's rules. Fact is, we live in a forest of symbols (Turner, 1967) and branding machines (Guralnik & Simeon, 2010). Ideology is a "lived relation ... in the constitution of a misrecognized subjectivity" (Goldberg & Sekoff, 1980, p. 41). Contra Laplanche's wish to contract the social as the broker of meaning rather than its impetus (Laplanche, 2011), the *socius* is a caste system (Wilkerson, 2020) that always already floods the subject's first enigmatic encounter with *beta elements*. The first other whose unconscious presses upon the neonate and launches the infant's prospective unconscious is just as likely a worker bee (a nurse, a physician, a lab tech, a nanny) as a parental King, Queen or Drone (Hartman, 2007). Wish as one might for psychoanalysis to offer "an irreducible realm of psychical representation, with its own specific form of articulation, interacting dialectically with other determinate infrastructures in the social formation" (Goldberg & Sekoff, 1980, p. 42), one can only gain a foothold in such a paradigm by imparting truthfulness truthlessly to a pre-representational realm without political qualities. Perhaps this strategy helps map the "symbolic floor," but it eludes the preexisting condition of race, gender, and ability politics. (Most nurses, nannies and lab techs are women and/or people of color. Fortunately, re: physicians, this is increasingly also the case. But, oddly, the enigmatic Other, like the psychoanalytic baby, is persistently White).

5

Truth be told, *truthlessness* in the guise of unrepresented experience has been colonized by psychoanalysis as a discipline to garner what ruthlessness is theorized to muster in infancy and, more recently, in political protest (Swartz, 2018): survival, recognition, and the power to stake a claim for ones' strategic version of the truth. I'm reminded of Mannie Ghent's favorite aphorism: "no one has a lien on truth" as I write, and yet I am overwhelmed by the degree to which psychoanalysts continue to cling to truthlessness in principle while they don the garb of truthfulness because it girds their functional expertise. Perhaps they don't catch Omar's sarcasm when he opines: "the game is out there, and its play or be played."

There are many historical examples of this ruse. Here is an example with contemporary relevance. In the recent debate about Rapid Onset Gender Dysphoria, psychoanalysts have taken positions on either side of the question, is transgender "real" or a fad? Are young people who suddenly declare the intention to re-establish themselves in a gender position different from the one they were assigned at birth truly transgender? (see Farley and Kennedy (2020) for review). This question comes to the analyst with all the more urgency because, historically, mental health providers have been required to sign affidavits affirming the patient's diagnosis of gender dysphoria before the patient was allowed to undergo "gender reassignment"[3] surgery (Latham, 2016; Saketopoulou, 2014).

No surprise, this debate on the truth of gender circles back to Freud's truthlessness gambit. Classical analysts were able to script a phantasmagorical Eden in the terrain of Freud's "primary bisexuality" with membership reserved for neurotic analysands whose forays in *poly* were tethered to "fantasy" rather than fact. By prioritizing the analysand's capacity for truthlessness over their attunement with a *felt sense of the body* (Salamon, 2010), sexuality retained its privileged perch atop psychic structure ensuring that gender variance emerges in a classical treatment as "transference" rather than trans. Over the years, the use of primary bisexuality to demarcate perversion lost credibility (see Layton (2011) for review). Still, the notion that an analyst can distinguish between the fact and fantasy of gender begets the notion that the analyst can distinguish between patients who are using gender to defer "the real work" on deeper structural issues from others who truly manifest gender dysphoria (Lemma, 2018). Such a claim tells us more about the analyst's omnipotent faith in the game of psychoanalysis than it does the patient's gender.

The arrogance of this claim finds its lineage in Freud's own flip-flopping about the status of pathology in "the perversions." Suddenly back to the shaky ground on which psychoanalysis launched, we can rest assured in our current forensic position. Truthlessness is justified by its purported clinical usefulness post hoc by the analyst who saves (or failed to save as the case may be) *his* patient from unnecessary adventures in body modification or "neosexualities."

Yikes! I definitely have my boxing gloves on. Ought I take the high road? I'm not entirely sure what that would be other than a clear path to greater inclusivity and equity in our ranks—and slow to prompt meaningful change that will surely be without some kind of shakedown (Hartman, 2020). Alas, should I play this one rogue and stand tall with Omar? Assume the role of editor-king and let them come at me? (I hate that enactment.) To escape this dilemma, perhaps I opt Machiavellian? Make friends. Build alliances. Maintain continuity. Keep the status quo pro quid ... That would require I work with a notion of truth that is *the truth that we would prefer truth to be*. After Omar, truthlessness can't be a ruse that allows gamers go on playing as we have always played: worked as we have always worked, and esteemed value as value has (fortunately) esteemed us. Is it possible to play both games: to champion a psychoanalysis that is both post-truth and accountable to truth at the same time? It's a paradox worthy of Ghent (1992). We will never be rid of the Dora Freud made and the Dora we were each willing to become in order to practice our vocation with Doras; and we owe Dora, but not ourselves, an apology because, truth be told, we have consented to consort with truthlessness.

6

The analyst's reparation to "the patient" is a step beyond what most psychoanalysts might consider necessary to the survival of psychoanalysis. Khan's (1989, p. 17) insight that: "the analyst has to make the reparation so that differentiated personalization can begin to operate" would have the analyst begin a process that the idolizing patient cannot tolerate. Ostensibly, the analyst's reparation for their own idolization of the profession (Hartman, 2013) allows the watchful patient, mimicking the analyst's high and mighty, to summon the moxie to knock the analyst off his high horse (thus becoming "idealizing" and "devaluing" rather than simplemindedly idolizing and "perverse").

Strategic reparation as clinical strategy cannot, however, account for a sordid legacy, nor take account of the survival rate of Rotten Apples (Dimen, 2016) in a guild that tolerated then purged Masud Khan for being, himself, a dubious exemplar of *Us*. It is quite difficult for psychoanalysis to wrangle with the painful fact that our bedrock is pretty crumbly. For reparation to be collectively meaningful, I'm afraid there may yet need to be a mudslide.

COVID-19 demonstrated that the economics of candidacy (and the Ponzi scheme that approves "training analysts") is self-selecting and elitist yet more than a bit fungible when push comes to shove. Rules that govern the royal road to the unconscious were suddenly rewritten when technology turned out to be destiny. Factor in the upsurge of race politics that is changing the game and frame after the murder of George Floyd, and a recruitment scramble ensues as if a demographic solution could foster diversity, equity, and inclusion. Any senior colleague of color who should have been on journal advisory boards a generation ago is suddenly invited to be on six. I owe my late mentor Muriel Dimen (and my gracious colleagues of color who are willing to accept such belated appointments) at least this: some structural intervention that features truthfulness and destruction rather than vetting truthlessness as collateral in a conservative transition to repair. We were not unaware of how white psychoanalysis was; we just didn't want to worry about it. Dismantling privilege is not so easy to achieve in a field where the analyst (even if only provisionally) commands *The Real* as holder of the frame. As my colleague, Francisco Gonzalez often says (in a nod to Fanon), "it's gonna have to get messy."

Massive overhaul of how we imagine ourselves is not easy to achieve. As Ta Nehisi Coates (2018) explained in his case for reparation, Americans will have to accept that our founders were slaveholders and our most cherished myths (be they Federal or Oedipal) are just not true. Psychoanalysis is neither about knowing or knowing that one does not know (which is more or less the same thing). It is a domain name that hyperlinks strange bedfellows to clunky passages and ruthless beginnings. Clearly, the fear of things falling apart gets in the way when one hears about efforts to "integrate" diverse voices into our practices and cannon. Fear of breakdown prevents the dismantling of shibboleths that quietly ensconce a truthless status quo.

Over 100 years ago, Weber (2012) wrote that "politics is the slow boring of hard boards." Psychoanalysis, one might say, is the slow boring of hard truths. But, "Omar don't scare." Psychoanalysis has to confront its truthless scaffolding in some truly meaningful way to impact how and when we practice, who practices where and whether, and whom we serve. I am not alone in calling for this kind of structural change and like my colleagues who do (See Gonzalez, 2019; Knoblauch, 2020; Leavitt, 2018; Merson, 2020; Sheehi, 2020) I cannot cart this solution before the horse that will draw it. I can only welcome it and offer a commitment to personal change that is as true to my profession as I can understand such a claim to be.

Notes

1 All quotes for Omar Little can be found at https://www.goliath.com/tv/the-10-greatest-lines-from-omar-in-the-wire/

2 https://www.nytimes.com/video/opinion/100000007026836/hysterical-girl.html?action=click&module=Opinion&pgtype=Homepage
3 A term that comes with its own legacy of coloniality, "gender reassignment," implies the gender binary that many trans theorists wish to subvert leading to the preferred use of the phrase "gender affirmation surgery."

References

Bion, W. (1962). *Learning from experience*. London: Tavistock.
Crews, F. (2017). *Freud: The making of an illusion*. Berkeley: University of California Press.
Dimen, M. (2016). Rotten apples and ambivalence: Sexual boundary violations through a psychocultural lens. *Journal of the American Psychoanalytic Association*, *64*, 361–373.
Farley, L., & Kennedy, R. M. (2020). Transgender embodiment as an appeal to thought: A psychoanalytic critique of "rapid onset gender dysphoria". *Studies in Gender and Sexuality*, *21*, 155–172.
Ghent, E. (1992). Paradox and process. *Psychoanalytic Dialogues*, *2*, 135–160.
Goldberg, P., & Sekoff, J. (1980). Ideology and the question of the subject. *Canadian Journal of Political and Social Theory*, *4*, 23–43.
Gonzalez, F. (2019). Necessary disruptions: A discussion of Daniel Butler's "racialized bodies and the violence of the setting". *Studies in Gender and Sexuality*, *20*(3), 159–164.
Grunbaum, A. (1984). *The foundations of psychoanalysis*. Berkeley: University of California Press.
Guralnik, O., & Simeon, D. (2010). Depersonalization: Standing in the spaces between recognition and interpellation. *Psychoanalytic Dialogues*, *20*, 400–416.
Hartman, S. (2007). Class unconscious: From dialectical materialism to relational material. In M. Suchet, A. Harris, & L. Aron (Eds.), *Relational psychoanalysis volume 3, new voices* (pp. 209–226). Mahwah, NJ: The Analytic Press.
Hartman, S. (2013). On making reparation to the analyst's idolized countertransference: Commentary on paper by Dana Amir. *Psychoanalytic Dialogues*, *23*, 408–417.
Hartman, S. (2018). When we frame. In I. Tylim & A. Harris (Eds.), *Reconsidering the movable frame in psychoanalysis* (pp. 141–163). New York: Routledge.
Hartman, S. (2020). Binded by the white: On Steven Knoblauch's Fanon's vision of embodied racism for psychoanalytic theory and practice. *Psychoanalytic Dialogues*, *30*, 317–324.
Khan, M. M. (1989). *Alienation in perversions*. London, UK: Karnac Books.
Knoblauch, S. H. (2011). Contextualizing attunement within the polyrhythmic weave: The psychoanalytic samba. *Psychoanalytic Dialogues*, *21*(4), 414–427.
Laplanche, J. (2011). *Freud and the sexual: Essays 2000–2006*. Ed.J. Fletcher. New York, NY: International Psychoanalytic Books, pp. 159–180.
Latham, J. R. (2016). Making and treating trans problems: The ontological politics of clinical practices. *Studies in Gender and Sexuality*, *18*, 40–61.
Layton, L. (2011). On the irreconcilable in psychic life: The role of culture in the drive to become both sexes. *Psychoanalytic Quarterly*, *80*, 461–474.
Leavitt, J. (2019). Plea for a measure of un-belonging. Paper presented at the winter

meeting of the American Psychoanalytic Association on the panel, "The analyst's anxiety in a skeptical culture: Do we still believe in what we do?" New York, NY, February 9.

Lemma, A. (2018). Transitory identities: Some psychoanalytic reflections on transgender identities. *International Journal of Psychoanalysis*, 99, 1089–1106.

Merson, M. (2021). The Whiteness taboo: Interrogating whiteness in psychoanalysis. *Psychoanalytic Dialogues*, in press.

Quijano, A. (2007). Coloniality and modernity/rationality. *Cultural Studies*, 21, 168–178.

Saketopoulou, A. (2014). Mourning the body as bedrock: Treating transsexual patients analytically. *Journal of the American Psychoanalytic Association*, 62, 773–806.

Salamon, G. (2010). *Assuming a body*. New York: Columbia University Press.

Sheehi, L. (2020). Talking back: Introduction to the special edition: Black, indigenous, women of color talk back: Decentering normative psychoanalysis. *Studies in Gender and Sexuality*, 21, 73–76.

Swartz, S. (2018). *Ruthless Winnicott*. Karnac.

Turner, V. (1967). *The forest of symbols*. New York: Cornell University Press.

Weber, M. (2012/1919). Politics as a vocation. In H. H. Gerth & C. W. Mills (Eds.), *From Max Weber: Essays in sociology*. New York: Routledge.

Wilkerson, I. (2020). *Caste: The origins of our discontents*. New York: Random House.

Chapter 25

My Psychoanalytic Search for Freedom: Do we need it twice?[1]

Ilana Laor

To begin his journey into the analytic field, to be able to meet his patient, the analyst, then, needs to be close to himself. The clinical situation creates an intriguing and unique experience, fashioned by the analyst and the patient: the inner world of the analyst has its impact on the field, while the field also has an impact on the analyst's inner world. Thus, closeness to one's self is a good starting point for the psychotherapeutic endeavor. This chapter will turn to several clinical vignettes to demonstrate this particular and unique experience.

When I was an intern, I had a very strict supervisor. Each meeting was the same. I read the verbatims of the meetings, she would ask me questions, and I would answer. It seemed to me as though I could never get her approval; she was never satisfied. I felt like I was in a never-ending examination, and that made me deeply angry. Yet, she never showed any interest in what I was going through; and I was left exasperated. When I tried to communicate my feelings, she disregarded my experience as anxiety. I felt that she blamed me for my anxiety, so in my guilt I kept silent. Although I could not articulate, even to myself, my wish for more mutual relations, I thought that if only my supervisor had asked me to share my experience of our interaction with her, we could have had very fruitful conversations and reach a new level of understanding. Yet, she had a different idea about the "solution" to our difficult interaction. She believed that she had the right interpretation—and maybe that I needed to remain silent and accept this truth. Thus, we really achieved very little together. She remained inaccessible; there was no room for dialogue or change. However, I believe that my anxiety in these meetings could have served her as an indication for a different path—a path I would like to call psychoanalytic freedom.

We can define psychoanalytic freedom as a way of listening to our inner experience (feelings, bodily sensations, images, thoughts, beliefs, etc.) at a given moment in time. This freedom is indicated by the possibility of recognizing some of our self-states (Bromberg, Stern, Davies) as well as our limits; that is, what I would like to call "being close to ourselves." If we speak from this place of closeness to ourselves (I will expand on this later), in an attuned yet not too calculated manner, we risk misunderstanding or ruptures with our patients and supervisees. However, at the same time, analytic freedom involves the profound belief that should rupture occur we will be able to acknowledge and repair them (Safran & Muran, 2011). This freedom requires us to replace judgment with observation, which, of course, cannot be achieved without the help of our patients or supervisees. The more we are attuned to ourselves, the more we can be attuned to our patients. My supervisor, for instance, could have stopped and examined her inner experience with me, she could have examined her own self state, thus opening a different kind of space between us and a different dialogue, that would have led us toward a different path. That is, as I would like to show, when the analyst is attuned to herself and her own self-states, without letting the "superego" take hold of her, she invites her patients and supervisees to share the same approach and space.

As a relational analyst, I see the clinical situation as an evermoving field (Baranger & Baranger, Stern, Bromberg). The field is fashioned from several elements: the analyst and the patient, the interaction between them, and what they create together and are hence embedded in (sometimes called the analytic third by Ogden, 1994). Our task as analysts is to meet our patients within this ever moving field. To begin my journey into the analytic field, to be able to meet my patient, I need to be close to myself. My inner world has its impact on the field, while the field also has an impact on my inner world. Thus, closeness to one's self is a good starting point for the psychotherapeutic dialogue. This dialogue is achieved through verbal and non-verbal communication; for instance, responding to the patient's words with smile, surprise, sometimes laughter or tears; sharing with the patient images that I encounter within myself even when I do not understand their meaning; sharing a story I made about their life, them, and of course more articulated interpretations when I feel it is necessary.

I make use of a wide gamut of ways to reach my patients: from primal and sometimes nonsensical ways of communication to the more complex interpretations. The field moves in many directions and I try to let myself move within it. Moreover, when I feel it can help the analytic process, I also generate this movement.

Let me turn to an example from the clinic. A new patient was trying to figure out if psychotherapy would be good for her. Her husband recommended it to her since he thought she was too nervous. It was difficult for me to reach her. It was our third session; and as it was coming to an end, she began to explain to me, in great detail that people do not change, hinting that she has nothing to gain from therapy. She said this in a cheerful tone. She is a successful engineer and very loveable. She was so cheerful and convincing in her tone that I thought to myself that maybe she could do well without psychoanalysis. I felt, in a way, detached and was a little annoyed, even my tone of voice began to sound impatient. And yet, as I encountered these parts of my inner-state, I also found myself challenged to reach her. I told her that in our sessions we will explore her inner world so as to understand her deeply cherished and pessimistic view about people's inability to change. I felt that her cheerfulness is a mask she places between us. I offered her my understanding that her pessimistic view was connected to her stubborn, hard-working and unreachable parents (this was how she described her parents in the previous sessions). She answered that she is a pessimistic person and her facial expression changed, she looked somewhat lost and said it was difficult for her to figure out what I was talking about. I suddenly felt sorry for her. I encountered my anxiety and my guilt. Was I too harsh with her? Maybe she was much more fragile than my initial impression? I encountered not only her anxiety but also my own. I did not expect my intervention to be so destabilizing. I felt a change in myself and in our connection. I was closer now to her than in the previous sessions. By listening to the movement between my self-states (Bromberg)—from confidence to frustration and then from detachment to anxiety, and from guilt to caring—I was able to meet my patient and begin our work together. By exploring my self-states, which were slightly dissociated to me within the context of this interaction, I was able to help my patient encounter her own otherness.

In my psychoanalytic work, I try to focus on helping my patients encounter otherness (Bromberg, Stern, Davies, Bass); the otherness inside them and the otherness outside of them, and help them with their inner and outer movements. In the case of this patient, she was able to encounter her pessimism and anxiety. I would suggest that moving closer to ourselves and our inner world is also achieved by encountering our own "otherness" which, in turn, helps us to be more attuned to the otherness of our patients. Facing our own otherness makes it possible for us to better understand both inner and outer situations in the clinic.

We may encounter many obstacles on the way toward psychoanalytic freedom; for instance, our daily insecurities, our need to feel secure in our profession, the need to be loved, feelings of shame and the way we feel toward our parental figures (Loewald)or our "psychoanalytic police." We are in an intriguing profession that helps keep us alive and stimulates our intellect. Yet, we can also sail too far with freedom. We can get lost exploring our own inner world and forget why we sailed in the first place. How, then, do we place a limit to this freedom? How do we keep the focus on promoting the well-being of our patients? Turning to theory allows me to organize what I feel, think, and do at the clinic. I love to read and think theoretically. I love relational thinking; I feel at home in the knowledge and atmosphere of this field. However, while theory is my consultant, the clinic is my guide: during treatment, I do not consciously think in theoretical terms and I do not plan my steps according to theory. After the meeting with my patient or supervisee, I can think about what took place in the meetings through a theoretical prism, through terms such as enactment (Bromberg, Stern, 2013 Davies, 2004), impasse (Aron, 1998; Benjamin, 2004), doer-done-to (Benjamin, 2004), defenses (Anna Freud), recognition (Bromberg, Benjamin, Aron), projective identification (Klein, Bion, Ogden), dissociation (Bromberg, Stern, Chefetz, 2004), empathy (Kohut, 2009; Ornstein & Ornstein, 1985; Slavin, 2013; Hazel Ipp), free floating associations (Freud), and many other theoretical terminologies in order to make sense of what happened (Bass, 2007; Laor, 2007).

Much has been written on the subject of freedom, from many perspectives and in many disciplines. In this chapter, I wish to articulate my inner understanding of what freedom means to me in our profession and how I strive to achieve it. My understanding of this freedom is drawn not only from the theoretical field but also, and mainly, from my clinical work.

Let me present a few more examples of this freedom. A supervisee presents a clinical hour. We both could see that she was in a very good mood during that hour and listened mostly to what resonated with her good mood. I was struck by the fact that although she had made many "mistakes" during the treatment hour and the patient had even acknowledged this—some important changes took place in that hour. We went through the vignette again to find out what we thought took place in that hour. She presented a case of a child who was very aggressive in the way he played. However, no matter how aggressive he became in his games, she did not react to his aggression and kept smiling. She was not, in any way detached, she simply did not react to the violent dimension in his game. Toward the end of the hour, his aggression seemed to fade. We could have looked only at the: "mistakes," at the misattunements, at the partial mirroring; in other words, at what was "right" or "wrong," but what was most important to me was to ask ourselves what had happened (Stern, 2013a; Laor, 2007) during that hour that created the change. I was very surprised with what took place during this hour and I followed my own surprise. We went through the vignette again and tried to give words to what else had happened that was so meaningful, we tried to give words to her way of being with her patient. We discovered that the way she smiled, that is, her facial expression of delight, made it possible for her patient to introduce more of his self-states into the meeting. As I was following my surprise, I opened a space to articulate more of what happened in that hour between my supervisee and her patient. In the supervision hour, we opened a space of freedom which enabled us to listen to my supervisee's self-states and mine as well. I shared with her my surprise and enthusiasm and she followed the thread. The inner world of the analyst has an effect on the analysis. This effect lies beyond any single theory. It is hence important to be attuned to this inner world and its impact.

There is no formula for understanding our inner experience. In a way, this is sometimes different from what students would like to have in their classes and supervision. Although we tend to use formulations to understand the world around us, what I would like to emphasize is that there is no ready-made formula for how to discover our inner selves. As a supervisor and analyst, then, I do not feel that I have all the answers, on the contrary, I explore the analytic situation with my supervisees and my patients. And when I encounter an impasse between us, I can turn to them for help. Their own understanding of the situation can help us move beyond the impasse. Exploring the dynamics between the supervisor and supervisee also helps deepen the ability to reach our patients since it helps us reach more and more of our inner world.

No universal path leads us to encounter our inner selves. It can take us by surprise, if we let it. Sometimes, as I mentioned before, this path can move through our physical body. For instance, on my way to my Pilates class one morning, I found myself in a strange mood, a little anxious about some decisions I had to make. There was nothing in the real world that prevented me from making the decision I wanted, and still I felt that I was not free to decide. During class, my teacher told me that she felt my movement was rigid. Although she was only referring to the physical dimension, something in me moved. I realized that I also felt rigid in respect to a decision that I was supposed to make. It was as if I had only two options: to do or not to do something. I understood that this rigidness was not only in my muscles, but also in my mind, and I tried to find the reason for it. So, I can say that the first step toward being free is looking at my inner state of being, or even more than that—searching for it within the physical dimension as well. Being close to myself is not a cognitive experience, and we can meet some self-states that we may not particularly like. When it feels right, we can communicate all this: our rigidity, our inner change, and our uneasiness.

Freedom does not mean no conflict. I believe that we sometimes "fight" with patients for their own sake, and they know it and appreciate it (it is worth noting that not much has been written about the freedom to "fight"). We know that raising children involves a lot of conflicts and we know that even with very young children, it takes time to know what is good for our child and even when we think we know, we have to negotiate with them. It is not the ruptures that create the difficulties, but the inability to repair them.

One of my other supervisors set a very different example to the one described in the beginning, and "fought" with me to write a paper, which later turned out to be very important to me. When I finished the psychotherapy program, I thought that writing the final paper would be a waste of time. We psychologists study so hard, and these papers do not give us any credit in the "real" world. My desire was to accomplish more by writing a dissertation, but that was not possible at that time. However, my supervisor opened a space for discussion about my writing. It was clear we did not agree, she thought it would be important for me to write this paper and I initially resisted. But she took the freedom to create a space in which we could meet an inner part of my desire that I was not aware of at the time.

In the end, I wrote a paper. It was the first paper I wrote as a professional therapist, and in this paper, I expressed my own beliefs about the therapeutic process. I liked working on the paper and I published part of it in a professional journal. I never stopped writing. My supervisor was not formally obliged to fight for me nor to try to promote my writing, but I very much appreciated her for doing so. I now follow her example in my own work with my supervisees.

Before becoming a psychoanalyst, I studied and practiced organizational psychology. For me, it was obvious to think that the organization we are part of plays an important role in our professional growth. This puts me back in touch with my first days as an intern. We may divide the work with interns into two main paths: we can treat them like young children in need of a parent, that is, we can take them by the hand and guide them; or we can create a space for more mutual relationships by asking for their point of view as well. Both situations can be beneficial; some interns find it helpful to be guided. As a supervisee, I found more mutual relations to be more beneficial and enjoyable.

How do we, then, promote mutuality without losing asymmetry (Aron) in our organizations? Or, in other words, how do we promote freedom in our organizations and in our students? This remains, for me, an open question. Relational thinking is an approach which, for me, cherishes questions within the right atmosphere, thereby paving the road to freedom.

Let me turn to a final example from my clinic. It was hard for me to reach Ella. Her way of talking was concrete; she spoke in very short sentences and with a lot of silence between them. She felt she had nothing to say and worried she cannot be understood because of that difficulty. In many of our sessions, I saw in my mind's eye a desert with no shelter. The desert was arid. The image of the desert scared me, and I could not figure out its meaning. Very hesitantly, I told her about my inner image. I also said that although I really don't know what that means I thought it is relevant to our connection. To my surprise, she was relieved by my image. She felt she could be reached. I was very surprised to hear that. She did not refer to the content of the image but just to the idea that she reached me by this special image (Laor, 2009).

Let me repeat myself and apologize if it may sound redundant for some, perhaps I am unsure about how I am reaching you. As freedom helps us move closer to ourselves and meet more and more of our otherness, we become more creative. We surprise our patients and are ourselves surprised by them (Bromberg). We create a space for mutual surprise. There is always a sense of anxiety when I encounter this surprise, yet it is the real opportunity to step toward a change.

Thus, for me, **the essence of psychoanalysis is freedom.**

Note

1 I would like to thank my colleagues and friends who provided their valuable feedback: Dror Gronich and Tamar Gerstenhaber, who also translated this chapter.

References

Aron, L. (1998). Analytic impasse and the third: Clinical implications of intersubjectivity theory. *The International Journal of Psychoanalysis, 87*(2), 349–368. doi:10.1516/15EL-284Y-7Y26-DHRK.

Baranger, M., & Baranger, W. (2008). The analytic situation as a dynamic field. *The International Journal of Psychoanalysis, 89*(4), 795–826. doi:10.1111/j.1745-8315.2008.00074.x.

Bass, A. (2007). When the frame doesn't fit the picture. *Psychoanalytic Dialogues, 17*(1), 1–27.

Benjamin, J. (2004). Beyond doer and done to: An intersubjective view of thirdness. *The Psychoanalytic Quarterly, 73*(1), 5–46. doi:10.1002/j.2167-4086.2004.tb00151.x

Bion, W. R. (1994). *Learning from experience*. Northvale, NJ: Jason Aronson Inc. Publishers.

Chefetz, R. A., & Bromberg, P. M. (2004). Talking with "me" and "not-me": A dialogue. *Contemporary Psychoanalysis, 40*(3), 409–464. doi:10.1080/00107530.2004.10745840.

Davies, J. M. (2004). Whose bad objects are we anyway? Repetition and our elusive love affair with evil. *Psychoanalytic Dialogues, 14*(6), 711–732. doi:10.1080/10481881409348802.

Freud, S. (1916–1917). Introductory lectures on psycho-analysis. *Standard Edition*, Vol. XVI: 15–16.

Klein, M. (1946). Notes on some schizoid mechanisms. *International Journal of Psycho-Analysis, 27*, 99–110.

Kohut, H. (2009). *How does analysis cure?* University of Chicago Press.

Laor, I. (2007). The therapist, the patient, and the therapeutic setting: Mutual construction of the setting as a therapeutic factor. *Psychoanalytic Dialogues, 17*(1), 29–46. doi:10.1080/10481880701301055.

Laor, I. (2009). The holy see: The individual and the group-intersubjective meetings. *Psychoanalytic Dialogues, 19*(4), 486–501. doi:10.1080/10481880903088583.

Ogden, T. H. (1994). The analytic third: Working with intersubjective clinical facts. *International Journal of Psycho-Analysis, 75*, 3–19.

Ogden, T. H. (2003). On not being able to dream. *The International Journal of Psychoanalysis, 84*(1), 17–30. doi:10.1516/1D1W-025P-10VJ-TMRW.

Ornstein, P. H., & Ornstein, A. (1985). Clinical understanding and explaining the empathic vantage point. *Progress in Self Psychology, 1*, 43–61.

Safran, J. D., Muran, J. C., & Eubanks-Carter, C. (2011). Repairing alliance ruptures. *Psychotherapy, 48*(1), 80–87. doi:10.1037/a0022140.

Slavin, M. O. (2013). Why one self is not enough: Clinical, existential, and adaptive perspectives on Bromberg's model of multiplicity and dissociation. *Contemporary Psychoanalysis, 49*(3), 380–409.

Stern, D. B. (2013a). Relational freedom and therapeutic action. *Journal of the American Psychoanalytic Association*, *61*(2), 227–256. doi:10.1177%2F0003065113484060.

Stern, D. B. (2013b). *Unformulated experience: From dissociation to imagination in psychoanalysis*. Routledge.

Chapter 26

The Risk of Analysis

Avgi Saketopoulou

> You hear a bird singing.
> As absurd as it may seem
> for a bird to be hanging in the balance in the desert,
> you are, nevertheless, obligated to build it a tree
>
> (Kiki Dimoula, 2012, my translation)

I have always told myself that I could pinpoint exactly when and how I fell in love with psychoanalysis.

I was 13 and the book was Marie Cardinal's *The Words to Say It*. I remember pulling it off a kitchen shelf, which is another way to say that it must have belonged to my mother. I spotted it first amidst her unused cookbooks and the self-help manuals, which were similarly pristine. Jammed amidst this odd virginal assortment, the blue book was different; it was marked by the passage of time, decrepit, as if it had been read again, and again, and again. My mother did not read, so, reason told me, the wear could not have been inflicted by her. Still, I pulled it off the shelf, dislodging it from its tight quarters to inspect it more as a curiosity, a kind of strange interloping object, than as something that was meant to be read. I was fascinated by this spent, soiled volume, by its dilapidated spine. Later, I would come to speculate that I must have been hoping that my mother had in fact engaged this object again and again, causing its deterioration, that I must have believed that it could therefore deliver some truth to me about her, about where she went when she was not with me, which was often. Its title intrigued me: in the original French it reads, *Les mots pour le dire,* which was translated in English as *The Words to Say It*. But in Greek, my mother tongue and the language in which I read it, it became *Εγώ και Αυτό,* which roughly translates as "I and It"—a locution that announces itself as intentionally mystifying. What did that "It" mean? Was I expected to know? I took the title as something between an address and a challenge, perhaps a provocation, and this transformed it from an object that likely belonged to my mother into a book that demanded to be read by me. I did so immediately.

Cardinal's novel is narrated by the main character, a woman who suffers from severe menstrual bleeding, a symptom that medical doctors can neither explain nor stop. In the opening pages, she has freshly "escaped" from a sanatorium, and we meet her on her way to first analytic consultation. The session unfolds with her recounting to the analyst the horrors of her bleeding, her deep despair, and her sheer incapacitation to take care of herself or her children. She is taken aback by how closely he listens to her. She ends up saying more than she had expected she would. At the end of this first meeting, he recommends a 3x/week analysis. He states declaratively that she should immediately stop all her medications. When she protests that she will bleed out without them, he advocates for the part of her that's speaking through her symptom, for the importance of letting what her psyche is trying to secrete flow through her body, so that it can be understood. She objects that she cannot afford analysis, that she is agoraphobic, and that she can barely leave her home. This does not deter him either. She will need to take a job, he replies; they can work out the fee. This stranger, whom she has just met, seems to understand the urgency of the crisis, but what he has to offer is entirely counterintuitive, by all tokens dangerous, even mad. At age 13, the intensity of this encounter astonished me. In this man's illogic, I felt, lay something beyond my understanding, a promise of some kind that excited me.

Surprising herself, the main character—and as it turns out the real person, too, since the book is actually an autobiographical account of Marie Cardinal's psychoanalytic treatment—agrees to an analysis. In the taxi on her way home from this first visit, she finds that her bleeding has stopped. The lifting of her symptom, of course, is not the end of the treatment; it's only the beginning. Or, to say it differently, she, and we as readers, only knows with certainty that the symptom would never return after the analysis was completed, only, that is, in the après-coup. If transference idealization was what initially chased the symptom away, the symptomatic relief only sustains over time because it is followed by deep analytic work. We, indeed, get a detailed account of that work: it is long, arduous, and life-changing. The rest of the book is not as phantasmagoric as that first enthralling chapter. There are no pyrotechnics, only the toil and tedium of hard work. As such, at a narrative close-up, the accounting of the analysis is, as far as novels go, rather boring. But by the book's end, the originally compromised person has become a pulsating human being. She acquires a sense of her own interiority without being persecuted by it. She can love and hate, be loved and be hated. She can have pleasure, aspirations, a future—in short, she can claim a life. She writes books, including the blue one in my hands.

As a child, I was transfixed by this extraordinary display of the spectacular powers of psychoanalysis. Notably, what most impressed me was the analyst's willingness to take the risk of treatment. This person, I marveled, must have surely realized that by offering so much to someone who had so little, that by inviting such a deep commitment from her at a time she could barely leave her home, he was also in some way seducing her. His seduction, in which one could sense the force of the analyst's conviction and desire, ethically demanded a matched-in-seriousness commitment of his own: a commitment to this seriously ill, inexplicably bleeding stranger who might never get well. I was nothing short of mesmerized by his steadfast belief in what he had to offer to this other human being, and by his own willingness to take on, and, thus, to risk so much. How could one person say so confidently, and to a virtual stranger at that, something so at odds with common sense and which incubated such risk? How could one person promise another so exorbitantly much?

This is how, at 13, I decided I would become a psychoanalyst, after having fallen in love with psychoanalysis, which at the time I understood as one person offering to a stranger something that was in equal measures strange and incomprehensible; as something that requires a certain kind of faith, the guarantor of which is a particular kind of benevolent seduction; as an offering that could only make sense long after the process started perhaps, even mostly, after it ends. This faith in something one does not understand enchanted me. I didn't have those words then, of course, but I felt all of what they describe. With some modifications, I, in fact, still hold onto this today: psychoanalysis starts with the analyst's ethical seduction (Chetrit-Vatine, 2012). This is not a sexual seduction in the sense of violated limits or boundaries that are not stringently protected; it's a seduction of a different sort: a lure, a mirage, even an alibi, for engaging in a relational process for which there is no equivalent in everyday life. The analyst offers to set up the conditions for the patient to take certain kinds of risks. These conditions establish the relative safety of the space, and I say "relative" because, in my opinion, and contrary to much psychoanalytic theorizing, the psychoanalyst's office is not a safe space. Not really. It may, in fact, be the most unsafe space one can find oneself in. It is not unsafe in the sense that it admits of retaliation, physical danger, exploitation, or abuse; it's unsafe because, even when these protections are ensured, or in fact, especially when those are ensured, it's a space where the pretense of the obvious is suspended. Where one comes against the limit of what one thought was possible. It is this crash against the limit that also procures psychoanalysis's gifts: coming to see that the manifestly irrational gets two votes when reason gets merely one; that temporality works backward and laterally as well and as often as it works in time-forward; that repetition marks not a stalling but the horizon of the new; that the wearing of defenses may feel like defeat, even humiliation, but is actually the soaring of possibility; that an unexpected turn of phrase can sprinkle on you an insight that awakens you to your desire and to how you have been caught up in that of others'; and that homes can still be built even if you grew up amidst ruins and lies. Psychoanalysis can help unhook you from the clear to deliver you to a journey into the obscure and the tentative.

The analyst forges the conditions for this risky undertaking by going first, by offering, that is, a risk of her own. She does this by conveying to a patient something she never puts in words, but which the patient nevertheless senses. If it were said out loud, it would sound absurd and look like this: "I will enter this relationship with you even though I don't know you. I will lower my defenses so that you may act on me *in almost any way you like.* I will surrender my armor and let you enter my being in ways that I otherwise defend against with almost all others. And when something happens between us, which I know it will precisely because I have made myself passible to you (Lyotard, 1988), I will try to bear this "something" however much it may demand of me. I will try to breathe through it, however much it pierces me. I will do so because I have faith that if I do, it may carry us somewhere important-even though I cannot tell you, because I don't myself know, why or how. I will do all this even though you are a stranger to me, just because you walked into my office."

The risk we take as analysts has to do with a radical exposure, not keeping ourselves safe in the sense of securing our psychic borders, an offering that, for us as well, "takes place precisely at the limits patrolled by the obvious" (Moss, 2017, p. 7). In my experience, and at its best, psychoanalysis is an experience of the limit (Pontalis, 2005; Zaltzman, 1979), which does not mean that it pulsates constantly at that level of intensity but that at its most poignant, it invites the patient's and the analyst's destruction. By destruction, I mean that it puts under pressure the very understandings of ourselves that constitute us, that make us feel safe, that reassure us that the world is known to us (e.g. that you don't go off meds if you are sick, that you can't go to sessions if you are agoraphobic). In my second year of undergrad, a teacher I loved and whom I credit with the foundations of my psychoanalytic education said to me: "every time an analyst sits with a patient, she risks her sanity." I remember being taken aback by a statement that sounded so hyperbolic, from a person who was usually so measured, about a profession that involves sitting and just listening. But now I know she was right. I have felt profoundly unmoored with almost every single patient I have worked with deeply. I am lucky to have been forewarned, to have been prepared that this wave, however alarming, eventually subsides, that I will not get pulled into some dark hole of insanity. That knowledge does not make it easier, but it does make it survivable. Still, the jolt always comes as a surprise.

Such undoings are, hopefully, of different magnitudes for the analyst than they are for the patient. For the patient, Scarfone (2015) writes, analysis comes down to a *crisis of representation.* Representations, the building blocks of the ego, have to come undone, to even shatter (Bersani, 1986) if any significant remembering (Scarfone, 2011) of the self is to occur. For De M'Uzan (2018), psychoanalysis produces a permanent disquiet. This may seem like a paradoxical claim given that patients (and I include the analyst here in her own experience as a patient) come to analysis imagining that what they need is to be relieved from their distress by quieting the disquiet. For De M'Uzan, however, it is the persistently stable stories we tell ourselves about ourselves, our hyper-investments in identity and in our self-representations, or, to put it more plainly, our commitment to maintaining them that leads to problems. The disquiet he is after is not a permanent state of turmoil, but the productive dysregulation that accompanies our having to contend with the strange in ourselves. This internal sense of foreignness, which Freud called *The Thing* (1915), and which Laplanche called the enigmatic core (1987), is the "It" that Cardinal was trying to find the words to say. This is an "It" that is captured by trauma but which extends far beyond it. Imagine, then, my surprise, when in a conversation about Marie Cardinal's writing with Dominique Scarfone, he mentioned that it is a well-known fact in France that the analyst who treated her, the analyst in the blue book that inspired my wish to become an analyst myself, was none other than the French psychosomatician, Michel De M'Uzan (personal communication).

Over the years, I have given a great deal of thought to this story of origins regarding my relationship with psychoanalysis. When I started my analytic training, I also learned that Cardinal's is the kind of clinical tale that appeals to a wider, if increasingly obsolete, psychoanalytic imaginary, one that has for decades shaped an ideality of what clinical work looks like: the analyst who knows, the patient who gets better. When I rethink this story nowadays, I am more ambivalent about it. The narrative continues to feel compelling to me, yet my idealization also feels naïve. It has a sentimentality that appealed to my youthful idealism, but it is too confident for my adult self, too certain, too hermetically self-contained. As an analyst myself, I see that conviction in psychoanalysis as a method earns its heft only if it is also countered by self-questioning and by doubt. Such are the incommensurabilities of analytic thinking. As a clinician, I also see Cardinal's treatment as a version of psychoanalysis that can be limited in scope, which has imagined the clinical dyad in a sort of enclosed "purity" that protects it from the impact of the outside world—its purview being the intrapsychic and the familial, but not the social conditions that subtend them. We have more developed and nuanced theorizing today, for example, about de M'Uzan's potential recklessness in advising a seriously medically ill patient he barely knew to go off their medications; about the top-down pronouncement which is announced *to* the patient; and about the powerful gender dynamic between a male authority figure delivering a treatment verdict to a fragile, female patient suffering from, well, it almost doesn't get more symbolic than that, dramatic, bloody overflows. Further, Cardinal's treatment takes place in France, unfolding between a French analyst and a French patient who, and this I learned as an adult, grew up in

Algeria; when Cardinal was growing up, Algeria was still a French colony, a colony where brutality and power abuses were not rare. The suffering caused by colonization, the issues of Whiteness's violence, you will not be surprised to hear, do not get mentioned in the treatment, nor do questions come up about how they may inflect the patient's hemorrhagic symptoms. Registering that absence, however, did not just take my knowing this information about Cardinal's life but, also, to integrate in my own analysis that half of me, the Cypriot part on my mother's side, is also a product of colonization.

Still, I have never quite given up on the other dimensions of this tale, about what the analyst's seduction can inaugurate in the patient. To this day, I passionately believe that there is something admirable in De M'Uzan's confident conviction in the therapeutic potential of psychoanalysis,[1] a conviction that I now also share. His unwavering belief in the value of what he has to offer was critical to why Cardinal accepted his "offer of analysis" (Laplanche, 1987), however unrealistic, impossible, and unimaginable to her. It is this belief, a secular kind of faith in psychoanalysis as a method that makes it also a seduction. When students or supervisees ask me how to get patients to come more frequently, I always say that it has to do with one's own relationship to psychoanalysis. If you don't feel that what you have to offer is exigent, that the psychoanalytic process will be worth what it will cost—your patient's suffering, her anguish, her time, and her money—it will be hard to feel authorized to invite anyone into the preposterous enterprise that it can appear to be from the outside. "[T]he degree to which the analyst believes in the special value of psychoanalytic treatment" writes Abend, "may determine what he advises as much as any other single factor" (1987, p. 34). No one in our field speaks better and more powerfully to the importance of the analyst's conviction and how this inflects her own resistances to starting/recommending an analysis than Ehrlich (2004, 2013).

Here's a brief but telling example from my personal experience: several years ago, a 24-year-old man came to see me. We agreed to a three-session consultation as is my usual practice before deciding if working together is a good idea. In our first meeting, he told me he had Lou-Gehrig's disease and that he expected he would be dying within the year. He was alone, having alienated everyone in his life—even his family. He did not quite know why he was coming to see me. A supervisor I greatly respected felt strongly that a young person with only a year to live should not be laying on anyone's couch, he should be out there trying to live their life. I was young and inexperienced and I strongly disagreed: what was possibly more urgent than analysis? After our second session, he called me and left a message, thanking me for a helpful link I'd made, telling me how much he enjoyed our time, and that he was not going to finish the consultation as he had just been offered a job for which he would be moving to another state. I suggested we meet. He came in. When we discussed the job offer, which indeed seemed promising, I told him that though I didn't know him well, I believed that my earlier interpretation had frightened him. He said it had. He asked me what I thought he should do. I heard myself say to him something I've never said to anyone before or since: "I think you need to stay here and do the work." The words came out of my mouth. It's not that I did not believe them, I did. But it was not my place to speak that way. It was an important and a terrible thing to have said: I did not know if it was the right thing for him. After all, I barely knew him. Further, he had not been in treatment before and had no idea what it involved. He was clearly lost, and my word carried too much influence. I was also acutely aware that I was signing on to get to know and work really closely with someone who would soon be dying a terrible death. And who had no other relationships than the one he might create with me. He thought about it. He came back, started a four times weekly analysis. I lost sleep over what I had said to him, agonized over what I had taken on. We ended up working together for eight years. The blue book had, no doubt, been pivotal in my intervention. The neurological decline slowed down. He got a job. He made a friend.

I am by no means proposing what I said to him as technique: what I am trying to do shows how when the analyst speaks from within her conviction in the work, she takes a real risk and that she does so by making a peculiar claim: the claim is that there is another regime, a regime beyond conventional reason where things are revealed to have shapes not visible to the naked eye, where the ordinary rules that order everyday life—rules of time, rules of causality, rules of logic—are suspended, yielding an alternate reality: a psychic reality. The analyst lays a claim to this alternate reality by presenting to the patient as a viable proposition a project that in the quotidian world is nothing short of preposterous. She offers a space to be inhabited privately, with everything else suspended for 45, or 50, or insert-your-session-length-here minutes at a time, several times a week. In so doing, she implicitly yet perceptibly offers an odd form of contentless promise, a care which comes with dangers that cannot be anticipated and, hence, cannot be knowingly consented to—ahead of time by either party. It is this surrender to unknowingness and its scrambled temporality that is so radical about what we do as analysts. It is radical because it contravenes common sense, because it is outlandishly intimate, and because it is on such strange terms with linear time.

Sometimes of the risks don't pay off. Any risk that is guaranteed to deliver is, after all, not an actual risk. But some of the time, enough of the time, we get to see someone claim a life. And that is no small thing.

Note

1 Of course, we don't know if he is indeed as confident as the patient reports him to be. All we have is the patient's experience.

References

Bersani, L. (1986). *The Freudian body: Psychoanalysis and art*. New York: Columbia University Press.
Chetrit-Vatine, V. (2012). *The ethical seduction of the analytic situation: The feminine-maternal origins of responsibility for the other*. London: Karnac.
Dimoula, K. (2012). *The Brazen Plagiarist: Selected poems*. New Haven: Yale University Press.
Ehrlich, L. T. (2004). The analyst's reluctance to begin a new analysis. *Journal of the American Journal of Psychoanalysis, 52*, 1075–1093.
Ehrlich, L. T. (2013). Analysis begins in the analyst's mind: Conceptual and technical considerations on recommending analysis. *Journal of the American Journal of Psychoanalysis, 61*, 1077–1107.
Freud, S. (1915). The unconscious. *Standard Edition of the Complete Psychological Works of Sigmund Freud, XIV* (1914–1916), 159–215.
Laplanche, J. (1987). *New foundations for psychoanalysis*. New York: Unconscious in Translation (translated by Jonathan House).
Lyotard, J. F. (1988). *The inhuman*. Stanford: Polity Press.
Moss, D. (2017). *At war with the obvious: Disruptive thinking in psychoanalysis*. London: Routledge.
Scarfone, D. (2011). Repetition: Between presence and meaning. *Canadian Journal of Psychoanalysis, 19*(1), 70–86.
Scarfone, D. (2015). *The unpast*. New York: Unconscious in Translation Press.
Scarfone, D. (2018). Personal communication, May 18.
Zaltzman, N. (1979). Η Αναρχική Ενόρμηση (The anarchic drive). Αθήνα, Βιβλιοπωλείον της Εστίας (translation from French by Γιώργος Καράμπελας, 2019).

Chapter 27

Credo: Relationality and the Collective—A Psychoanalytic Journey in Context

Chana Ullman

I am grateful for this opportunity to reflect and weave together thoughts about my professional development and my current views about fundamental issues in psychoanalysis. This chapter tells the story of my evolution as a relational psychoanalyst. It reviews the legacy of my family and of the sociocultural context in which I was raised as related to my professional development, and outlines the important influences on the directions I have taken. The chapter highlights three tenets of my theoretical and clinical credo: the intertwining of the collective in the intrapsychic and intersubjective, the centrality of relational trauma in psychic pain, and the therapeutic function of witnessing in psychoanalysis.

Education and Professional Affiliation

Born and raised in Israel, I completed my Master's Degree in Clinical Psychology at the Hebrew University of Jerusalem. I then traveled to Boston, where I received my Ph.D. from Boston University, followed by a clinical internship at Harvard Health Services and a clinical post-doc at Boston University Hospital. My spouse and I stayed in Boston for over a decade and, during these years, I pursued academic interests as a teacher and a researcher as well as clinical training, all the while being absorbed in raising our two sons.

For many years, I oscillated between academia and clinical practice. I loved the inquisitive pursuit of scholarship and debate in an academic milieu of intellectual excellence. Back then, the Hebrew University's Psychology Department was home to intellectual giants such as Amos Tversky and Danny Kahneman (who later received the Nobel prize) and inspiring teachers. But I was also drawn to the intimate encounter with others and to the matters of the heart. The title of my dissertation at Boston University, "Change of heart, change of mind? The psychology of religious conversion," inadvertently revealed this oscillation between what I experienced as two poles. My dissertation was based on an empirical study of religious converts, who transformed their lives by moving from one religious denomination to

DOI: 10.4324/9781003206248-27

another for intrinsic reasons. In my own Jewish modern-orthodox upbringing, religion involved a scholarly pursuit and a quest for answers to deep existential queries, but the converts I studied were moved and converted by a relationship. It was love that transformed them, not "knowledge" or ideas. This insight into the nature of such a deep transformation of the self came as a revelation to me and paved the way to deepening my clinical interests as well as my later interest in relational psychoanalysis.

Following a year of post-doc at my Alma Mater, the Hebrew University, in which I conducted research on adolescents' views of the "true self," we returned to Boston. I spent a remarkable and transformative year at the Boston University Hospital Trauma Clinic, headed by Bessel van der Kolk, where I became acquainted with the understanding and treatment of complex post-trauma and its devastating impact on the minds and hearts of those who suffer at the hands of their attachment figures. Understanding trauma became a cornerstone of my psychoanalytic understanding of psychic pain.

In 1992, we made our final return to Israel. Although Boston remained a home and a place we often revisited for professional and personal reasons, we recognized that our attachment to family, friends, the language, and the beloved, conflicted pressure-cooker that is Israel, would not allow us to feel truly at home anywhere else.

I started a private clinical practice in Rehovot and resumed my academic affiliation with the Hebrew University. I became interested in psychoanalytic training. I was drawn to the depth of the psychoanalytic inquiry into the human psyche and benefited immensely from my supervisors, who were mostly Kleinian and Winnicottian in their theoretical perspectives. I was, however, extremely ambivalent and put off by the classical training offered at the single IPA Analytic Institute in Israel, which I viewed as rigid and hierarchical. Once again, I found myself oscillating, sitting on the fence as it were, unable to commit myself to psychoanalytic training while continuing to admire and learn from my psychoanalyst-supervisors. I struggled with this ambivalence for a while.

It was during these years that Emanuel Berman, who was my analyst, first introduced me to the relational perspective. I read Mitchell, Aron, Ghent, Benjamin, Dimen, and others and immediately felt at home in this perspective. I felt that this was a psychoanalysis that I could practice; this was the kind of psychoanalyst that I could become. Luckily, by then, a new psychoanalytic institute was being established in Tel Aviv (initiated by Michael and Batya Shoshani and Gila Ofer) with the help of Stephen Mitchell. It promised a rigorous yet open and pluralistic psychoanalytic training. I joined the Tel Aviv Institute for Contemporary Psychoanalysis (TAICP) in 2002.

That same year, the newly formed IARPP, still in deep mourning over the loss of Stephen Mitchell, held its first conference in New York City, which I attended. It was an exhilarating experience. The papers (by Jody Davies, Neil Altman, Spyros Orfanos, Stuart Pizer, and others) were fresh, innovative, moving, and relevant. The ambience was generous, authentically friendly, and intellectually stimulating.

Three years later, at the 2005 IARPP conference in Rome, I was elected to serve on the association's board of directors and it became an intellectual and professional home. It was in tandem with my increasing involvement at the IARPP that I found my own voice. While I had already published a book (Ullman, 1989) and several papers in my capacity as an academic, it was only then—and with the help of my personal analysis—that I found a clinical psychoanalytic voice.

I completed my analytic training and, in 2010, was elected to serve as chair of the TAICP. My leadership position at the institute in which I was trained became a formative influence. I realized that leadership depends on recognizing vulnerability in self and others, that listening to contradictory voices, rather than suppressing them, enhances genuine authority and that it is possible to hold paradoxes without giving up one's commitment to action. This experience became particularly helpful as my affiliation with the IARPP board deepened. I was honored and pleased to continue contributing to the IARPP's mission in my role as president of the association, during the years 2016–2018, and by serving on the executive board until the end of 2019.

Family and Subjectivity

Professional affiliations and convictions develop in a context. For me, this context has been the multilayered politics (in the broadest sense of the word) of survival, of profound losses and past traumas, alongside the promise of a new start. My parents were both Holocaust survivors who lost entire families, which had been wiped out by the Nazis. I described in detail (Ullman, 2014) the impact of this legacy on my subjectivity, my theoretical and clinical choices. I see this second-generation history as inseparable from my work, from my ethical convictions, and from what I consider valuable in psychoanalysis.

My parents' message and, in fact, their entire lives epitomize the resilience that can be found amid unimaginable traumas and losses. Their ability to rise from the ashes and find vitality and even happiness in their intimate relationship and in their children, imprinted on me the power of attachment and witnessing as insulators from horrific traumas. Choosing to become a psychoanalyst felt natural for me, saturated with the ambitious aim of reparation, and striving to enable a new start. It also shaped my professional interest in the intertwining of the personal and the political, of autobiographical memory and collective memory. Coming into my own as a political subject, I rebelled against my religious upbringing, while at the same time upholding my commitment to my parents' legacy through my identification with those on the "wrong" side of power structures.

A powerful experience, which became a cornerstone in my understanding of trauma and witnessing in psychoanalysis, has been my involvement with "Machsom Watch" (Ullman, 2006), a human rights group of women who monitored IDF checkpoints, witnessing the daily traffic of Palestinians controlled by Israeli soldiers throughout the years of the Palestinian uprising (intifada).

Reflecting on my experience at the checkpoints, I am aware of complex links between my personal history, the collective context, and my theoretical convictions as a psychoanalyst. I am aware of my multiple self-states and the challenge of "standing in the spaces" (Bromberg, 1996). My presence at the *machsom* (checkpoint) not only bears witness to the trauma of the other, it is also born out of the shame and guilt of being on the powerful side. Moreover, it may reveal traces of the guilt of the survivor or of the child who could not cure her parents, as it has forced me to come to terms with my own inability to save the other. At the checkpoints, I am present both as perpetrator and victim. In my role as a witness, however, I resist identifying with either role. I become a Third, whose presence humanizes both sides of the barrier. It declares I refuse to take part in the "doer-done to" seesaw (Benjamin, 2002), of violence that disavowed and unwitnessed trauma may create.

As I will elaborate later, I consider witnessing an ethical imperative in our role as mental health professionals and a distinct psychoanalytic function. In retrospect, I am aware of how this theoretical and clinical emphasis is related to the child who was a witness to her parents' silent suffering. There is reparation in this repetition: turning passivity into activity, silence into speech. At the same time, reparation is limited; the witness tries to cross the distance to the world of the other, while inevitably remaining an observer of it.

Formative Influences in Relationality

While my roots were deeply connected to the vibrant psychoanalytic community in Israel and my colleagues at the TAICP, my involvement with the IARPP has brought far-reaching professional growth. It resulted in relationships with people whose writings I admired, with whom I collaborated, argued, or identified, and with some of whom I developed cherished friendships. My years on the board of the IARPP deepened my understanding and appreciation of multiplicity, as I listened to an international tapestry of voices, yet these years clarified my internal muddles about where I belong theoretically and clinically. My internalization of my Kleinian supervisors remained solid, but became a part of a larger whole, of curiosity about the manifestations of my subjectivity, of the mutual processes of enactment rather than unidirectional projections, and of attention to the context—gender, class, ethnicity, and politics—as an influential Third in the clinical encounter.

There were many who influenced this integration of my own voice. I will focus here on the two most formative thinkers who shaped my psychoanalytic perspective: Lew Aron and Jessica Benjamin.

I first met Lew Aron in person in 1996, when he spoke at a conference in Israel. For many of us who were then less familiar with the relational approach, his talks were riveting and unsettling. Since then, Lew gradually became an advisor and a friend to our local psychoanalytic community and to me personally. As we both share a similar Jewish Orthodox background, I found his Talmudic style familiar, and was fascinated by his constant search for underlying layers and for complicating matters, albeit with clarity and rigor. I found his early work in "Meeting of Minds: Mutuality and Intersubjectivity in Psychoanalysis" (1996) eye-opening. Along with Mitchell's work, it introduced a paradigm shift that felt crucial in moving away from the ideal of abstinence and neutrality. It uncovered and formulated what seemed evident to me as a clinician—mutuality in the sense of mutual influence and emotional engagement, underlies our work whether we acknowledge it or not, yet it is a mutuality that never shirks the responsibility that comes with asymmetry. I marveled at Lew's ability to create links between different concepts and different self-states, as in translating Kleinian concepts ("The internalization of the primal scene," 1995) to a relational understanding of the oedipal, which made it possible for me to use classical terms in a different manner. What seemed rigid and binary ways of thinking about gender, superego and identity, became flexible, playful concepts allowing varied trajectories of developmental achievements. Lew emphasized that both similarities and differences are needed for people and theories to develop, confirming and influencing my ideas about otherness as curative in the process of therapeutic transformations (Ullman, 2006). I also resonated with his later writings on critical dialogue (Aron, 2017), which challenge us to go beyond tolerance and respect for difference toward a "critical pluralism" in which the other perspective is appreciated for what it can uniquely contribute to us. This critical pluralism has been immensely important to me not only in thinking about theory but also in clinical practice as in listening to patients' different, sometimes appalling positions or acts, not as resistance that we need to overcome, but as communications about the relationship or about different contexts of which I am ignorant.

I consider the critical pluralism that Lew articulated for psychoanalysis both theoretically and clinically, as crucial too to our immersion in the Collective. It is a pivotal call to welcome otherness, to listen to a different and even hated narrative, and to attend to a suffering that we may be implicated in perpetuating, as psychoanalysts and citizens. In this view of otherness in its clinical and social manifestations, I have been greatly influenced by Jessica Benjamin's revolutionary ideas. Her notions of doer/done-to dynamics in the clinic and beyond, of mutual recognition as a developmental achievement, of the Moral Third and the failed witness, of the linking of Psychoanalysis and Feminism, and of embracing vulnerability, have been implicit and explicit in almost everything I taught and wrote. There are disagreements as well: I will clarify those by focusing on an experience. At the height of the second intifada (uprising, 2003–2004), Benjamin organized a mutual acknowledgment project (Benjamin, 2018, pp. 236–239). This project, which brought together Israelis, Palestinians, and internationals, was an implementation of Benjamin's views of the power of mutual recognition and of "going first" in repairing harm. This encounter remains in my memory a formidable heroic effort to bring about reconciliation when the trauma of the conflict is raw and alive. While it led to several insightful meetings and cherished personal moments, as a mutual recognition project it failed. For me, it has been a failure that I could learn from. There seemed to be in this project an *a priori* striving for a just world and for mutuality that I resonated with, but that had been simply unrealizable as the trauma was still bleeding. I realized that we all came up against the limitations of expecting mutual recognition within an ongoing power imbalance. While achieving some form of reconciliation seemed impossible, the project strengthened my understanding of the therapeutic power of witnessing when trauma is raging and mutuality or reparation are felt to be impossible. My own notion of witnessing in the consulting room and in society remained to accept the "face" of the other and her narrative, without demanding to be equally recognized, without assuming transformation, reconciliation, or justice.

Contemporary Thoughts on the Nature of Psychic Pain

So where has all this landed me today? I will briefly elaborate here on three tenets of my work as a psychoanalyst that together constitute my psychoanalytic credo.

First, the recognition that social forces interact powerfully with individual unconscious and object relations, and affect the therapeutic relationship, became saturated in my work. As is evident in what I have written so far, the intrapsychic, the intersubjective, and the Collective context are intertwined in the formation of my psychoanalytic identity. Similarly, those are intertwined in our patients' lives. When I sit with patients, I cannot contend with an investigation of their intra-psychic or the inter-subjective as divorced from reciprocal cultural and sociopolitical influences. In working with Israeli men, for example, the tensions of cultural myths of heroism, conflicts of group belongings, and the individual relational history, all come together to shape current distress (Ullman, 2020). I attempt to attend to all three registers of our experience as containing the seeds of psychic pain.

Given my background, I cannot disregard the ghosts (Harris, 2006) that sometimes enter the clinical process, completely unexpectedly and explosively. In the Israeli context, I am acutely aware of how culture, values, and politics enter our discourse, at times leading to painful clashes with "otherness" and to difficult dilemmas in the face of the evil and suffering associated with social violence. I am also acutely aware of the sociopolitical contributions to individual pathology, and hence of the need to apply our psychoanalytic wisdom to the powerful collective forces that shape our lives.

Second, the relational history of patients as played out, enacted, and repeated within the analytic dyad is a major focus of my work. In particular, an emphasis on relational trauma in contemporary psychoanalysis appears to me no less than revolutionary. While the concept of trauma existed since the early days of psychoanalysis (i.e., in Freud's seduction theory), it was only in the relational literature that it was given a primary place as the cause of psychic pain and distorted development. Toward the end of the 20th century, significant changes to the political and cultural zeitgeist joined theoretical trends and developmental psychopathology research, which attested to the prevalence of abuse trauma within families and to the long-term psychic harm it causes, reintroduced trauma into the psychoanalytic discourse. This change led to a different understanding of pathology and psychic suffering as stemming directly from actual and recurring injuries in one's primary relationships. Unlike other traumas, which are not "man-made" or which occur outside the context of interpersonal relationships, these "relational traumas" take place in the context of unequal power-relations—those between adults and child, between men and women, between authority, and those who depend on it. Relational traumas become woven into the psyche, creating complex consequences, dissociation and a combination of denial attempts and repetition compulsions. The perspective on traumas as common and present in everyday life, rather than as singular, exceptional events, demanded a broadening of one's outlook to include a wider social context. Trauma is directly related not only to one's inner world and to one's idiosyncratic history but also to the social-political history of the world as well, to the powers that allow and sustain it. While the insidious and chronic effect such traumas have on the psyche is potent, it is often invisible to both those who experience it and to mental health practitioners. It forces us, as psychoanalytic therapists, to confront alien and unknown social forces that act upon us as much as on our patients.

This means that our responsibility to our patients includes the acknowledgment and working through of the traumatic impact of such power structures and the espousal of a position of resistance or of "ontological ways of refusing" (Levenson, 2012) to these dynamics. This, again, is the beginning of a paradigm shift, from psychoanalysis that serves as an instrument of resignations and adaptation to social reality, to psychoanalysis that emphasizes agency and resistance.

Third, the understanding of trauma and its impact throughout one's life cycle leads to a greater emphasis on witnessing as a therapeutic function. For me, witnessing is a dyadic process in which a denied reality of evil and suffering becomes a narrative (Ullman, 2006). It is an attempt to speak the unspeakable, to transform absence into a loss that can be mourned, or to a recognized harm that can be protested. If trauma is "an event without a witness" (Felman & Laub, 1992), testimony restores humanity and dignity. Moreover, I view the major significance of testimony in therapy in terms of its role in manifesting subjectivity. As Oliver (2001) argues, subjectivity is born out of and sustained by the process of witnessing—the possibility of address and response—which puts ethical obligations at its heart.

Witnessing as a psychoanalytic function is more than an encounter with empathy, or with historical truth, and more radical than recognition. The encounter with testimony, about man-made traumas, inevitably raises political and epistemological questions regarding credibility, regarding whose suffering is worthy of empathy, regarding attachments and group identity. Witnessing highlights difference, rather than sameness, as the most valuable component of the encounter between self and other. In psychoanalysis, the analyst is the other who says that what had happened to you should not happen to anyone; the other who is willing to examine the way she is implicated in the suffering of others, albeit within the "relational bubble" (Ullman, 2014) of the psychoanalytic encounter that provides safety, insolation, and secure attachment.

In *Thoughts for the Times on War and Death* (1915), Freud claims that war, like psychoanalysis, reveals the true nature of man's primordial drives. But we also know that the urge to seek peace and resist war is just as persistent as outbursts of violence, in their various individual and social forms. Current research on altruism and empathy in babies and young children clearly indicates very young children spontaneously help those who seem to be in need and are happy to do so. It indicates that, alongside the primordial roots of fear and aggression, there is also an inherent human capacity to recognize the "good" and to engage in the ethics of care. Alongside the cruelty and brutality of the world that is at our doorstep, there exists resilience and a specific inherent human capacity to care for an other. I believe it is part of our responsibility as psychoanalysts to seek out the conditions that cultivate this capacity.

References

Benjamin, J. (2002). Guilt and terror. *Psychoanalytic Dialogues*, 12, 473–484.
Benjamin, J. (2018). *Beyond doer and done to: Recognition theory, intersubjectivity and the third*. NY: Routledge.
Bromberg, P. M. (1996). Standing in the spaces: The multiplicity of self and the psychoanalytic relationship. *Contemporary Psychoanalysis*, 32, 509–535.

Felman, S., & Laub, D. (1992). *Testimony: Crises of witnessing in literature, psychoanalysis and history*. NYC, NY: Routledge.

Freud, S. (1915). Thoughts for the times of war and death. In J. Strachey (Ed.), *The standard edition of the complete psychological works of S. Freud* (24 Vols; pp. 273–300). London: Hogarth Press.

Harris, A. (2006). Ghosts, unhealable wounds and resilience. *Psychoanalytic Dialogues*, *16*(5), 543–551.

Levenson, E. A. (2012). Psychoanalysis and the rite of refusal. *Psychoanalytic Dialogues*, *22*(1), 2–6.

Oliver, K. (2001). *Witnessing: Beyond recognition*. MN: University of Minnesota Press.

Ullman, C. (1989). *The transformed self: The psychology of religious conversion*. New York: Plenum Press.

Ullman, C. (2006). Bearing witness: Across the barriers in society and in the clinic. *Psychoanalytic Dialogues*, *16*(2), 181–198.

Ullman, C. (2014). The personal is political, the political is personal: On the subjectivity of an Israeli psychoanalyst. In S. Kuchuck (Ed.), *Clinical implications of the analyst's life experiences*(pp. 98–111). New York: Routledge.

Ullman, C. (2020). The Hero transformed: The dialectic of heroism and psychoanalytic process in working with Israeli men. *Psychoanalytic Inquiry*, *40*(7), 478–486.

Index

A
Abend, Sander 231
abortion 148
Abraham, Nicolàs 22–23
absence
  psychically absent 14–15
acknowledgment 100, 108, 129, 144, 219
  dependency, their 97; injuries, of 102; mutual acknowledgment project 239; unacknowledged truths 103; violations 99, 101
adaptation 108, 240
  modes of 106
adherence, rigid 72–73, 74, 132, 139, 142, 146, 235, 238 *see also:* dogmatic attitude, models
adolescents 155–158, 235
afraid *see fear*
aggression 117, 221, 241
aliveness 124, 158, 164, 178, 179, 180, 182, 200
Algeria 231
American Psychoanalytic Institute 66, 67, 140n
American Psychological Association 65
analyst's memory *see Bion, Wilfred*
analysts of color 173, 215
analytic bracketing 131, 143, 144, 145
analytic frame 58, 122, 130, 143, 161–162, 170, 215
  spontaneity within 74
Analytic Institute in Israel 235
analytic process 63, 64, 124, 129, 179, 180, 181
anti-intellectualism 189
anxiety 218, 220,
  crisis 17
apartheid 201–202

après-coup 22, 78, 227
association *see free association*
Aron, Lew 54, 147
  Meeting of Minds: Mutuality and Intersubjectivity in Psychoanalysis 238
attunement 98, 100, 143, 204, 213, 219–220
  good enough 133; mis-attunement 138, 144, 221; own experiences, to my 111; safety and 102
  see also: holding, containment
Austen Riggs 10
authenticity 58, 182, 196

B
Balint, Enid 81–82
banishment 42–43
Baranger, Madelaine 32, 157
Baranger, Willy 32, 157
beta elements 212 *see also:* Bion, Wilfred
biology-versus-culture 57
Bion, Wilfred 124, 158, 178, 180, 181, 212
  being-at-one with the psychic reality of the patient 187; "Without memory or desire" 25; waking dreaming and container/contained 157
Bionian see Bion, Wilfred
Black Lives Matter 119 *see also:* racism
Blackburn, Simon 46
Benjamin, Jessica 239
  Bonds of Love 202
bits and pieces 107, 110 *see also:* Winnicott
Blass, Oren 76
Bleger, José 18
Bollas, Christopher 27, 189

The mystery of things 187
Bornstein, Melvin 39
Boston Change Process Study Group 186
Boston University Hospital Trauma Clinic 235
boundaries 142
    violations 146, 148
Bromberg, Phillip 138
Buddhism 99
Butler, Judith 115–116

C

cancer 94
canon, psychoanalytic 169, 202
Cardinal, Marie 226–227, 230–231
Cezanne's Doubt see Merleau-Ponty, Maurice
Change of heart, change of mind? The psychology of religious conversion 234
Chicago Psychoanalytic Institute 62
child abuse 196, 198 *see also:* trauma
civil rights 33 *see also:* racism
Civitarese, Giuseppe 117, 179
    Mentioned 116
Coates, Ta Nehisi 215
coconstructed 58, 144, 146
Coetzee, J.M. 202
Collective, the 238
colonialism 155, 202, 212, 216n
Columbia Teachers College 70
comparative psychoanalysis 55, 65, 66, 67
complementary 97–98, 99, 157
conscious *see unconscious*
conflict 48, 62, 92, 94, 103, 105, 148, 222 *see also:* Oedipus complex
confrontation 39, 97, 125, 147
containment 110, 122, 144, 145, 147, 178, 179, 180, 181, 202
    cannot contain 17; capacity to contain 101, 125; container/contained 157; containing-searching 162; maternal 177; perfect container 100 *see also:* holding attunement
conviction 118, 129, 131, 193, 228
    ethical 236; theoretical 237; work in the 230–232

countertransference 25, 58, 81, 100, 101, 106, 108, 109, 210 *see also:* transference
couple work 73
creative 50, 110
    capacities 178–180, 181
Creativity and the Erotic Dimensions of the Analytic Field 181
Credo quia absurdum 187
"the dance" 98

D

Davids, M. Fahkry 201
Davies, Jody 54, 116
deadness *see aliveness*
defenses 37, 57, 119, 182, 203, 228–229
    obsessional 187
depressive position *see Klein, Melanie*
derailment 136, 145
desire 60, 61, 97, 101, 171–172
destruction, analyst's 185, 229
development 176–178, 180, 181, 182, 193–199, 238, 240
    analytic 78, 80; gender 202; interruptions 136; psycho-development 45 *see also:* analytic process
dictatorship 34, 38
Dickinson, Emily 184
Dimen, Muriel 54, 116, 202, 215, 235
disorders of the self 13
dissociation 100–101, 119, 136, 203, 220, 240
Division of Psychoanalysis (Division 39) 65
Dodgers, the 59, 60, 61, 69
doer and done to 98–100, 102, 103, 237, 239
dogmatic attitude 34, 36, 72 *see also:* adherence; rigid
dramatize 100, 101
dream 16, 17, 43–44, 114, 122, 124, 125, 157
    "dream the session" 123; work model 42, 48–49
drive 42, 43–44, 137, 195, 241
dyadic 98, 101, 135, 138, 176, 180, 185, 197, 230, 240, 241
    conversation 178; dyadic "dance"

144; movement 99; structures the 184

E
early caretaking 118, 131
ego 42–43,
  position 49; psychology 45; unconscious ego 41, 188
  see also: Freud, structural and topographic model
Ego kai auto [εγώ και αυτό] 226
Ehrlich, Lena Theodorou 231
Eisenbud, Ruth-Jean 137
elasticity of psycho-analytic technique 81, 105
Eliot, George 160
Emmy von N [Fanny Moser] 79
empathy 75–76, 106, 132, 241
enactment 100, 109, 138, 143, 145, 146, 166 *see also:* transference; countertransference
enigmatic core 230
Enriquez, Michelene 22
epistemological approaches 39
Erikson, Erik 10
Eros 163, 176
erotic 163, 176–178, 180–181
  feelings 158
ethics 47, 50, 118, 148, 149n, 166, 203
  course 114, 117; labor 173, 174; non-indifference, of 131; obligation 49, 237, 241; relation 132–133; seduction 228
evenly suspended attention 46, 79, 82, 173, 187
expansion 101
  experiencing, of 165; personality of the 181–182; psychic 203

F
Faimberg, Haydeé 139n
Fairbairn, William Ronald Dodds 51, 53, 55, 97, 123, 137
faith 228, 229, 231
  omnipotent 213 *see also:* conviction, *work in the*
family romance 36
Fanon, Franz 114
fantasy 146, 165, 189
  fantasized affiliations 36; games 200; gender, of 203, 213; group 33;

unconscious 110, 157 *see also:* gender; unconscious
father 15, 16, 17, 61, 70–71, 89, 123–124, 148, 156
fear 84, 93, 99, 118, 157, 162, 178, 189, 215
Felix Holt the Radical 160
female psychology 71, 76, 97, 116, 137
feminism 96–97, 116, 143, 148, 195, 202, 239
Ferenczi, Sándor 102, 115, 130
  confusion of languages 20; 'The elasticity of psycho-analytic technique' 81–82; therapeutic acknowledgment 100
Ferkauf/Yeshiva University 90, 128
Ferro, Antonino 117, 157, 179
Field theory 157, 179–180
Floyd, George 215
Fraiberg, Selma 196
framework, theoretical 14, 35, 38, 46, 137, 147, 220–221
  learning 49, 80; polarization 145
  see also: models
the Frankfurt school 96, 195
free association 17, 25, 37, 41, 47, 49, 73, 84, 106, 138
  process of 42
  Freud's theory of 46
freedom 34, 71, 80, 83, 93, 97, 142, 170, 180, 191, 218–223
  dream, to 122; mental 161–163; think, to 124, 138; thought, of 33
Freud, Sigmund 26, 35, 41, 47, 67, 72, 139n, 178, 197, 212
  actual style of clinical engagement 75; American psychiatry 9; *Civilization and Its Discontents* 71; Community around 116; Developmental theorizing 178; dialoguing with 91; doctor, the 79; Dora, and 211, 214; dream work 42, 48, 49; evenly suspended attention 82; evolution of Freud's thinking 11, 65; Ferenczi's struggles with 115; free association, Freud's theory of 46; Freudian supervisors 89, 142; "fundamental rule" 122; "Instincts and their vicissitudes" 19, 23; Loewald's love of 56; "Mourning and Melancholia" 74, 137; Primary

bisexuality 213; psychic conflict 92; revisiting 17; structural and topographic model 43, 44, 45, 135; *Studies on Hysteria* 79, 84; study 51–52, 129, 136, 161; *Thoughts for the Times on War and Death* 241; time 55, 57; "Totem and Taboo" 36; tragic vision 59, 60–61, 63, 64, 69; writing about women 76, 96, 128 *see also:* aggression; conflict; countertransference; defense; dream; ego; erotic; evenly suspended attention; free association; model, classical psychotherapy, model of; mourning; transference; unconscious
Fromm, Erich 51, 55, 64, 71
Fromm-Reichman, Frieda 75, 130

G

game, the 209–212, 213, 214, 215
gender 116, 202–203, 213, 216n
   see also: fantasy; identity; transgender
generations
   links between 21–22; telescoping of 14; trans-generational attachment trauma 139n; transmission 135, 138
George, Sheldon 114, 120
Ghent, Emmanuel 99, 113
"Ghosts in the Nursery" 196
Gill, Merton 58
   Analysis of Transference 65
glischrocaric position *see Bleger, Josè*
Glover, Edward 81, 82
Gonzalez, Francisco 215
Grand, Sue 146
Great Hunger, the 155
Green, Andrè 166
Greenberg, Jay 52–53, 91, 185
grief *see mourning*
Grossmark, Robert 133
growth 103, 105, 174
   authentic 13; growth-promoting 123, 176, 177; personal 80; professional 223, 237; psychological 122
guerrilla movements *see human rights*

H

Harris, Adrienne 202
have-not 171
Hebrew University, the 234, 235
Herman, Imre 24
hierarchical 89–90, 139, 197, 210, 235
   hierarchical system 11; repressive and oppressive 166
holding 100, 109, 110, 142–143, 144, 147, 163
   failures in; holding-mutuality binary 145; silence is a form of 58
   see also: containment
human rights 33, 237

I

Id *see Freud, structural and topographic model*
idealization 145–146, 147, 227, 230
   motherhood, of 143
identity 36, 161, 166, 230
   gender 202; psychoanalytic 31, 36, 78, 80, 82, 146, 148, 169, 171, 185, 239; true 13 *see also: gender*
identifications 102, 116, 148, 155, 174, 237
   alienating 20, 22; projective 180; unconsciously identified 21, 27
idolization 214
illusion 47, 58, 144, 146, 163, 164, 166, 216
imagination 81–82
immigration 202
impasse 100, 222
incommensurable 37, 39
infant-parent work 177, 196
injustice 102, 103, 118, 130
Institute of Argentine Psychoanalytic Association 25, 32
the Institute for the Psychoanalytic Study of Subjectivity, New York 129
International Association of Relational Psychotherapy and Psychoanalysis (IARPP) 235, 236, 237
interpersonal psychoanalysis 37, 57, 63, 65 *see also: intersubjective*
International Psychoanalytic Association 65
infantile sexual phantasies 43, 163–164, 177, 178, 192
injury 99, 102
   class injury 211
inner life 105–106, 108, 110, 111, 202
internalized 45, 48, 49, 72, 97, 100, 108, 109, 111, 135, 136, 237–238 *see also: object, internal*

internal dialogue 17–19
internal space 203
interpretation 17, 73, 102, 105, 106, 111, 161–162, 165, 187, 219, 232
  Absence, the 14; association, on the basis of an 25; correct 63, 218; efficiency of 81; emotional contact, the 37; interpreted in different ways 35; non-saturated 26; patients do not need 75; transference 58
interior 57, 81, 144, 197, 227
interrupt his treatment 14–15
intersubjective 73, 97, 98, 100, 138, 139, 143, 145, 148, 176
intrapsychic 146, 230, 239
  conflict 172; life 202; repair 100
Israel 211, 234–235, 237, 239, 240
I-You relatedness 131

J

Jewish 89–90, 92, 95n, 201, 235, 238
jouissance 114, 120

K

Kahneman, Danny 234
Kalinkowitz, Bernie 11, 51
Katharina [Aurelia Kronich] 79
Khan, Masud 214
Klein, Melanie 50, 185
  depressive and paranoid-schizoid position 23, 45, 46, 189; hegemony 32, 35; psychic processes, elaboration of 201
"Know thyself" 72, 129
Knowing 15, 16, 21, 25–26, 48, 50, 108–109, 133, 144, 162, 193, 194, 202, 203, 215, 229
  analyst's 212, 230; common vulnerability, of 103; interpretation 161; 'not-knowing' was respected 18–19; other minds, our ability to 99; parents, our 92–93; resistance to thinking and 119; surrender to unknowingness 232; unknowable feelings 135; unknown, the 157, 174, 204; want to be known 94; "yet to be known" 110, 134, 136, 138
Kohut, Heinz 12, 13, 35, 66, 75
van der Kolk, Bessel 235
Krause, Rainer 74–75
Kristeva, Julia 176–177

L

Lacan, Jacques 18, 19, 27, 49, 50, 92, 98, 114, 161, 196
  Symbolic, Imaginary, and Real 45–46
  see also: Third, the; jouissance
Laplanche, Jean 177, 212, 230
  mentioned 129, 172
lawful world 99, 100, 101
Les mots pour le dire 226
Levenson, Edgar 58
  The Ambiguity of Change 56
Levinas, Emmanuel 131–132
libido 163, 177–178, 181, 182
  libidinal engagement 176, 180; libidinal turbulence 163
Lillescov, Roy
limit 44, 50, 105, 106, 109, 125, 229
limitation *see limit*
listening 28, 45, 110, 138, 182, 204, 218, 221, 227, 237, 238
  block 16; capacity 84; contradictory voices, to 236; deep 182; interior 81; listened to 79, 161, 239; listened for 135, 136, 162, 166; listening to listening 19, 21; movement, to the 220; position 25–26; resistance to 17; struggling to 108
Little, Omar 117, 209–215
lived experience 42, 48, 131–132, 171, 173, 197
Loewald, Hans 55–56, 74
Løgstrup, Knud 131–132
loss *see mourning*
Lou-Gehrig's disease 231

M

Machsom watch 237
Maci, Guillermo 19
Mahler, Margaret 12
Marcuse, Herbert 71
Marty, Pierre 18
Massachusetts Institute for Psychoanalysis 172
Marxism 96, 191, 195
masochism 107, 131, 137
  see also: perversions
mental state examination 79
Merleau-Ponty, Maurice 169
mirror transference 35
Mitchell, Stephen 91
  "big tent" approach to theory 137–138; common ground 90;

critique of Winnicottian maternal tilt 143; dialoguing with Freud 91; guiltiness 119; *Object Relations in Psychoanalytic Theory* 65; openness and intellectual curiosity 185–186; panels at the American Psychoanalytic Convention 66–67; relational matrix 135
models 24
classical psychotherapy, model of 12, 42, 44, 74, 81, 147–148, 213, 238; ideal 34; psychoanalytic 37, 38, 48–49, 50
mother 15–16, 43, 61, 70–71, 89, 91, 93, 148, 156–157, 163, 176–178, 181, 226–227
maternal loss 135; maternal order 43
mourning 23, 74, 102, 105, 135, 137, 166, 236, 241
aborted, has been 136; accountability, and 113; barrier to 119; born into 139n; fruitful 172; play of 107, 109, 110
movement 98, 99, 100, 109, 219, 220, 222
Munro, Alice 186
mutuality and asymmetry 90, 97, 98, 99, 132–133, 145, 223, 238
de M'Uzan, Michel 230–231

N
Nacht, Sasha 81, 82
Nachträglichkeit *see après-coup*
narcissism 12, 13, 24, 26
narcissistic position 35; narcissistic resistance 16–17
National Institute for the Psychotherapies (NIP) 65
nature-versus-nurture *see biology-versus-culture*
Nazism, psychic consequences of 21
negative capability: *see Bion, Wilfred*
negation 99, 100, 102
neutrality 47–48, 58, 157, 173, 178, 238
New Left 195
New York Psychoanalytic Institute 11–12
Nieto, Marta 35
NYU Clinical Program 10
NYU Postdoctoral program in psychoanalysis 11, 129, 137, 202

O
Object
bad 162; internal 107–111, 163, 188
Object relations 56, 66, 137–138, 166, 239 *see also:* framework, theoretical
Object Relations in Psychoanalytic Theory 65
Oedipus complex 24, 25, 60, 177, 178
Oedipal configuration: see Oedipus complex
Ogden, Thomas 98, 110, 116
mentioned 55, 117, 135, 155, 179
Oliver, Kelly 241
omnipotence 97, 188
one-person theory 96, 98
oppositional *see rebellion*
oppression 97, 102, 138, 155, 203
see also: racism; dictatorship; Black Lives Matter
organizing
authority 161; experience 100; principles 129, 131
other
othered, being 102, 139; otherness 57, 220, 238, 240

P
pain *see suffering*
Palestinian uprising 237
paradigm shifts 53, 57, 135, 137, 139, 238, 239
parallel 177
process 82, 101, 202
paranoid-schizoid position *see Klein, Melanie*
parentified (It) child 132
Parsons, Michael 106, 162
Patient stories 14–17, 25–26, 148, 162, 200–201, 219–220, 221, 223, 231–232
Paul, Campbell 176
Peasant in the Analyst's Chair: Reflections, Personal and Otherwise, on Class and the Forming of an Analytic Identity 169
people of color 114, 212 *see also:* analysts of color; racism
perversions 12–13
perverse pact 119 *see also:* masochism
Pharmaceutical-industrial complex 13, 188 *see also:* psychotropic drugs

Pichon Rivière, Enrique 18, 24, 25
play 108, 111, 157, 163, 166, 181, 182, 187–188, 210, 214, 221
   capacity for 106, 107, 162; content 164–165; deep 117–118; erotics of 180; metaphor 105; mourning, of 109, 110; mutuality of 99; or be played 213; player 209, 211, 212; symmetrical experiences of 101; together 164
pluralism 31, 34–35, 36, 38–40, 65–67, 68
Poland, Warren 125, 129
postmodern
   poststructuralist and postmodern positions 39; relativistic postmodern perspective 38; theory 211
power 202, 209
   abuses 231; dynamics 173, 210, 240; inequities 195, 239; structures 119, 237
pragmatism, American 128
privilege 114, 118, 130, 173, 212, 215
primary bisexuality 213
primitive agonies 125, 164
projection 47
psyche 20, 57, 201, 202, 227, 240
   analyst's 81; development of the 181; erotic dimension of the 180
psychic 14, 21, 25, 42, 45, 46, 50, 80, 92, 96, 109, 125, 201, 212, 213, 229
   changes 17, 48; forfeit 109; life 82, 180; pain 178, 180–181, 234, 239–240; reality 187, 188, 232
   see also: expansion, psychic
Psychoanalytic Association of Uruguay 32, 33, 34
Psychoanalytic Collisions 145
psychophobia 189
psychotropic drugs 12
   see also: pharmaceutical-industrial complex

Q
queer 161, 192, 202, 209, 211

R
racism 113–114, 118–120, 139, 140n, 170, 173, 201, 203 *see also:* oppression; whiteness; Black Lives Matter; Floyd, George

Rapaport, David 10, 63–64
rapprochement 98
rebellion 71, 73, 93, 130, 236
receptivity 50, 106, 110, 173, 182, 187, 203
reciprocity 98, 132, 176, 181
   reciprocal cultural and sociopolitical influences 239 *see also:* mutuality and asymmetry
recognition 26, 96–97, 166
   mutual recognition 98–99, 100, 101, 102, 239
regression 109, 142
Reik, Theodor 71, 72, 73
   Reik-Fenichel debate 75
relational
   bubble 241; communities 115; early influences 129; excess 145, 146; holding 144; practice 98, 99; psychoanalysis 53–56, 57, 63, 75, 77, 91, 100, 102, 138, 143, 147, 148, 237–238; track 137; trauma 136, 234, 240; turn 96, 135, 139, 195
Relationships in Development: Infancy Intersubjectivity, and Attachment 194
religion 89, 130, 234–235, 236
repair 98, 99, 100, 101, 102, 103, 118, 219, 222
   reparative impulses 116, 119
repetition 89, 99, 103, 105, 110, 165, 228, 237, 240
representation 99–101, 179, 198, 202, 212, 229–230
   unrepresented 107, 213
Research Center for Mental Health 63
resilience 236
resistance 16–17, 98, 100, 106, 109, 129, 147, 162, 240
respect 19, 28, 76, 111, 173, 182, 238
responsiveness 76, 97, 99, 105, 110, 111, 132, 196
reverie 110, 181
revolution 54, 91–92, 96, 97, 135, 240
   revolutionary concept 202, 239
Rollo, Edgardo 18
rupture 99, 100, 101–102, 219, 222
   see also: repair

S
sadomasochism *see perversions*
safety 134, 136, 228, 241

scaffolding 98, 210, 215
Scarfone, Dominique 229–230
Schafer, Roy 59, 60
    The Analytic Attitude 65
schema 100
School of Dynamic Psychiatry 18
Schools of psychoanalysis 49–50
Searles, Harold 93
seduction 43, 58, 178, 228, 231
self
    care 115, 118; other, and 99, 100, 109, 136, 204, 241; self-analysis 37; self-disclosure 58, 77, 94, 145; self-states 107, 118, 135, 136, 138, 145, 218–219, 220, 221, 222, 237, 238; self-to-self negotiation 203; true 49, 136, 179, 203, 235
shame 101, 108–109, 144, 145, 171, 172, 174, 175, 237
    class 170
silence 19, 47, 58, 122, 171, 204, 223, 237
slavery 119, 139, 140n
    slaveholders 215
snark, the 27
Snitow, Ann 116
social class 170–171, 173, 174
    see also: shame, class
social frame 160–161
South Africa 200–202 *see also:* apartheid
Spence, Donald
    Narrative Truth and Historical Truth 65
Spielrein, Sabina 116
Stein, Ruth 119
Stern, Daniel 97–98
structural model *see Freud, structural and topographic model*
Structural-Functional sociology 195
subliminal stimulation 10
submission 99, 130, 202
suffering 96, 107, 124, 125, 230–231, 237
    attachment figures, at the hands of their 235; attempt to understand this 132; bear our 74, 124; implicated in their 201, 203, 238, 241; painful feelings, relief from 62, 131; psychic pain 178, 180, 181, 234, 239–240; recognizing 98; reliving of 136; unrealized 101, 103
    see also: trauma
suicide bomber 211

Sullivan, Harry Stack 51, 55, 58, 64
superego *see Freud, structural and topographic model*
supervision 35, 49, 64, 221
surrender 99–100, 101, 132, 203, 204, 229, 232
survive 103, 109, 118, 213, 214, 229
    destruction 98, 102; failing 100; history of 203; Holocaust survivors 236, 237; survival is of the fittest 209

T
Taragano, Fernando 18
Tel Aviv Institute for Contemporary Psychoanalysis 235, 236, 237
tension 80, 92, 99, 107, 193, 197, 239
    dialectical 51, 103; generative 68–69; unspoken 61
therapeutic action 98, 100, 164
Therapy experience [as a client] 33–34, 61–63, 72–73, 74, 93–94, 117, 134–136, 170–172, 174
The Thing 230
Third, the 98–102, 203, 204, 219, 237, 238, 239 *see also:* Lacan, Jacques; Ogden, Thomas
Third ear 135
Thomson-Salo, Frances 176
Torok, Maria 22–23
traif psychologist 66, 69
trauma 99, 124, 135, 136, 138, 139, 236–237, 239, 241
    cultural 138, 139; prior generations, from 135; relational 136, 234, 240; war, of 9 *see also:* child abuse; racism; suffering
truth 71, 77, 102, 103, 119, 124–125
    emotional 134, 181, 182, 184, 187, 209–215; personal 178; self, of 201, 203
tolerance toward uncertainty 34
topographic model *see Freud, structural and topographic model*
transference 16–17, 58, 62, 73, 100, 109, 110, 227
    British school's view of 47
    see also: countertransference
transformation 103, 176, 203–204, 234–235, 241
    experience 97, 101; genuine, demand for a 120; intimacy that itself is

187; openings 166; painful affect 179, 180, 181; patient, for the 46, 82; power 102; relationally 132; therapeutic 238; thinking 122
transgender 202, 216n
   Rapid Onset Gender Dysphoria 213
transitional space 162–164, 165
triangular relationship 24
   see also: narcissism; Oedipus complex
tripartite model *see Lacan, Jacques*
Tversky, Amos 234

U
Ulysses [The Odyssey] 39–40
unconscious 25, 46–47, 79, 81, 102, 124, 125, 184, 192, 197, 202, 239
   conscious experience 63; consciousness 49, 101, 204, 212; denial 119; efforts to comprehend the 187; evading 123, 210; family inscription 26; fantasy 110, 157, 189; fears 118; group 156; identification 27; issues, movement of 48; life 45, 50, 82; meaning of theories 36; made conscious 161; parental transfers 164; pre-reflective 129; primitive elements of the 43–44, 57; process and content 41–42; processes 75, 83, 162, 163; roots 114
unitary psychoanalytic theory
   see pluralism
Universidad de la República 32
University of Witwatersrand 201
unlearning 79, 80, 128

V
violence 130, 237, 240, 241

racial violence 114, 119
   see also: racism
vulnerability 74, 103, 125, 204
   derailment, to 145; embracing 239; mutual 100; our own 99, 102; recognizing 236; social class, of 171; undefended 178

W
wait
   capacity to 81–82, 134, 162, 165, 173
waking dreaming *see reverie*
Waldenfels, Bernhard 131
Wallerstein 37
whiteness 114, 118, 119, 209, 231
   Unraveling Whiteness 203
William Alanson White Institute 52, 54, 55, 64
Winnicott, Donald 107, 109–110, 189
   adolescence 158; affective attunement 143; *The Child, the Family and the Outside World 142*; creative function 180, 181; "going-on-being" 136; good enough 163; holding model 144, 177–178; interprets to show his patients the limits of his understanding 105–106; outside other 97–98; playing 164–165, 187; *Playing and reality* 82; surviving destruction 102; true self 179, 203; "The Use of an Object" 12
witness 74, 99, 100, 101, 102, 118, 134, 145, 146, 236–237, 239, 241
Wire, the *see Little, Omar*
The Words to Say It 226
Writer's block 17

Professional Credos: What Contemporary Critics Believe They Are Doing in Their Work

Printed in the United States
by Baker & Taylor Publisher Services